Acting in Their Favor

John Seidel

ISBN: 978-0-9858282-1-9

Published by:
CONVERPAGE
23 Acorn Street
Scituate, MA 02066
www.converpage.com

Chapter One

When he was a younger man, he felt the spirit dream had hold of his heart. His love was often confusing, broken and violent. For awhile back then, he was drinking a lot trying to make the dream let go. But now, as a brittle fisherman just brushing the grave, he realizes that for all this time, it wasn't his heart. The spirit dream has had his soul.

Charlie Bay's chest ached as he sat forward. Rolling left he felt the moist sheets peel from his skin. He raised his arm and took a quick breath, then another, slower, deeper. As his lungs filled he eased back onto a damp pillow. He knew the smell. He knew the sound. Like so many times before, he inhaled ocean air and listened to waves until the chest pain ended. Charlie Bay Burningwater had a pretty good idea of how his life was going to end. He saw it coming. Waking from the spirit dream more often than ever, he was narrowing in on when.

After collecting himself, the combination of gin and a weak bladder forced him up. He struggled off the edge of the bed, knees and lower back cracking. His wiry body of somewhere around eight decades was stiff but most parts still worked, worked well enough for Charlie Bay to keep going. He expected nothing less and refused to acknowledge that he had to shuffle in the dark to keep his balance.

On his way into the hall, Burningwater turned a passing glance to the alarm clock on the nightstand. He was safe for a while. The darkness was with him for a little longer. The luminescent arms of his wife's wind up clock read ten to three. Through the years of waking from the dream, he came to find this a time when darkness consoled him. More often than not, he was sober and he was alone. He didn't have to face the dream or face the day. He liked the darkness but was ambivalent about being alone.

Charlie Bay lived by himself for the last thirty years in a house built by his grandfather. It had been that way since his wife traveled to visit her sister in Lewiston and didn't come back. She died six years after leaving him. Telling those who asked that the "sugar" got her, Charlie Bay said no more. To this day, he refused to accept that she never planned to come home and thought sometime she'd just show up. She had before, but she didn't. He was angry the last words they exchanged were about buying fruit. He was angry she died. Still, he knew he had his chances.

Their son's first photograph of the two of them was tucked in the corner of the mirror above the bureau in their bedroom. The black and white snapshot, with its scalloped edges, was curled and faded. He hadn't looked at the picture for years, but had no intention of taking it down.

Unable to go back to sleep or start his morning routine, Charlie Bay walked to the window at the top of the staircase. A slice of light separated the half drawn shade from the oak molding. Pulling aside the dark green paper, he looked out from the second story of his frame house onto Spruce trees dotting the northwest acreage. The gray hue of a full moon and its moon shadows over the landscape eased the knots in the muscles of his back. The stillness relaxed him.

It was the seven folding chairs that always lingered from the dream. Seven empty chairs scattered between those seated in a circle stuck with him. He figured they were the seats of the missing. The empty chairs broke the circle. They nagged him.

To distract himself from the spirit dream, he considered the dozen or so trees that he planted with his grandfather a few months before the old man died. The cone shaped moon shadows of thirty-foot Spruce trees were dark enough to hide a lacrosse player during a nighttime game. With his eyes darting from tree to tree, shadow to shadow, Charlie Bay remembered his grandfather, Bat Player. He was a long legged and fiery man, who, on a fall night with a full moon, ran from shadow to shadow and played the lacrosse game of his life. It was a story that Charlie Bay heard many times as a child. He looked down onto the field and imagined Bat Player dashing one shadow to another, into legend.

As his eyes drifted to the western sky, Charlie Bay thought in the moment why lacrosse captured so many of his ancestors' hearts.

In the Casco Nation, the game of lacrosse was the Little Brother of War. It was his Tribe's celebration of speed and bravery. Lacrosse made Casco boys, men, and Casco men, warriors. Season after season it was the chance for victory. It was also the chance to show off and impress women.

His grandfather's story was so much a part of Charlie Bay it was as if he played in that game. But he never played the game of his people, he never got the chance to show off and he was never that good with women. In just one generation, there was no one left to run among the moon shadows, listen to the legends or marry. Charlie Bay found a wife outside the Casco Nation. She was a second generation Irish American housekeeper. She was beautiful and she grew to hate him.

Keeping the presence of Bat Player with him, his thoughts drifted to the hour of moon low tide, of how cold the east wind was on the sand flats this early in April and how digging clams was the focus of his days. Back on the dream, he wondered if one of the empty chairs belonged to his grandfather, Bat Player.

The skiff sat stern first in Burningwater's pickup. The truck's rear wheels were in about six inches of water on the beach next to the fish pier. Wading the ten feet to a dock piling with the bowline, Charlie Bay watched the light air paw the harbor's surface. There was a ritual for the skiff during the winter digging season complete with prayer and common sense. His body was old. If things were done in rhythm, the clams knew he was coming. They expected to be taken and he expected his bones to give him another day. Tying the skiff to the pier on the outgoing tide and driving the pickup from under it was the opening. Dragging it up the beach behind his truck to a perch in the dunes was the closing. In more recent years, the ritual was known by the local fishermen to mark the boundaries of Burningwater's livelihood. The last time he fished on the water was coming onto a third season. He called himself a lobsterman but he dug clams for a living.

This Maine morning on the waterfront felt no different to Charlie Bay than any other in early spring. The half dozen Downeast lobster boats that dotted the river harbor rode with the tide. There was heavy water moving through the moorings; the combination of runoff from melting snow, four days of rain and the full moon. With his gear onboard the skiff, Charlie Bay studied the current. As usual, his tack was perfect to ease across the tidal river basin that fishermen had used as a harbor for generations. Rowing fifteen yards up one of the shallow feeder streams, he was on a sand bar he had worked for a lifetime. It was an island uncovered by the outgoing tide that had remained through years of dredging and landfills, digging and dumping. And, each time Charlie Bay set foot on the sand, it was new.

As Burningwater stepped from the skiff into the boot high water, the bar showed only a few lumps and bumps as evidence of yesterday's digging. He noticed the southern edge was remodeled to a little sharper curve with the stronger current. He felt the cold creep inside his boots as he waded through the shallows to set the anchor center stream. And as Charlie Bay trudged to wet sand, just like every other day, he wondered how long he could last.

In the warmer weather, digging clams meant finding a good crop of squirt holes, pounding the ground with a clam hoe and watching for the clams to spew. Once a spot was found, Charlie Bay would sit on his bucket and work just one hole. This time of year, digging was more work, more holes over more territory. The extra effort was compensated by higher market prices and fewer fools on the sand. Today he was one of five.

After digging for about four hours, Charlie Bay's back told him no more. At the turning point of his workday, the choice was quit now, maybe buy some gin and drink. Or, force himself to hang on, go two more hours with the tide and then drink.

Most of the folks who lived and worked around the harbor thought Burningwater drank to kill memories, memories of a family and an Indian Nation destroyed. The locals knew him as an Indian who belonged to the Casco Tribe, what was left of it. He was someone who never said much, worked hard and spent his time on the water or the sand. Because of this, he was accepted and left alone.

Charlie Bay Burningwater was a full-blooded member of the Casco Nation and he did drink. But it wasn't to kill memories. He drank to remove a circle of time. The purpose of alcohol for Charlie Bay was to eliminate his time at night in the spirit dream and his time in the day thinking about it. He wanted to get rid of both. With gin he thought he was good at it.

Without much consideration, Charlie Bay chose to keep going. He stretched his back and moved a few steps to start a new hole. Burningwater spread his legs, bent forward and drove the claming fork into the sand. With the thrust, he felt a hard object shatter. Thinking that it was just another empty quahog shell, he turned over the ground. As his eyes focused, he recognized the sand-covered fragment of a human skull. He froze staring at the bone. Falling to his knees and reaching into the watery hole, Charlie Bay pulled the skull to his chest. The top was broken. The two eye sockets, despite being packed with sand, were unmistakable. Burningwater rolled to the ground. His eyes clamped shut. The moist sand glued clothes to skin. The fragmentary skull fused day and dream. Lying with knees pulled to his chest and looking skyward, he cradled Casco bone.

"Uh-kosisco, Uh-kosisco rising above me.
Look down upon a son of the Nations...
call to Earth and Sea that I might be forgiven.
I make this prayer to you Uh-kosisco.
Uh-kosisco, Uh-kosisco rising above me.

Look down upon a son of the Nations...
call to Earth and Sea that I might be forgiven.
I make the prayer to you ..."

His voice tailed off behind clenched teeth, *"and call to Sea that I might be forgiven."*

Charlie Bay Burningwater fought it hard but failed. He cried an old and deep cry.

Thirty-three thousand feet in the air, six hundred miles per hour, satellite TV that included CNN and it was all for a fare just a little more than driving. The trip from Philadelphia to Maine was at least eight hours by car. The choice was easy. TV was a bonus.

Margaret set her laptop on the seatback tray but avoided turning it on by scanning through the forty-eight channels on the headrest screen in front of her. An elderly couple in the adjacent two seats had settled into the flight with headphones and an early afternoon soap opera. As Margaret searched for CNN the woman leaned toward her during a commercial, "Isn't this great! I don't have to miss my story."

Margaret nodded with a smile and considered how she called the soap her "story". She turned on her laptop and entered the expression under dialog notes at the bottom of a long list in the file.

This was the fascinating part of writing for Margaret; listening to a phrase and catching a glimpse of a story line in some everyday event or conversation. The challenging part was to sort through the files, the dictation, the plot lines and integrate them into dialogue and a story that worked. Her first play took two years to complete by writing around part time jobs. Margaret turned out grant proposals for a university consulting firm and a few nights a week, waited tables in a small South Philadelphia bistro. She wrote the rest of the time to finish it. Although in her mind, now working on a third play, the first wasn't done.

Margaret's first play was sparked by a thirty second national news spot on the fiftieth anniversary of Brown v. Board of Education. The Supreme Court's decision in the case of Plessy v. Ferguson and Jim Crow legislation for separate but equal education was the story line. Her ignorance of the law and her ignorance of supposedly separate but equal education embarrassed her. After college, she never stopped reading, researching and writing about Plessy, later Thurgood Marshall and overturning Plessy with Brown v. Board of Education. Her play, *Overturn* with all the key players, chronicles the journey. It is two years of historical research and two years of writing. It is thorough, accurate and boring. It reads, even to her, like a history lecture.

So Margaret is on her way to Maine to connect with actors and a director, all doing summer stock somewhere along the southern Maine coast. She plans to schedule a workshop for *Overturn* and to rewrite it. Not discouraged, Margaret sees writing as process and believes in an improved play. She is determined to keep at it.

Keeping at it was not easy when it involved Maine and her family. Margaret fought for independence after college. She lived in a studio apartment in South Philadelphia, maintained her own finances and established herself as a writer. But in returning home, she was always weary of getting sucked back into the old ways, ways frozen in time. The trouble was she needed some of the old ways when she returned to Maine. For this visit, she needed a place to stay and a car. Fortunately, her parents were away on an early May golf holiday in the Carolinas. She had the keys to her father's SUV and the house was empty for the weekend.

During this trip, Margaret was scheduled to meet a director to view some rehearsal sites she lined up by email in Kennebunk and Ogunquit. She also needed to line up actors and digital recording equipment. Her hope was to set up dates to workshop the play and record at least one complete run-through sometime during the last two weeks in May. Then it was back to Philadelphia for the summer, rewrite *Overturn* and keep writing her current play, *Shadowcatchers*. She considered the holes in her plan as the plane landed.

With the lingering evening sun, Margaret had no trouble finding the backdoor key under an eve of the porch roof. Her leather sandals against the tile floor were the only sounds in the kitchen as she set down her carryon and opened the refrigerator, looking for nothing in particular but taking a bottled water. She glanced at the home phone out of habit and then to the photos on the door as it closed. Her eyes drifted to the granite-topped island in the center of the room. There was a note and what looked like a shoe box wrapped in brown paper sitting on the counter. Margaret read the block letters in two lines on the box. They were a mix of caps and small case, printed with childlike quality, names spelled correctly. "Margaret" was the first line and "Charlie Bay Burningwater" the second. The note alongside was from her mother.

"I'm off to meet your father at Hilton Head-please give me a call when you're settled in. Bud Walker dropped this package off for you. He's much better looking than I remember him when you were in school together. Maybe you should call him. Love, Mom".

Margaret mumbled, "Bud Walker was always good looking... Charlie Bay Burningwater...what's going on...?"

The box was light, well wrapped and tied with twine. She got a knife from the draw below, cut the tie and tore off the paper. It was a shoe box but an old one. Margaret didn't recognize the brand and growing up surrounded by retail, she knew shoes. Inside was a single audio cassette tape, standing upright and supported on all sides by crumpled white tissue paper. There was no note and no label on the cassette. Margaret was stunned. She hadn't seen or spoken to Charlie Bay in what had to be a dozen years. As Margaret tumbled the tape from hand to hand, she flashed back to sitting in Charlie Bay's lap and her view up onto his weathered chin speckled in white stubble. She thought about the high cheek bones that sheltered his squinting eyes and the brown stain filling the cracks of his worn teeth. He smelled like peanut brittle. She was amazed. This tape was from Charlie Bay Burningwater; the Storyteller.

"Where can I play it?" Talking to herself, "What am I supposed to do with this... it's a tape... what am I going to do with...tape?"

Margaret knew there was nothing in her room to play the cassette. At one point, her brother had a boom box that she remembered seeing stacked in the basement storage room. It had a tape player but she had no idea if the huge thing was still around or worked.

When she got to the storage room, it was apparent most of the boxes in there were hers. She saved everything. The first carton she saw was labeled "my so called high school life or something like it, #2 of 5." She was tempted to dive in but passed for another time. There was no boom box and she was on to the garage.

From time to time, her father was known to recycle old TVs, stereo consoles, any obsolete appliances, to his work shop in the third bay of the garage. The shop was separated from the rest of the inside space by a double sliding door. As Margaret slid one panel far enough to slip in and hit the light switch, she saw it, a 1983 red Cadillac Seville with a full Cabriolet roof. She forgot the fake convertible garaged for preservation. She forgot her father's pride and joy but, she did see the boom box.

Margaret checked the plug and hit the on button. AM talk radio was a good sign from the speakers but when she pressed play on the tape deck, the heads didn't move. She inserted the tape, selected the tape button and hit play again, nothing. Leaning back against the Seville she bumped the antenna. The Delco Bose Stereo Cassette was factory built into the Cadillac. He called it a must have option, "Just listen Margaret, just listen to this stereo!"

She did and she remembered the cassette player. It should work. She needed keys. They fell from the visor as she remembered again. Dean Martin singing *Volare'* came from all four bulging door speakers before she ejected the tape. He was consistent, "Dean Martin's Greatest Hits", long a favorite on record, tape and CD. She inserted the unmarked cassette and settled into the smooth leather driver's seat.

"It happened along the coast pretty far from here... a seal hunter in search of a wife..." Charlie Bay's voice was tentative and there was a pause. He cleared his throat and began again.

"He wasn't having any success... was restless and often long on the water...hunting harbor seals." Charlie Bay gained strength and volume.

"One day, hunting the ledges at Bass Island, he saw a beautiful woman standing on shore. He paddled closer, his heart taken, he knew this woman to be his wife. Her heart also captured... knew the hunter to be her husband."

Charlie Bay continued, his voice now with rhythm. "Following the custom of his people, the hunter wished to meet the family of his new wife... to give gifts in return for their daughter as his bride. But the hunter's wife said her family lived far from his village. She asked him to be patient and promised one day she would take him there.

Many days past until...it was time. She told her husband with the coming morning they would travel to her family. At sunrise, the two paddled their canoes back to the ledges at Bass Island. Once on the rocky shore she asked her husband to dive three times into the waves. The hunter obeyed and dove...one...two...and on the third surfaced, not as the hunter, but as a harbor seal. Then the hunter's wife dove three times into the waves and she too surfaced as a harbor seal... together... they swam to her family.

When they arrived at her seal herd, she was quick to find her father, a seal chief. He was pleased to see such a fine husband for his daughter and asked that they spend their remaining days as harbor seals."

Charlie Bay chuckled, his voice livened. *"The hunter did not want to live his life as a harbor seal! He wanted to return to his village...as a human being...as a hunter!*

She again asked her husband to be patient and appeased her father by suggesting a contest to determine their fate. The chief, confident of the outcome in his favor, agreed to his daughter's proposal. They could return to the hunter's village if her husband swam faster than the fastest seal bull in the herd. The hunter had never raced a seal and sought his wife's counsel. She told him to use the tide and the waves to his advantage, never to swim against the current or into the surf. He should allow the ocean to carry him whenever it was willing. Always remember, seal bulls are stubborn and proud...they will swim into anything, even if it slows them down. Following his wife's advice the hunter easily out swam the fastest seal. For now...the seal chief had to accept his loss. He bid farewell to his daughter and her husband...hoping that they might reappear someday to stay with him for good."

Charlie Bay's voice had grown hoarse. There was a pause. Margaret thought she heard a clink. She recalled the sound; glass colliding with the blackened pipe ashtray that sat beside the storyteller's chair. Seconds later, she listened to a metal cap twist off the bottle. A few gurgles and the burp confirmed it. She was annoyed with the interruption. Another few gurgles and Charlie Bay continued.

"Returning to the ledges at Bass Island, they dove into the waves three times. Back to human form, she asked her husband to tell no one of their journey. In the days that followed, the love between them grew. Soon they shared their lives with a son.

Through the coming years, the hunter provided meat and skins for his people. But...there was a grandmother in his village who was very suspicious about how well he knew the heart of the harbor seal. She often told him that there was more to his hunting success than he let on. Of course...she did eat well, food was plentiful and life was good.

Over time...Mother Earth changed. The ocean darkened and the bait fish disappeared. Where the hunter and his people had known harbor seals, they found only crabs and snails. Without seals came hunger. Now more than ever, the people depended on him for food. Seals were nowhere to be found. The hunter told no one, but he knew without seals starvation was near. He hunted long and far.

On one such trip...while the hunter was away, his son and the other children of the village were playing in the surf, acting out the seal hunt... some pretended to be hunters, others the seals. The hunter's son played the seal, dove three times in the waves and without warning surfaced as a harbor seal. Nearby, his mother saw this change from human form to seal, ran after him, and dove three times into the waves to join him as a harbor seal. Mother and pup swam side by side back to the ledges at Bass Island... all this did not escape a watchful eye of the suspicious grandmother.

When they arrived at the ledges of Bass Island mother and pup rested in the sun. Searching the very same ledges, the hunter caught sight of two harbor seals on the rocks ... his heart soared like an eagle. The hunter paddled hard toward the seals... at water's edge...they faced his deadly harpoon...

Heading home, he was proud and happy... these seals would feed his people. When everyone saw the hunter's canoe towing harbor seals, the village celebrated. Wanting to share with all, the hunter kept only a small portion for himself and his family. As he searched for them in the excitement of the feast, he saw only the suspicious grandmother waiting to tell him what she had seen. He heard the tale and a loud cry leapt from deep in his heart...he knew..." Again Charlie Bay's voice grew weak. "...a loud cry leapt from deep in his heart...he knew he had taken his wife and son...in heartache he left the village and paddled his canoe to open ocean until he could paddle no more."

Hearing the sound of his deep breathing, raspy throat and the click of his recorder, Margaret pressed stop. She needed a break. The voice was a little thinner but the words were without hesitation. She sighed, looked around the interior of the car and let her head fall back to the red leather rest of the driver's seat. Margaret stretched out her right arm without moving her body and held her finger on the chrome play button. She closed her eyes before she pressed it.

"After days of drifting, unaware of the world around him, the hunter washed up onto a shoal. He was tired, thirsty and thought it was a dream. He saw an old woman standing on the rocks. He went before her lost and told his story. As the old woman listened, she grew restless with the hunter's self-pity. When he finished, she scolded him for believing that it was he who brought food to the village. She reminded him that by diving three times into the waves his wife and son could've turned ... *back to his loved ones!* The old woman pointed a finger in his face and told him that he was a captive of his own sorrow and not thinking clearly about what had been given.

Humbled by the old woman's tongue, the hunter asked what he could do that his wife and son might live. The old woman told him to return to the seal chief and he would direct his future. So the hunter dove three times into the waves and swam to the herd.

The chief greeted his son by saying he understood from a dream the hunter had spoken to the Old Woman of the Shoals. He told the hunter that in order to act in the favor of his loved ones, he must return to his people and gather the bones of his wife and son...the bones must be brought to the ledges at Bass Island... be covered in seaweed on a rising tide. The chief warned that if the bones had been burned or broken...then all hope was lost ...the hunter was to spend the rest of his days alone. But even if he did as asked, there was one condition for his wife and son to live again...the hunter must come back to the herd and spend his remaining days as a harbor seal.

The hunter swam back to the surf near his village, dove three times into the waves and surfaced as a human. He searched everywhere for their bones...no bones to be found...none...his heart ached.

Preparing to spend his remaining days without his wife and son in heartache, he gave away what little he had and readied his canoe to drift on the tide...go wherever it may take him. But, just before he was to leave...the suspicious grandmother told him that the Old Woman of the Shoals came to her in a dream. She asked her to gather the bones of the hunter's wife and son before they were burned or broken and hide them. Old Woman of Shoals had a sharp tongue and the grandmother did as she was told...gathered the bones.

Ha! The hunter's heart soared like an eagle! He bundled the bones and returned to the ledges at Bass Island... covering them with seaweed on an incoming tide.

The hunter spent the next two days watching from his canoe... hoping to catch one last glimpse of his wife and son as human beings. It never came. He knew that for the circle to be complete he must fulfill the conditions of the seal chief. He dove three times into the waves and surfaced as a harbor seal... swimming for the herd to spend his remaining days.

When he arrived, the seal chief reminded the hunter that he had always hoped to have him live as a seal.

"It is the call of harbor seals...your call...to provide food and clothing for the Nations...my son, as a harbor seal, it is good to have a growing heart and not one stopped by heartache...

... to have a growing heart, you must choose your place on Earth and once chosen, hold what is yours... this doesn't often take the form one might expect."

Turning to the East, the seal chief looked toward his daughter as she slid from a ledge into the water, son by her side.

And so it was, the hunter, wife and son spent their remaining days on this Earth in a proud and noble manner."

Charlie Bay laughed, "Storytellers know many legends my child, and are always eager to tell one."

To the hum of the tape player Margaret wondered why after all these years Charlie Bay Burningwater sent her this story. There was no note, no explanation. "Heartache of the Hunter" was her favorite. After listening to it two more times, she took the tape up to her old room and tucked it in her nightstand drawer under some expired Bloomingdales' coupons.

When Margaret's head hit the pillow, she was tired

but her mind occupied by Burningwater, Long Neck Island and Molly, the woman who brought her there.

"Let's ride to Charlie Bay's ocean!" was Molly's call. Together, in the huge old American car with ash trays everywhere and push button everything, they rolled to Long Neck Island. With every window down and Molly's long salt and pepper hair dancing in the breeze, the two of them headed across the marsh for Charlie Bay's as the rest of the world melted away.

Margaret fought sleep with images of Molly tapping the wheel and staring over the dash as the blue Mercury rumbled its way toward three mounds in the middle of the marshland. She remembered crossing the narrow railroad tie bridge, turning up the sandy road and passing the blueberry patch to park just shy of Charlie Bay's backdoor. From the age of about seven, for five or six years, Margaret rode at Molly's side to Burningwater's Island.

The recollection of days spent with Charlie Bay brought her mind's eye to the Casco Point beach at half tide and her never ending search for star fish. Near sleep, Margaret was there; feeling the sun, hearing the waves and seeing the fixed silhouette of Molly staring to open ocean. Visit after visit, she and Burningwater waited without measure in Charlie Bay's beached dory for Molly's ocean time to pass. Nestled between the high walls of the dory's bow and dosing in a bed of salty orange life jackets, time and again, Margaret listened to the Storyteller's "Heartache of the Hunter".

She took a deep breath, slid further under her blankets and considered the smell of Charlie Bay's pipe tobacco, the small pieces of peanut brittle that collected on flaps of his shirt pockets and the feel of curling deep into the Storyteller's lap to sleep.

Margaret knew Harry, now directing, better than most of the men in her life. They became friends in college and worked as interns together on Broadway shortly after graduating. Harry was a director's assistant on the revival of a tried and true musical and Margaret was on the second run of August Wilson's *Fences*. Harry had a title, Margaret, a much better play. Wilson's cycle of works about African Americans in his home town of Pittsburgh was inspiration for her. The chance to hear *Fences* performed every day, she considered an extraordinary gift. It was because of August Wilson that Margaret wrote any time she wasn't doing any job asked. Harry networked all of the time.

On Saturday, Margaret was the beneficiary of Harry's extensive contacts. She found excellent rehearsal space and met old friends and understudies willing to workshop her play. Harry connected her with free tech support and a condo to house sit at the end of May for as long as she needed it. He would do anything for her and down the road he wanted one of her plays. They both would know when and which one.

Margaret had the feeling Harry had already passed on *Overturn* by his persistent questioning about *Shadowcatchers*. He was glad she shelved the first draft of her adaptation for the stage of Dee Brown's *Bury My*

Heart at Wounded Knee. Despite her passion for injustice, the history of Native American genocide became so heart wrenching, even she thought it was too much too soon. In the meantime, a nineteenth century love affair between a female photographer and an older publisher eager to work with glass plate techniques kept Harry interested. The irony with the project was Margaret's uncertainty about love. She had fallen in love but wondered if she had ever been in love. When she was unsettled with love, *Shadowcatchers* stalled. It was presently stalled. But today, *Overturn*, thanks to Harry, was moving with a lot fewer holes in the plan.

Driving back to her parent's home, reviewing it all, she was ambivalent about the day's successes and it surprised her. Charlie Bay's hold on her with "Heartache of the Hunter" did not. The new plan was to change her flight from Sunday to Monday and find Burningwater.

Chapter Two

It wasn't Molly's big Mercury that turned onto the dirt road next to the abandoned railroad tracks, but with the windows down, the saltwater marshland smelled the same to Margaret. As the SUV bounced in and out of the sand ruts on the only route to Long Neck Island, she was forced to slow down and appreciate the contrast of the pale blue sky against the brown sea grass in the May sun. Margaret was happy returning to this huge, flat open space. Acre after acre spread in front of her until the corner of her eyes caught the marsh blending with the woodlands to the west and the tidal Casco River melting with the ocean to the east. All the while, straight ahead and due north rose the island home of Charlie Bay Burningwater. Her heart was pounding.

Charlie Bay lived on the ocean side of three mounds known collectively as Long Neck Island. They were elliptically shaped patches of farmland that ran from east to west across the marsh. Each eighty acre plot, joined by two causeways, was part of the Casco Indian Reservation's northern third. The whole reservation, including a landfill to the west along Rt. 1 was dominated by about three thousand acres of sand flats and marshlands. The middle third of the territory was comprised of the sea grass islets and marshes that shored the Casco River. The southern third was a series of sandbars and clam beds. At low tide, mile after mile of corrugated sand and at high tide, a ten foot bay of saltwater poised to turn and rush back to the ocean. This was a federally recognized Indian Reservation and land which at the end of the 1960's, nobody wanted. It was the last remnant of the traditional homeland of the Casco Nation.

At the beginning of the nineteenth century about eight thousand acres of woodland to the north was also Casco land. The tribe's main settlement bordered the Casco River to the south and was the center of fishing activity for the Casco people. In more recent generations, Charlie Bay's family drifted from the village on the mainland to occupy the three mounds of Long Neck. For a good part of the 1800's his grandfathers shared with other members of the Casco tribe in the resources provided by sea and marshlands. At the turn of the twentieth century, thousands of acres, once home to the Casco Nation, were parts of two small Maine towns and all of a State Park.

The bumpy road seemed to go on forever before Margaret approached the narrow bridge crossing the Casco River. Easing the SUV up to the succession of rail ties that formed its surface, she glanced down over the edge into the rushing out-going tide. Margaret held her breath, aimed the truck to the center of the bridge, skipped a second look at the churning current and headed for the other side. Once on solid ground, she turned east up the hill to Charlie Bay's and exhaled.

The grass in the center of the winding road to his home was a brown stripe bordered by white sand tire paths. The truck surged side to side as she made the climb. To Margaret, the road and the island appeared so much the same, so unchanged. She drove past the collapsed walls of the hay barn and beyond was the single, loan-standing chimney, anchored to the fireplace by its beach stone mantel, beauty intact. She never saw the farmhouse but heard the story of the fire many times. The sharp and straight vertical line of the chimney cut the sky to the hill crest and to Charlie Bay's. After parking the truck on the near side of the house, Margaret shut off the engine and listened to the distant muffled rhythm of rolling waves. As she opened the truck door and looked back to the west, the marshland unfolded almost at her feet. It was different, very different. Her memory held the image of large sandy white patches strung together by narrow blue waterways. The white islets of her past, produced by years of dredging, were now completely overgrown with sea grass. The tiny meandering streaks of blue had also disappeared, leaving only an enormous stretch of golden brown marshland, bordered on each side by the North and South branches of the Casco River. The straight running ribbons of blue pooled at the western end of Long Neck Island. A view that Margaret remembered as a maze of sand and grass, scratched with estuaries, now ran before her as a solid swath of land straight to Rt1. She considered the difference until she felt the east wind, moist and cold, off the water.

Margaret didn't head up the steps to the backdoor of Charlie Bay's home. Through force of an old habit, she passed the plum rose bushes and walked around the south side to the front porch. She climbed the stairs, pushed the wooden screen door and eased inside. The brown wicker furniture and the high back rocker were exactly the same. Margaret remembered musty cushions, Charlie Bay rocking, puffing his pipe, dull thumping sound of wood on wood, rickety rocker to rickety floor, salt air and pipe smoke.

As Margaret moved to knock, she noticed the shade was up on the front door window. Peering inside, she saw Charlie Bay's home unaltered in time. The center staircase was dark and bare with a small braided rug at its base. To the left of the stairs, an end table topped with Charlie Bay's pipe ashtray was just arms length from his stuffed chair, stained and worn. Shifting to the right, she scanned past the oak rocker next to the fireplace and on to the blue sofa. She froze. It wasn't a full view but it was enough; the pile of work clothes on the floor, the pint gin bottle next to the clothes and the naked wrinkled bronze body next to both. She remembered; Charlie Bay slept when he was tired, where he was tired and without clothes.

Margaret first heard the clicking spring cushions and then the shuffling footsteps on the hardwood floor. In an instant, a naked torso flashed across the window. No sooner than the unclothed form passed in front of her, it reappeared, headed in the opposite direction. Without warning, once again, a bare Charlie Bay dashed by the door. This time, he was carrying pants.

Just seconds after disappearing from sight, Charlie Bay reappeared, wearing baggy khaki work pants, without a belt or shirt. He opened the door slowly. Only his left arm moved. He was locked on Margaret's face. Recognizing her large dark eyes and auburn hair, Charlie Bay knew exactly who stood before him. In a soft hoarse voice, he was the first to speak "I'm a little slower than I used to be ... you know...the pants." Without changing his expression he continued, "I, ah, I...."

Thinking he had no idea who this was at his front door, other than someone who had just seen him dash naked across his living room, Margaret reached to say something, anything to break the moment. "I...I'm older. It's me Margaret, Margaret Garret...sorry I should've knocked."

"I know...it is you." Charley Bay responded not caring if she knocked, still focused on her eyes. "Come in." He opened the door a little further and turned toward the clothes that remained scattered on the floor. As Margaret stepped into the house she immediately noticed the skin on his bare back was scarred. The scars ran from the base of his left ear, at an angle across his neck, to just below his right shoulder blade. From there the light and irregular skin covered his back, only to disappear at the waist of his pants. Charlie Bay bent over, picked up his shirt and faced Margaret to expose additional scars on his arms and the left side of his stomach. Hesitating for a second, he saw her stare, "My legs also got burned...too."

Margaret didn't remember the scars. Charley Bay didn't want to lose her. He did what he did best; he told the story.

"When I was about twelve...I was named Seal Swimmer. The name came in the summer while I was working as a tailman...a lobsterman's helper."

Continuing to talk, Charlie Bay put on and buttoned his shirt. The buttons and holes weren't matched and he only tucked in the front. Unaffected by the mismatch, Charlie Bay motioned for her to sit in the rocker as he eased into his stuffed chair.

His voice had the same rhythm and tone as on the tape, raspy at first, then stronger. She slid into the rocker.

"It was a hot day in August...not a breath of air. Looking back on it, ol' Abe Jordan was a little hung-over... never spoke much anyway. But on this day, he didn't say a word. At around mid-morning, with no wind and no current...he just went below and to sleep. I sat on the fantail of his thirty foot Friendship sloop...beautiful boat...we drifted in the sun for awhile...until I got so boiling hot that I finally decided to strip down and jump into the biggest, coolest swell I could find. When I popped my head up out of the water and opened my eyes... about fifteen feet away, a harbor seal had come up with me. We just floated there...face to face for a few seconds until without so much as a ripple...the seal slipped back under water. I put my face into the water, opened my eyes...floated dead man's style...watched that seal swim right under me...big dark eyes, watching me, watching him. When I came up for air there was two or three more of them...right there in front of me. As soon as I'd dead man float...they would cross underneath me...but an arm's length away. And when they would pass...their big round eyes rolled right back to the top of their brow without a blink. Before I knew it, I was surrounded by harbor seals. At my next breath I found myself in the center of a circle of seals...each focused on this scrawny naked little human being...not of their world...giggling in boy's pitch...no fat to keep from shivering and treading water...working hard to stay afloat. I have often thought of how curious a being I must've been to them."

Charlie Bay paused and considered the event, distant from Margaret. Catching his own drift, he cleared his throat, looked at his gin bottle and chuckled, "Well it didn't last for long...Abe came topside...called me Seal Swimmer and mumbled about getting back to work. The seals were gone in a heartbeat but I was called Seal Swimmer...'til the fire."

Margaret was puzzled by Charlie Bay's reference to the fire. Recalling the fire story, there was never a mention of him burned or injured when flames took his uncle's farmhouse to the ground. She watched as Charlie Bay settled deeper into the Storyteller's chair for another go-a-round. She had never heard this one.

"At that time...I was working my own boat...bought from Abe's brother, Sparky Jordan. He was given the name because he installed engines in fishing boats. It was sunrise...just a few boats had left the harbor. There was no air...quiet. I was starting to salt bait...make room for more red fish...I brought'm with me in the skiff. I figured I'd let her warm up a bit...pushed the starter. Out of nowhere...I heard a thundering boom. My ears blocked. The bones of my legs got jolted and the cold... cold water was all I felt around me. When I finally came to the surface everything was burning...including me. I was surrounded by flames...couldn't see a thing 'cept up. When the fire got close...I'd duck under...look through the water for sky then pop up again for air...trying to find a way out. They say I was among the burning water as it moved with the current...the whole length of the harbor. I don't remember being pulled into a skiff by my Uncle William, but when they finally reached me, I was laying on my back...my stomach burning...gasping for air. It was right then and there...my Uncle William changed my name."

Looking at the gin bottle, Charlie Bay squinted to see how much was left. He looked back to Margaret knowing two quick stories had broken the passage of time. Grinning, he rolled open the palms of his hands with a warm welcome expression. It was a reception that she knew well. He looked to her eyes, "Bay Burningwater to this very day. Charlie was added a little later...as a first name for the American folks...outside the Casco...make it easier for the locals to call me an American name...don't know where it came from."

She smiled. After a moment, Margaret leaned forward in the rocker, curious about the fire but even more curious about the tape.

"Why did you send me "Heartache of the Hunter"?"

Charlie Bay continued to grin. He appreciated her directness. He was happy she came.

"I can't write. But...I heard you do...heard you were good at it.

I need a writer...you're from university. You know university people...how they write back and forth."

The words, "I can't write", came from his mouth with a matter of fact quality that expressed no guilt or shame; he simply stated a just reason for a common sense way to meet his need. In her everyday world of e-mail, texting, blogging and all the others, the ability to write was never a question. She glanced toward the small oak table next to Charlie Bay's chair. Not a book, magazine or newspaper was in sight. There wasn't and, in her recollection, there never had been a lamp in that corner of the room. Charlie Bay followed her response.

"Can't read either...but I can print my name. Bud helped me with yours."

She sat back in the rocker.

"I don't have a telephone...address. I don't have a driver's license or a mail box."

The list of don'ts and didn'ts progressed through all of the state and federal institutions he knew. He made his point by ending with, "...in the American world, I don't exist."

But practicals aside, she sensed that there was another reason he sent her "Heartache". For his part, he was aware his choice to send her favorite story was more than a charming use of an electronic device in an old storyteller's attempt to reconnect with a relationship of his past. But for now, in his own way, he chose to be blunt and pragmatic.

"And I need your help with the university Americans."

Margaret whispered, "university Americans".

Without speaking, he stood up, walked to the staircase and climbed the stairs. She watched his bare feet shuffle against the oak steps and his left hand slide along the rail. For a few moments after he left the room Margaret didn't move. She considered his phrase, "university Americans" and reached to dictate into her cell. She stopped; no need.

When he returned, Charlie Bay was carrying a small wooden Clementine crate containing an unopened box with a picture of a portable radio on the outside and a pair of binoculars without a case. The printing on the side of the wooden crate was faded but the orange stencil of the fruit was clear. Sitting back in his chair, he set the box gently across his knees.

"Years ago, as I became a young man, the mound of Long Neck Island closest to the setting sun was called the western door."

Hesitating for just an instant, Charlie Bay glanced at the pint gin bottle and then returned to her face.

"The western door is the burial ground of my people. For as long as I can remember, a grandfather, one who kept the dead, would bring me with him whenever he traveled to tend this place. As my grandfathers died, on a certain day, I became one who kept the dead." He paused, his voice cracked, "The circle of the dead has been broken." Then in words never spoken, "I am the one who broke the circle."

Charlie Bay dropped his head in shame. Burdened by guilt built over decades, he sat slumped and motionless. Margaret was lost.

"What do you mean? What happened?"

Feeling some relief in finally speaking the words, Charlie Bay raised his head, took a deep breath and began another story.

"The marsh...sand flats, the tidal water...all are beautiful places...rich and fertile places. They had been so for many generations. Two generations ago these places were thought to be useless...just places to dump waste from factories...from humans. Places to bury old cars and oil drums, to leave old boats and barges...to rust and bleed into the river...until they were no more. The fish left, the birds left, the clam beds closed and the marsh became like it was thought to be...useless. All that remained was the harbor in the Casco River...but it was filling up with sand and mud and the boats of summer people. Some of the people...people who make decisions about these things, decided to dredge the river to make the harbor better for the summer people...for the fisherman. The marshland to the west and the north, the homeland of the Casco Nation, was the chosen place to dump the mud and the sand."

Margaret hung on each word.

"Decisions were made by American men and money. It was no good then."

Charlie Bay's explanation touched her passion for injustice. She was right where he expected her to be.

"The dredging piped all the sand and mud that they sucked up from the bottom of the river and harbor...pumped it...took it to the western end of the marsh, filled it all in to make land along Rt.1...where the golf is?"

She knew the area and businesses along the highway and nodded.

"That's where they began dumping everything and from there...they worked their way east, back toward the island. The western door of Long Neck Island used to be shaped like the tip of a harpoon...with prongs sticking out on each side and waterways and eddies running on both sides like this."

Balancing the Clementine crate on his thighs, Charlie Bay held up his hands before his face. With arms outstretched, he spread his fingers apart, palms toward her and touched his index finger tips together but not his thumbs. Peering through the opening, Margaret saw the pronged shape he formed.

"After about eight months of filling up the marsh the engineers and the dredgers said that to hold the sand and keep the water away, all of these little rivers must be made into one river with branches from the north and south and the western door reshaped like this."

Bringing his fingers together, he tucked his thumbs over against his palms. This altered the shape to a narrow wedge and formed the western tip of the island as she saw it today.

"When they widened the channel on the north and south by cutting into the western door...the bones of my ancestors were torn from the earth. After the very first morning of digging and dredging, there were pieces of Casco people sprinkling the sand...burping up from the ground. They stopped only long enough for university Americans to come. Then the scrapping and probing began, by groups with shovels...picks...brushes. But it was digging all the same...like dogs scratching in the dirt for the bones of my grandfathers. It happened very fast, the tents...the bags...the boxes of bones...papers and the promises to return everything to this place, their rightful place...with their people.

But that's not what happened. The work that was to put the bones in proper order...make a record for my people passed from months to years. More promises came with gifts and more letters with promises.

The circle of the dead has been broken. Too much time has passed...I no longer trust any of them. Theirs is not my world. And that's why I need your help. You are of university. You know them. You are a writer."

In formal fashion, Charlie Bay stood up, walked over to Margaret and handed her the Clementine crate. In it she saw an unopened portable weather radio, out of date, binoculars, unused and some sheets of stationary with the letterhead of the Anthropology Department for the State University. Removing the letters from the bottom of the box, she skimmed their contents. One came with the gift of the weather radio. The patronizing tone annoyed her. She searched through more pages for the name of the individual in charge of the Casco field research and found it. The head of the excavation project was Dr. Sandra Walsh. Without returning to his seat, Charlie Bay stood straight, his pants sagged and he followed her survey of the papers. As she lifted her head, he spoke, "Walsh, she's the university American you want...Walsh."

Margaret had no sense of how difficult, complex or political the request was from Charlie Bay. All she had was an instinctual urge to leap, to do whatever he asked. But, she was aware that the distance between where she was as a playwright and what he needed, an attorney, was a big gap. The big gap didn't stop her from saying yes.

Less tense, Charlie Bay eased back in his chair, mindful of his urgency and her hesitancy. He became cautious. At least for today, he was not going further. He didn't say a word to her about his spirit dream.

"I was chosen by my grandfathers to keep the dead of my people...I lost sight of my gift and let it slip away."

He let his hands rest on his thighs, body still. They considered one another for a few moments in silence.

Charlie Bay was the first to move. He slapped his knees in unison, leaned forward and stood. As his back straightened, there was first a crack and then a moan. Gesturing for Margaret to set the crate on the floor and at the same time jerking his head toward the back door, he motioned for her to follow. On the back porch, he slipped his bare feet into his shin high clamming boots, hobbled out the door and down the back steps with Margaret in tow. The fresh salt air felt good to both of them and was quick to renew conversation.

"How did you make the tape?"

"Bud Walker."

Margaret smiled. "He dropped the box off at my parent's house."

"You know, he graduated high school with you. He works on the fish pier at the Co-op and fishes. He sure remembers you...it's your figure he remembers anyway ...because I could tell by the smile on his face...the glint in his eyes. He was right, you turned out pretty good."

Charlie Bay mumbled to himself about sex and love.

"He also let me borrow the tape recorder... gave it to me really. He said he didn't use it anymore. Learning which button did what wasn't easy. I almost gave the damn thing back to him or the ocean...but, I got use to it...buttons ...batteries..."

As they walked past the south side of the house, out onto the bluff at the end of the island, Casco Point and the open ocean stretched eastward. Charley Bay removed his pipe and tobacco pouch from his breast pocket. Before packing the bowl he reflexively offered small pinches of tobacco to the four directions, then to the sky and to the earth while whispering an inaudible prayer. The ground leaves were carried on the wind. Studying him, Margaret saw a spiritual side she knew but didn't remember. Uneasy with her focus on his movements, he turned away and into the wind.

"The wind's 'bout to shift southwest...third day in a row... pretty early for May. If this holds the water will warm...the lobsters will be running on shore a week or two sooner come the end of July."

It wasn't often that Charlie Bay made conversation about the weather. Margaret wanted to talk but, not about the weather. She eased off. Facing east and both squinting into the horizon's reflected light, they made their way down separate paths onto the rocky beach.

As the eastern tip of Long Neck Island narrowed, it seemed the focal point in every view was a large solitary boulder. It was a waist high, arm wide rock with a concaved top among less than foot size sea worn flakes of slate and granite. Misplaced, unmatched and just barely licked by the ocean during storm surges, it was the bow pulpit of the island. It was where Molly spent hour upon hour, still and staring seaward. Both their thoughts recalled her silhouette against the water.

"How's she doing? ...haven't seen her in a long while."

Margaret was surprised Charlie Bay hadn't seen Molly. She turned to his face. He had his pipe clenched between his teeth, the same spot as always, notched and brown.

"I'm not sure. It's been a long time...saw her only a few times before high school...none since then."

"Hmmm", Charlie Bay murmured and let it drop.

A few moments later, they turned away from the Point and walked along the northern shore of the island, side by side, slices of sun and puffs of wind, now at their back. As they left the sea worn stones behind and meandered onto a sand-covered beach Charlie Bay spoke.

"For years, when I would walk along this beach...the sand flats too, I found those damn yellow golf balls from the driving golf. I'd dig them up all over the bars...never picked 'em up...after awhile I got used to it. Never liked it...but got used to it." He spoke with a troubled voice. "You see the ocean doesn't care. She is an indifferent being who will pick up and drop off on the tide. It used to be golf balls. Now...it is the bones of my people."

She stopped walking, so did Charlie Bay one step later.

"At the beginning of last month, while I was digging on the bar...I uncovered the skull of one who came before. I pierced the bone with my hoe...I broke it more ...than it had already been broken.

The dead from the western burial ground are once more burping up from their earth...this time from cutting tide waters instead of scratching people. I can never accept ...either the ocean or the university Americans... scattering the bones of my grandfathers. They're both too indifferent beings." He took a deep angry breath. "I've taken the bones that I found...moved them to a new place. I pray that it will be a safe place for all those who are to be returned to it. Now you and I must gather the missing...make sure that they are reburied."

Dignity and determination continued in his gate as they walked the shore line up to his fishing shack.

The shack was set on a small dock and work platform a few feet off the sand. It was scattered with barrels, stacks of wooden lobster traps and red and blue buoys. Next to the work dock was his beached dory. Its' light tan hull and red bottom were as she remembered. Entering a path marked by a large tree stump that served as the anchor for the dory, they made the steep inland climb, back toward the house in single file. Margaret let Charlie Bay walk ahead. A short distance later, she caught him standing on a small rise near some blueberry bushes and looking west. It was a beautiful place.

"This is it."

There was no response from Charlie Bay.

"I'll help you Charlie Bay...I'll help you get the remains of your people back here...back here to the island."

Charlie Bay dipped his chin and squinted without a word.

Instead of heading back to Rt. 1 and her parent's home, Margaret found Rt. 9 and wound her way to the fishermen's Co-op on the Casco River. She parked in the town lot and walked the half mile through the dunes to a public beach and open ocean. Rewriting *Overturn* had somehow fallen from the top spot on her list of summer priorities. She wasn't sure why. Sitting on the cool sand, she considered Charlie Bay. She said yes to his request but she wasn't sure what yes meant. She watched the water. Charlie Bay was in the one spot.

That evening Margaret returned to her parent's home by default. She had expected to be on an early Sunday afternoon flight and taking a Bistro evening shift. Because of Charlie Bay, with a couple of rescheduling calls, she was out on the 8:05 in the morning and tonight crossing paths with her parents.

During the Philly years and on her own, she learned that her ability to dive into a situation on instinct alone took its emotional toll; generally fatigue and collapse. Charlie Bay Burningwater exhausted her. Having no idea of how or why, she took the physical drain as an outward sign of an internal bull's eye. Her capacity to integrate was on overload and sleep was her answer.

Passing the refrigerator in the kitchen, Margaret remembered her parents planned to return in time for her mother's monthly Sunday night dinner date with friends from the nail salon. "Nail Gossip" was the notation written on the calendar stuck with a banana magnet to the freezer door. She assumed that her mother wasn't home, decided to leave on the microwave night light and shuffled toward the staircase.

As she approached the top of the steps, she saw the light in the hallway shining from the half open door of her father's study and heard the hum of his computer. Listening for the keyboard, she wondered if with luck, he was out networking at his golf club. He called them "Moose Hunts" and they usually coincided with "Nail Gossip". Tonight, she wasn't in the mood to be interrogated. She moved into the hall and found the gatekeeper at his post.

"Hey Margaret, how are you doing?"

Her head dropped, just what she hoped to avoid. But, it was still good to see him and she resigned herself to the inevitable. The thought that she was twenty-five and entitled to some measure of adult equality was her hope. She pushed open the six-panel door and peered inside, her father already moving to the doorway. Margaret stepped into the room. They hugged and with her chin on her father's shoulder, she looked around his space. It hadn't changed for years.

A large antique oak desk and leatherback swivel chair faced the door. Next to the desk was a tall oak bookcase filled with file folders, binders and portfolios. There was not a hard cover, paperback or magazine anywhere in the room. On the floor was a red Oriental rug with one of its corners fixed by a leather chair and a brass floor lamp. A half dozen or so manila folders were strune at the circular base of the lamp. This room always made Margaret uneasy. It was not neutral territory. It was not the kitchen table and her mother was nowhere to be found. Her father kissed her cheek.

Jim Garret, a stocky man, with jet-black hair, drifted back to the swivel chair and pointed to his computer, "Brand new laptop...not perfect but it's the best on the market...wireless with the fiber optic cable in downstairs....plus it's got that where...wherever card...you know. The thing runs like a rocket ship."

She smiled, expecting nothing less of her father than a rocket ship.

Jim Garret had a physical presence exuding strength and energy. His outstanding business instincts kept him where he enjoyed it most, behind the scenes, watching and building. And within this strategy of quiet construction regardless of the venture, he never exceeded the bounds of simply buying the best and routinely updating ahead of the competition.

Wondering out loud, "What happened to your old laptop?" were the first tired words that tumbled from Margaret.

"Donated to St. Mary's school...same as every year... why, are you looking for a new one?" He didn't wait for a response. "Because you're due..I could order online for you and have it sent down to Philadelphia. I think it's about time for a new one...yours has got to be almost two years old."

Again, she smiled at his words, words which always indicated an eagerness to solve a problem, to buy something, to do something, to go somewhere and in a heartbeat make everything better for one of his children. She shook her head no.

Without hesitation or any indication of disappointment, Jim reached down behind his chair next to the bookcase and picked up a plastic shopping bag from the floor. "I got this today...for you...if you're around this summer." As he spoke, he removed a top of the line GPS from the package. "The truck is a little old and the only vehicle without a GPS...I thought for travel it should have one. It has all the location features and if you end up commuting to the State House Offices...." He was uncomfortable and his words trailed off, knowing the plans were still undecided. "I downloaded the satellite info and had the adapter put in the truck...it's all set to go...you just have to plug it in." Reaching over his desk, he handed her the box. Margaret didn't have the heart to tell him she had voice activated GPS on her phone. So, she stepped up to the desk, took the gift to make him happy and understood it required her to talk. Questions were to follow.

"So what did you do today? You stayed the extra day." was his first, a subtle start for him.

Margaret was waking up. "I drove out to Long Neck to visit Charlie Bay Burningwater."

Taken aback, Jim left the thought of directing the conversation to Margaret spending the summer on a law school resume builder. Despite calmness, he was annoyed.

"Charlie Burningwater? Why did you go to see him?" Jim shook his head. "What in the world would you have to talk about with him?"

Within the ambiguities in the taxonomy of sin, Margaret was always very clear on this one; the Sin of Omission. GPS or not, she had no intention of telling him much about anything.

"It had been so long since I'd seen the ocean...I thought I should. I ended up at the Casco River Co-op so

I drove over to the island...saw Charlie Bay. He and I talked for a while...a little about the old days when I was a kid...visiting him. He asked about Molly...how she was doing?" She hesitated, "Where is Molly...what ever happened to her?"

For days Jim Garret had been having this conversation in his mind hoping he would see his daughter. For days he had been planning how to get her permission, to make the one phone call it was going to take to place her with the Governor's legal team, boost her resume and focus her career goals on law. Being a playwright was all well and good but, for Jim Garret, his daughter needed a profession. In his scenario, this was a key meeting. Now, it was a conversation headed in a direction he never could have anticipated. Now, he wasn't prepared. But most of all, with the mention of Charlie Bay Burningwater, he wasn't happy.

Walking around to the front of his desk and motioning for his daughter to sit down, he leaned the back of his thighs against the oak edge and folded his arms across his chest as she sat in the winged back chair. His voice was soft, serious and loaded with emotion, "First of all, you need some background on Charlie Burningwater...he's one of a long list of people that Molly cared for...who misused her kindness. Molly was like that...she tried to help a lot of people like Burningwater...people who were just lost souls. She always seemed to attract them...people she felt needed her. She built a social circle of these kinds of people; all these lost souls...Charlie Burningwater is a manipulative drunk who only took from Molly and never gave to her in return."

Jim paused. Margaret didn't see such anger in his eyes very often.

"When your mother and I found out Molly was taking you on her trips to see these folks...ah, when she was taking you to see Burningwater...when we thought she was taking you to the ocean...well, that's when she stopped taking care of you. That's when we hired someone new." Jim Garret was also familiar with the Sin of Omission.

"But what happened to her?"

Accustomed to her unrelenting tone, Jim stood still and silent. He had lost. He wanted to leave without saying more but it wasn't possible. It was time.

"Margaret, Molly was a sick women...depressed... confused. She became one of her own. She was broke, on and off medication...alcohol and in and out of the hospital. Finally I had her placed in a psychiatric hospital in Bangor."

"You had her placed...what does placed mean...you had her commit...?"

Jim, interrupted, "I had to...she stopped eating. Stop talking...she wouldn't get out of bed." After pausing, he spoke softly, "She passed during your last year of college". His eyes looked to the floor.

"What? She died over four years ago and I never knew?" Her father didn't respond. "How come you didn't tell me Molly was...dead?"

Waiting for her to finish, he answered in a low monotone "You had been away...I didn't want to have to explain why I was taking care of everything...." He raised his head, face flooded in guilt, "Margaret...there are some things I never told you...Molly was my half sister."

Looking into her father's watery eyes, Margaret knew, despite all her unanswered questions, their conversation was over.

Jim rolled open his palms, "Sorry Margaret."

Without another word, he left the room wondering what had just happened.

Chapter Three

One-way streets always gave Margaret trouble. It was routine for her to see a destination, so close, disappear in the rear view mirror because she was following directions. Margaret watched in frustration as the Social Science building faded from view and section after section of metered visitor parking was filled. Anticipating the meeting with Dr. Walsh, she was anxious. The poor planning with campus directions and the GPS telling her that it was recalculating wasn't making it easier. Moving further away and almost late, she decided to return to a faculty lot next to Dr. Walsh's office. She was prepared to take the ticket and pay the fine. Margaret parked in a spot reserved for an Assistant

Dean and wiped her moist palms on a napkin from under the driver's seat.

The meeting with Sandra Walsh was set up without deception but some ambiguity. By identifying herself as a researcher from the University of Pennsylvania and interested in the Casco skeletal collection, both true, she responded from experience to the questions from Dr. Walsh's secretary. Despite her vague and general answers, Margaret was given an appointment that matched their overlapping schedules. Sandra Walsh planned to leave for the State of Washington and a summer research project in five days. This was her only day for office hours before the trip. Margaret planned to be in Ogunquit, starting tomorrow, for at least a week working on *Overturn*.

As preparation, Margaret decided once the usual introductions were exchanged, she would be direct and ask up front for the immediate return of the Casco skeletal collection. Nervous but confident, she believed the less she knew about the political and academic aspects surrounding the situation the better. Charlie Bay Burningwater wanted the remains of his ancestors returned now. Her strategy was to keep it simple. For she and Burningwater, it was simple.

In the lobby, Margaret checked the directory and found Sandra Walsh's office in the Anthropology Department on the seventh floor of the eight story classroom high-rise. As she stepped into the elevator, the universality of academic life gave her security. Charlie Bay was right, she knew this world. He did not.

When the elevator doors closed a sense of loss hit her again. It came in waves, sometimes fast and without warning. She missed Molly. She missed someone who had been dead for more than four years. The measure of time meant nothing to Margaret. Her experience of Molly's death was the moment she heard the words. She was angry and edgy. To engage Sandra Walsh for the return of the Casco ancestral remains was welcomed.

In the Anthropology reception area, she announced her name to the secretary and apologized for being a few minutes late with the excuse of a parking problem. Dr. Walsh's secretary was cordial and told her in a loud voice that parking was always a problem. Hearing Margaret's answer to her question of a final parking spot, she laughed and joked about towing. As the secretary escorted her into Sandra Walsh's office, Margaret forced a polite smile and was thankful the small talk ended. She worried about the towing.

Margaret sat in a wooden straight-back chair next to a round maple table and was told to make herself comfortable. Determined to remain focused, Margaret refused coffee but used the smell of a fresh pot. As the secretary left the room, Margaret's eyes followed her through the open door with painted block letters: Sandra Walsh, Ph.D., Chairperson, Department of Anthropology, Maine State University. From the door, she scanned the room.

It was not a large office but, it did have an alcove. Three of the walls were masked by oak and maple bookcases stacked with hard covers and paperbacks.

Loose journals and bound periodicals were scattered among the shelves and any available additional space was lined with artifacts and photographic memorabilia documenting a lifelong academic career. Dr. Walsh's desk was a rectangular wooden table with another straight back chair. The center of her desk was buried by a mound of papers. Behind the desk, the fourth wall was a series of glass panels framed in aluminum casings. The most curious piece in the room was a library card catalog, apparently well worn from years of use, now recycled to Dr. Walsh in obsolescence. It was set at a right angle to the desk and within reach. About six of the fifty or so catalog drawers were open and marked with index cards tipped vertically. Without a computer, printer, scanner or some other everyday generic box of technology that does something remarkable, this office was of a different time.

The alcove, between two bookcases of one wall however, was home to two desktops, multiple laptops, printers, cameras and carts all strung together with a bird's nest of cable and wire. It was a technical walk-in closet and it looked dangerous.

Sandra Walsh separated her two worlds without a door. As Margaret sat in the oak and unplugged, it appeared to her that the digital world Dr. Walsh tolerated but the analog she cherished.

Edging closer to the card catalog, she read the labels on the drawers. Casco was printed on the front of two rows. One drawer was open and marked by a vertical card. As she leaned in for a closer look, she heard someone enter the room behind her. Margaret sprang up, turned and came face to face with a woman carrying a canvas tote bag that looked half full and heavy.

Her right hand extended, Sandra Walsh burst toward Margaret, bright blue eyes darting from side to side, lips parted in a smile. Margaret shook her hand and watched the pear-shaped anthropology professor speed around the room to deposit printed material, most of it journals from the tote. Along the way, she spoke a quick personal introduction. As she placed the last collection on the table and the bag on the floor, she gestured for Margaret to be seated.

"I miss paper...bound journals...hard to find. If I hear from one more jackass publisher telling me this or that journal is going paperless, I'm going to horde...horde every bound journal I can get my hands on! These piles are going to get a lot bigger that's for damn sure."

Sandra was an individual of intelligence and intensity. Margaret liked her immediately.

"So Margaret, I'm glad we could get this meeting scheduled. As you may have heard from my secretary, I'm headed away from all this administrative chaos for the summer...thank God." Sandra slapped the pile of papers as she spoke and then mumbled audibly, "I'd like to get away from it for good. But, that's another matter.

What's your interest in the Casco Collection?" Sandra sat down to listen.

Surprised at how fast she came to the point, Margaret removed a letter-sized envelope from her leather briefcase and leaned toward Dr. Walsh.

"I come at the request of Charlie Bay Burningwater to formally ask for the immediate return of all the bones of his ancestors...bones that were removed from their burial ground on Long Neck Island."

At the end of her statement Margaret maintained eye contact and handed her the letter. It was the same message as a formal written request and signed by Charlie Bay. The block letters, in pen, were much larger than the text. As Sandra Walsh read the letter, Margaret perceived a change in the pallor of her unmade cheeks from rose to white. Margaret's cheeks were flush.

After lingering on the signature, Sandra Walsh folded the single page, inserted it into the envelope and placed it on the table. She collected her academic demeanor, sat back in her chair and delivered a direct professional response. It appeared to Margaret, she had given this speech before.

"The policy of this University...as well as the anthropological research community in general, has always been one of repatriation considerations in the context of active ongoing research. If a collection housed at this institution was affording scholars and students the opportunity for continued study and publication...then the retention of the collection in question was more than justified.

I have a personal and professional affinity for the Casco Collection. I was a part of the excavation...the occasion yielded a specification that has defined my career. Along with colleagues...I have written numerous papers...designed many research projects focused on the investigation ...reconstruction of various aspects in the lifeways of the Casco. The Casco skeletal material has been a resource for many significant contributions to the literature. The difficulty has been...as new investigatory methods and technologies are developed, productivity increases. The advances in CAT scan availability...3-D cone beam technology...DNA analysis...SEM techniques make the sample even more valuable than it was forty years ago."

Sandra was successful. Margaret was intimidated. She was clearly out of her discipline. She did the only thing possible; she bluffed.

"The request is a simple one and despite all that you've said, it stands. Should you choose not to respond immediately and favorably, we are prepared to take further actions."

Margaret raised her eyebrows and implied in her tone and body language that there was a team of legal professionals supporting them with a specific, well-planned strategy. Margaret and Charlie Bay had neither. Thinking only about leaving before her stage presence collapsed, she knew this wasn't going any further.

From the other side, this late in her career, Sandra Walsh also had no choice; she bluffed. But she wasn't as good an actor.

"I am not in the position to make the decision. It will involve all of the powers that be in the University system...so...we will need to talk again. Call me on Friday. I will be at this number all day."

Margaret nodded, took her card and left the office betting that Sandra Walsh could do whatever she damn well pleased. A pensive Dr. Walsh closed the door behind her.

Sandra Walsh received her doctoral degree in the early sixties, as the only woman in a strong anthropology program. She was the first to admit her dissertation amounted to nothing more than a very long and dry biography of Ales Hrdlicka, a founder of physical anthropology. First and foremost, Hrdlicka was an avid collector. Collecting human crania and skeletal material from burial sites all over the world, he maintained a primary focus in material from North America. At the time of his death in 1943, some fifteen thousand Native Americans had their skeletal remains housed at the Smithsonian as a direct result of his efforts. Sandra Walsh's insight into Hrdlicka's contribution to anthropology spawned the clarity and direction in her own vocation. She recognized at an early stage of her career that it was necessary to collect and archive as many specimens as possible. From the bones of those who preceded us, she believed that there was the potential to reconstruct past lifeways. Her affection for the Casco Skeletal Collection was genuine. It was her opportunity.

Sitting alone in her office, Sandra remembered the day she received the call from the Corps of Engineers like it was yesterday. At the time, she was the only anthropologist in the Sociology Department of Maine State University. Placed in charge of the excavation of the remains from the Casco Nation burial site by default, she was given the task of harvesting, cataloging and archiving the skeletal material. The Corps of Engineers outlined the boundaries for their reconstruction of the western tip of Long Neck Island and she had ten days in which to clear the field of human bones. They were ten days that began a forty year journey linked to the Casco.

In an academic climate of publish or perish, she thrived with the Collection and produced a succession of well received papers on the diet, diseases, and lifeways of the inhabitants of the region surrounding Long Neck Island. With academic success came advancement. Her ease in many arenas, with diverse groups of colleagues did not go unnoticed. In nineteen-ninety Dr. Walsh was named Chair of the Anthropology department and a year ago she was offered an Associate Deanship. All of this she took in stride, never letting administration disrupt the primary focus of her career, her one true passion; the Casco Collection.

Recently however, she came to realize, the work recognized as her greatest academic strength, was a source of personal anguish. The Casco Collection troubled her. With increasing frequency, she found herself searching for a means to address the haunting responsibility for and the possibility of, Casco repatriation. Margaret's request from Burningwater was now a part of the search.

Dr. Walsh slid to the edge of the straight-backed chair, opened the door a few inches and called to her secretary.

"Connie, get Max Sorensen on the phone. I have to speak with him today...I want you to keep trying until you get him...try Boston first."

Closing the door, she sat back in her chair. It was time to repatriate.

After Margaret turned off the engine, she picked up the fifty dollar parking ticket she had shoved into the center console cup holder. Folding the ticket into her pocket, Margaret was uncertain about how much to tell Burningwater. She had spotted his truck at fishermen's Co-op and knew he had to be around somewhere. Walking to the pick up, she was replaying her meeting with Dr. Walsh. She toyed with different angles in the presentation to Charlie Bay, each positive. But, she was unsettled and thought a backup plan was needed if Sandra Walsh continued to stall. Backup plans implied lawyers and she thought it was best to leave lawyers for another time. Margaret knew Charlie Bay wanted no part of another plan. It wouldn't come up, not today.

The afternoon sun felt good on her face as she leaned against the truck's warm hood and searched the harbor for a sign of Burningwater. The air was easy to breathe as it bounced off the river. Unfamiliar with the schedules of the waterfront, she decided that finding his pickup was enough for now and sat on the bumper to watch for him. Margaret used the break to consider the library cabinet in Sandra Walsh's office and dictated a description into her cell recorder. She rambled on about the piece as a prop until Burningwater's battered blue skiff appeared off the stern of a much larger lobster boat. With oars gently breaking the surface Charlie Bay was guiding the small skiff to shore. He sat with his back to the bow, his face away from hers. Seeing the labors of a workday in two five-gallon buckets as the boat slid onto the beach, she waited to approach him. When she stepped away from the truck, her movement caught Charlie Bay's eye and he nodded. The compressed and curved body of the clam digger was all business as he pulled the bow up onto the sand and walked to the pickup. After backing the truck down the beach, he looped the eye of the bowline over the ball of his trailer hitch and dragged the skiff grinding its way above the high watermark into the dunes. He was loading the two buckets of clams into the back of the pickup when she gave him the condensed version.

"I saw Sandra Walsh this morning and gave her your letter. I am supposed to call her back on Friday for an answer."

She waited for a response. There was none. Charlie Bay was an angry and impatient man. His eyes squinted out onto the harbor. His lips pursed as he took his pipe and tobacco pouch from his breast pocket. Clenching the stem between his teeth, he pinched a small bit of tobacco with his thumb and index finger and made an offering in the four directions, then to sky and earth. The prayer was inaudible and she waited. As he filled his pipe and lit it, Margaret continued with more difficult news.

"The other thing I have to tell you is that Molly has passed away." She looked up toward his eyes, still on the water. "She died four years ago. I'm sorry that you didn't know sooner."

The muscles in his cheeks flexed repeatedly as he bit down against the pipe stem. He asked, "Where's she buried?"

Margaret's eyes began to tear. For the first time sorrow overcame anger. She had no idea where Molly was buried. She turned her head away from Charlie Bay.

"I don't know."

Chapter Four

It took Sandra's secretary three days to find the elusive Maximilian Kolbe Sorensen. Sandra Walsh was not happy. The delay meant she had to reschedule her flight west. When she finally spoke with Max on Thursday night, she arranged to meet him the following Tuesday at her home in Maine. She gave him no information other than it was important. As ridiculous as it seemed to her, he was entrenched for the Memorial Day weekend with his son somewhere in the Mid-Atlantic States for the NCAA Lacrosse Tournament. She had very little patience with Max and his distraction into a game that was a complete unknown to her. However, Max was the biological anthropologist she wanted for the reburial and waiting for him was her choice.

There were no clear reasons why Sandra Walsh picked Max Sorensen to implement her abrupt decision to repatriate the Casco. No reasons other than he was an expert in the field and he owed her. There were concerns. One recurrent problem was a characteristic of his personality Sandra perceived as both a gift and a curse. Max disappeared. In his nature, without conscious choice or intention, he was often so taken by a concept, a project or his passion that the world around him no longer existed. It was invisible and irrelevant. She identified this trait as the primary factor in the disintegration of his personal life and in his inability to obtain a tenured track university faculty position. As for the repatriation of the skeletal collection that comprised her life's work, she needed him to use the gift, disappear and get it done. Like it or not, she waited.

Heading north on the New Jersey Turnpike, Max was a half hour behind the morning traffic into the City. He was relaxed and reliving the weekend with his youngest son, Paul. It was a good weekend; with laughter, tailgate food and friends. He enjoyed the tournament, even though his knowledge of lacrosse was acquired by observation. Max never played. But, Paul did. On occasion, Max felt the athletic experiences of his son came close to being his own.

This was the second consecutive year they attended the Lacrosse National Championship weekend. Max hoped this and other tournaments around the East Coast were now father and son traditions. Anticipating the chance to watch his son play in regional games, he was looking forward to the summer's Connecticut Lacrosse Tournament and in October, Baltimore's Fallball Tournament. All of this made Max, the fan and the father, smile as he drove the highway in his faded Volvo sedan.

Just shy of the City, he was approaching a well-established family tradition, sometimes bittersweet, but always a necessary stop; the Vince Lombardi Rest Area. Glancing at his watch, he calculated his estimated time of arrival at the Lombardi, how much time he had for food and when to be back on the road to make the late afternoon meeting with Sandra in Maine. For Max, time was linear and segmented. Today he knew a twenty-minute block to eat but he was unsure about Sandra and his remaining ten weeks of summer.

When Max turned onto the ramp for the Lombardi, without his wife and their two boys of younger years, reality hit. He was alone. But still, it was a family tradition and this stop in New Jersey gave him the constancy he sought, even now, in solitude. Stepping out of the car, he stretched, tugged at his sagging pants and started across the hard top to the entrance of a familiar place.

Max had reached the stage in his life where he was getting soft in the middle. From time to time, he made halfhearted attempts to keep his weight in check but didn't. Like other baby boomers, his chin fought gravity and his hips rolled at the crest enough to be noticed even by his own subjective standard. Describing the color of his thinning gray hair as brown, he thought of himself as much closer to thirty than seventy.

The sun was warm as he leaned against a brick wall at the entrance to the Lombardi's Georgian Colonial building. He ate his first hot dog faster than he should have and then watched. People passed before him, diverse human beings surrounded him. His love of the Vince Lombardi was renewed. He was the anthropologist, the participant observer, planted at the entryway of a turnpike stop and watching people. For Max this rest area was a remnant of an American assimilation lineage. It was a link to Ellis Island. Travelers were passing through, headed for somewhere, anywhere in America. It didn't matter. He finished eating his second hot dog and watched some more. To him, participant observation was almost as good as skeletal material. He delighted in observing America's ethnic faces, a country with people from all over the world, looking like they came from all over the world. People seeking something: opportunity, education, belief, wealth and most of all American stuff. He studied the physical characteristics of the passersby and thought of great American stuff: land, homes, cars, debt, credit cards, lap tops, flat screen LEDs, tablets and smart phones. Revisiting an old and favorite hypothesis, he considered how rapidly generational assimilation homogenized cultural diversity and American stuff was the medium. He thought about the irony in Coach Lombardi's drive to win, how much these individuals milling around him were driven to win and whether or not the great American mean was a victory. He was distracted. Walking back to the car disturbed by the drift, he was at least full. He settled back into a worn driver's seat and wondered what was on the mind of his mentor and his friend, Sandra Walsh. He continued to wonder what the summer held.

The route from the highway to Sandra's home was like other parts of the Maine coastline, fixed with landmarks from four centuries of European settlement and fresh with the promise of new enterprise. Even though Max hadn't visited Sandra's for four or five years, he remembered the way until he was sidetracked by the smell of the ocean. The sea breeze renewed his tired body. As he rolled down the window and drew in the salt air, he lost his focus and missed a turn. But, he kept going along the shore road because he was early, restless and six hours after the hot dogs, hungry. Scanning the streets, a seasonal front yard fried clam stand caught his eye. Maybe it was the salt air or maybe it was the anxiety forever associated with the chair of his dissertation committee, but fried food was the solution. With a pint of clams in crumbs and a side order of onion rings, he wove his way through the narrow roads until he found an access to the beach. It was a long day's drive and he hadn't been to the ocean for almost a year.

The cool, white sand felt good against the soles of his bare feet as he walked to a large driftwood log and sat down cradling two grease spotted containers. No drink, no ketchup, no utensils, just salt and he ate the contents of both boxes. Full again, he stared toward the open ocean; eyes fixed on the horizon. The beach on a weekday, late in the afternoon and so early in the season was deserted in every direction. He burped freely and wondered if he should have taken an antacid before the food. Then he wondered if he should take one before the meeting with Sandra and his part in a project unknown.

Regardless of what Sandra had in mind, Max was concerned about being committed to more writing. Writing didn't come easily for him. He acknowledged its necessity, but found it to be a task. Max didn't like to write. He had been putting off writing all year. The summer was supposed to be scheduled as a time to catch up, complete two research papers on his work with Nubian skeletal collections. The one redeeming aspect, in generating these publications, was their focus on a location and skeletal material he enjoyed. The core of his academic career was Max's research in the Nile Valley. The lives and social organization of the people of pre-dynastic Egypt intrigued him. The attraction to understanding the lifeways of individuals with a stratified society existing seven thousand years ago remained constant in an otherwise meandering professional life.

Currently, his Nubian study was focused on the physical characteristics of the region's inhabitants and the presence of an elite ruling class in place as precursors to the dynasties of the pharaohs. An aspect of the research that excited Max was the change in methods afforded by skeletal DNA. The unique characteristics on the bones of individuals identified as evidence of a ruling class, had the potential to be traced with DNA. All the years of recording and analyzing the lumps and bumps on bones were verifiable with ancient DNA. For Max, it was a great time to be a scientist. His mind was racing with new research, but he knew all too well the principle that was so often his downfall; he had to finish one project, including the writing, before he was able to start another. Troubled by the sense that he was about to be interrupted, he rubbed his distended belly, burped again and considered how food, at this point in his life, was becoming the focus of his days.

Two large suitcases stood adjacent to the front door as Max entered the winterized cottage. Sandra Walsh had called this small frame house, just one block from the ocean, home for the last forty years. The water was visible through a row of cottages from the backyard but you had to stand on a chair to see the waves. On the inside, Sandra's home was well worn and comfortable. The first floor was dominated by a large main living area decorated like an early twentieth century reading room, oak cases and cabinets, every available space filled with books, journals, and papers. Bolstered by Sandra's warm embrace, in this environment Max was at ease before the door closed.

As Sandra led Max to a stuffed chair in the combination living room-study-office, he felt good, even relaxed. Without any hesitation, she sat opposite him in a rocker only feet away. She made no offers of cordiality and came right to business. He was neither surprised nor offended.

"Max, I don't know if I ever told you or anyone else the whole story of the Casco excavation. I know it was along time ago... I probably only gave you pieces of the Casco story...what you remember doesn't matter...the key is you recognize how much that skeletal collection has meant to me. It has been my life's blood and it is time to find a way to put those bones and all that goes with them to rest."

Max was lost but didn't speak. He knew she wasn't going to stop until he got all of what was on her mind. Without any expression of confusion, he listened, no longer relaxed.

"I'll never forget that first day...Max, there were bones everywhere! When the Army Corp of Engineers took off the sea grass on the northwest corner of Long Neck Island...it was like they were jumping out of the ground. My heart was pounding hard as hell. All I could think was gather. Gather like Hrdlicka and record when you can. We had so little time. The engineers gave us only a few days and it was a frenzy of collecting with whomever I could roundup on short notice...you have to remember...it was the late sixties, the methods were weak, protocols varied and people were scattered all over the place...but the harvest...the harvest was wonderful.

And I knew it was going to be great from the moment I laid my eyes on the tip of that island. In that instant, I saw what that collection could become...what it could mean. From then on, my career has been dedicated to the fulfillment of our obligation to those bones; to insure that the Casco story was told. I had to tell the story of a people who were basically rubbed out.

The problem is; I am not done. But, it's done. It is done because of the law...the law Max."

Sitting back in her chair, Sandra wondered whether she made any progress in convincing herself, let alone Max Sorensen, a colleague and more importantly a friend that the law was the reason for her forthcoming request.

For his part, Max wasn't sure what was going on and he wanted more information. He was certainly familiar with the Native American Grave Protection and Repatriation Act and its five-year compliance deadline to return skeletal collections. Using the acronym, he figured he'd let her go some more.

"NAGPRA?"

"Yes and I have a request for reburial...and yes it has been well over five years...I've sat on those bones for a long time. The request comes from a remnant...one member of the once large Casco Nation.

When we were doing the excavation, with trowels and shovels...disorganized manpower and all sorts of equipment, he was one of the few Casco in the area. He sat poised on top of the island knoll watching us harvest his past. And there we were bustling around full of ourselves...flush with scientific promise for the future.

He was there day after day; Charlie Bay Burningwater. Last week he made a formal request for the return of all the Casco skeletal material. The man is a known lineal descendant."

The Native American Grave Protection and Repatriation Act required the expeditious return by Federal agencies, museums and institutions of Native American remains and associated funerary objects when requested by lineal descendants, by tribal members or by other individuals asserting some degree of cultural affiliation. The NAGPRA legislation gave the strongest recognition for repatriation to lineal descendants. In the years since the law's enactment, litigation delayed the return of material from some institutions by exploiting the ambiguity of the term cultural affiliation. However, the courts were quick and consistent in their support of return based upon lineal descendantcy. The precedent established in the judicial system made Sandra's legal options non-existent and Max knew it immediately.

"Max, we don't have a leg to stand on. Without an immediate and definitive response this will be costly and a public relations nightmare for the University. I am committed to the Washington project for the summer so here is what I want...I want you to handle the skeletal inventory and the reburial for me."

Sandra didn't give Max a chance to respond. "The lab space was set up on Friday...you can stay here for as long as needed and I am only a call or an email away. All my numbers: cell, office, email ...all of it's on my desk." She paused and then continued in a very unbusiness-like tone. "Max I need you to do this for me."

The look on her face expressed the reciprocal relationship, which existed between Max and Sandra. He owed her and it was time to repay. He got the message but his debt was not to be repaid without an argument.

"It's like burning books. I love books."

The words shot from his mouth. As always, he spoke before he considered the depth of her request and the depth of their relationship.

Expecting him to vent about the implications of repatriation, she sat back and let Max go. He didn't disappoint, Max was on a tirade.

"Sandra you know that this contradicts everything that I believe as a scientist. How in the world could you ...you of all people, ask me to do such a thing? You can't be serious....I abhor the thought of putting those bones back in the ground. You're asking me to torch a library."

Max leaned forward in his chair, his face wrinkled into an incredulous expression and his outstretched arms begged for an alternative.

"Sandra, just think of the wealth of information that material holds...with the right technologies...in the right hands...new insights into a people that will jump out at us again and again. Those bones still have a lot to tell...you and all the researchers to come after you. You've just begun to uncover the secrets of the Casco lifeways and now you are willing to bury them away.

Think of the bigger picture here; we are a part of the European migration that ruthlessly wiped out millions of

Native Americans. Our European ancestors destroyed their homes, their traditions, and their lives. We have exterminated culture after culture.

It's only been four hundred years since a way of life that existed for maybe three or four thousand years was ruined. You've only been working with that collection for forty years...think of what we'll learn in the next forty or eighty or the next hundred years from those bones. We've an obligation to reconstruct and understand what our ancestors destroyed. How can you turn your back on such a responsibility? Hell, now we're, because you're dragging me into it, we're going to rub it out again." He took a breath but wasn't done. "Sandra, you know laws are just social constructs. They can be changed, amended, skirted, or even broken but this...what you have and what it can be...this is an irreplaceable treasure of human existence. This is something that, once in the ground, will be no more."

She loved his passion. The driving force in Max's life was a quest for understanding; an understanding of those who came before, who they were. How they lived. As she listened to his plea, she took consolation in his passion, a search for understanding in the process of human existence. It was also her passion but it was a different path.

Before Sandra responded, Max began again. "You know all this skeletal material is simply objective data, signs in the archeological record like any other artifact." He was less emotional and more logical. "The spirit which gave the organic components its humanness departed with death. The remains are inanimate... quantifiable material. The skeletal remnant is this objective vessel that once housed the being. Now, it simply endures to tell the story. Don't forget...the techniques for replicating DNA sequences have opened the door...in just the last five years or so...for me to trace Nubian lineages in ways that I never dreamed possible...from archived skeletal collections. Think of what lies ahead for the Casco Sandra...please...don't ask me to bury it away." Max was annoyed he was in her debt and that repayment superseded science.

Sandra responded in the context of her initial position; the law. But, she didn't repeat the NAGPRA requirement for repatriation, she gave him a different tack.

"Max do you remember the Settlement Act of 1980, that whole land dispute and claim with the Passamaquoddies and the Penobscots, the one made against the State of Maine? How the Tribes laid claim to thousands and thousands of acres of Maine land based on past treaties...and how, in most people's mind, they won; coming away with land, money and among other things Federal Recognition as Tribal Nations."

Max was familiar with the case and the resulting Settlement Act. He smiled affirming that some Native Americans finally got compensation for long-standing injustices. Remembering that the two tribes received considerable amounts of land, money and only lost gambling privileges, he nodded.

"Well, with all the notoriety and recognition afforded the Passamaquoddies and the Penobscots, it is important to remember that there are three Federally Recognized Tribes in Maine...don't leave out the Casco.

Because of their continuous presence in the region since European contact, on land which nobody else wanted, they argued successfully for federal recognition, but a few years after the Passamaquoddy and Penobscot Settlement Act. They used the same strategy in citing the Non-intercourse Act...that somehow the State of Maine either took land or brokered land deals of Indian Territory illegally. But the Casco, very shrewdly I might add, went through the Bureau of Indian Affairs for federal recognition. There was no cash or land claim. It was interesting...that whole thing. It's kind of a mystery how that all happened so quietly, no press, no publicity.

The Casco population numbers were much higher in the first half of the twentieth century...then dropped dramatically. By the time of their federal recognition, whole family lineages had died and there were just a handful of Casco left. You know, it was the same old story...they were relocated, assimilated into other Native American groups or the State's mainstream. The small number of Casco who chose to remain through those years were politically and legally passive...almost non-existent. The only exception was this BIA federal recognition that came out of the blue.

But to the point...the Casco have always been considered as impoverished fishermen...the remains of an indigenous group of predominantly marine hunter-gatherers destined to disappear...become extinct. Because they were in such a dramatic state of decline in the second half of the century, the Settlement Act, along with all those attorneys arguing for money and land, passed them by. But their federal recognition stands as powerful as any other tribe's, even though they haven't used its strength until now...until Burningwater. The law says that as federally recognized...they get the bones back no matter what the size is of the tribe...even if it's just this one member...Charlie Bay Burningwater. Max, that's all it takes."

Twirling his wedding ring with the thumb and index finger of his right hand, Max slumped in his chair with a facial expression and the body language of a man defeated. Sandra, familiar with the look, was quick to take advantage and outlined her plan.

"The lab space for the inventory has been set up at Gerald Wallace's old office and archive on the South campus. It will be quiet and away from the summer school traffic. The buildings aren't much, surplus Quonset huts donated to the University, but all the equipment that you will need for the inventory and packaging is in place. The portion of the collection from my lab has already been moved...all the other lab site locations, specimen ID numbers per site and contact people are on the Casco CD file waiting for you. I need you to round up parts of the collection that are under study in various labs around the Northeast. Most will be shipped...one or two you might have to pick up. Once you have all the material logged back in...it's the usual packaging...bones wrapped in unprinted newspaper...you know the routine. There's really nothing new, Max. The problem will be compliance with immediate return during the summer. You'll probably have to do some traveling to make sure it all comes together. So you stay here, sit the house and I'll leave you a credit card for the house and road trips. I realize that it's probably too much to ask for you to keep receipts, but please try...we'll settle up when I return for the reburial."

He smiled when she noted his poor reputation with credit, but otherwise, he waited.

Max was waiting for the reason why she chose him to perform a task better suited to a grad student or post-doc. Sandra also knew this look. For a mutually uncomfortable moment she didn't respond until the quiet obliged her to speak. Leaving the rational of the law and searching in areas of herself, rarely visited, she struggled with her words.

"Maybe it's guilt? I stretched the ambiguity in the relationship with Casco...the use of the Collection many, many years...to the point where maybe I believed they wanted us to keep...keep it indefinitely. Ah hell, it's guilt I have done something wrong, I'm guilty. Of course they wanted the specimens returned and I should have done it years ago. I made a mistake and I need protection. This repatriation has to be smooth and without incident, political or otherwise. I need you to resolve this for me."

Sandra Walsh had never addressed or expressed her guilt regarding the Casco. She was relieved. Confession had its place, even to Max. She lowered her head and went deeper.

Dr. Walsh knew that she stretched and manipulated the NAGPRA law in her study of the Casco bones. She recognized that she exploited the passivity of the Casco people, what was left of them. But, it was her most recent insight that has touched her soul. She obviated Casco beliefs. She denied them. Sandra Walsh violated a part of the Casco she chose not to understand. Casco beliefs exist; she has known it and she has repeatedly chosen to desecrate them. This she has confessed to no one. It was for the resolution of such quiet and ironic atrocity that she needed help. To persevere in her search for reconciliation, she needed, of all people, Max Sorensen.

The extent of Max's perception into her turmoil was the simple misplaced thought that self-doubt was not a sole possession of middle aged men. With very little compassion for Sandra's torment, he gave it another try from a different angle.

"Did I ever tell you my plan for my body when I die?"

She was confused by the tangential response, shook her head no and implied she didn't care.

"If I'm physically interesting enough I plan to be dissected. But, if it is an ordinary run of the mill death, I'd like to go straight to having my flesh boiled off. You know, my bones cleaned and bleached, put in a box and sent off to join a skeletal collection somewhere...maybe here."

Sandra burst into nervous laughter. Max continued.

"I'm serious, because when I'm dead, it doesn't matter. I know what's left is not me. It's just data."

Controlled, she answered, "Max, you mean you believe what is left, is just data."

He stared at the now demanding expression in her eyes and twirled his wedding ring.

The early arrival of Sandra's cab to the airport was a welcome sight to both of them. He never said yes to her request but no was impossible. Their good-bye was genuine and heartfelt with Max assuring Sandra he planned to keep the appointment already scheduled with Margaret Garret for the next morning. She also gave him very specific diplomatic instructions for what was expected to be a follow-up meeting with Charlie Bay Burningwater. He listened but had no intention of taking her direction and she knew it.

Alone in the house, Max sat at her desk and set up his laptop. He scrolled through the files on her memory stick and a CD for all of the information necessary to repatriate the Casco. Also on the desk was her credit card. Sandra was organized. He thought of her as an intense, focused and singular thinker: one direction, full throttle, no brakes. And that quality, he knew to be a saving force in his career and in his life, somehow always roaring in when he needed it most, grabbing him for the ride. Picking up the plastic card, he smiled at how difficult it must have been for her to leave him with uncontrolled access to money. Everything Max owned was borrowed and Sandra knew it. To leave the credit card was significant; to leave the data files was leaving her career.

Early that evening, Max took a long walk on the beach and distracted himself with the moderate northwest wind and small curling waves. Wading in the shallows made his feet numb. When he returned to the house he performed his usual ritual in the face of confusion. He got a beer, always in Sandra's refrigerator, a jar of pasteurized cheese spread, purchased for him, a box of salted crackers also for him, and the TV remote.

Two hundred and seventy-three channels and not one held his attention. He was searching for a Barbara Stanwyck film on old movie channels without luck. Gazing at the food on the coffee table, he thought of how repulsive the combination was to his wife. Max had not seen Linda in almost seven months. He drifted through the divorce a few years ago to clarify the monetary chaos, but viewed their marriage as continuing in separation. He kept wearing his wedding ring with no intention of taking it off. Max didn't know what happened in the dissolution of their relationship, other than he was impossible to live with, never satisfied, too quick to jump to the next project, the next town or the next thing that was going to turn his life, their lives around in a weekend. The phrase, irreconcilable differences, was haunting. For the longest time, there were the two boys and the bills. Then everyone and everything went away, including most of Max and Linda's wants and desires for each other.

Thinking about the work ahead, all in the next ten weeks, Max reached for another beer, cracker and more cheese spread.

Chapter Five

The Casco seated in a circle around Charlie Bay were silent. As before, some eyes fixed to his, others stared away. Charlie Bay faced the Ancient One and didn't back down. He met him eye to eye with strength and an edge of arrogance. Charlie Bay held firm to his choice as the right one, the only one he could have made at the time. But it wasn't the Ancient One that countered his defiance; it was shattered by the seven empty metal chairs staggered between his Casco ancestors. The vacancies haunted Charlie Bay. They were seats of the missing, spirits whose dream journey had been halted. Each empty chair bore witness to his choice and each chair pressed his obligation to act in favor of the missing.

Charlie Bay tried to retell his story, speak in defense, but he had no air.

Burningwater woke up choking. His pillow was soaked and his moist hair was matted to his neck. Twice he gasped raw and wheezing gulps of air. As he sat up, the skin of his back separated from the damp sheet. Charlie Bay labored, savoring each breath until he caught enough air to relax.

The window on the north side of Charlie Bay's bedroom rattled with the surge of a strong northwest wind. Lying back down in bed, he listened to the howl and felt the vibration of the outside wall against his headboard. Some gusts were higher, but he figured it was blowing twenty-five to thirty. Remaining still, he waited on the rain. The sheets of water rapping the glass panes had their moments but he knew the weather was more wind than water. In this breeze, with the moon high tide, Charlie Bay also knew trouble for the fragile water sculpted sand walls of island's western door. Today, he was not going to be digging clams. At high tide, with this air, waves were going to carve into the sacred ground of his ancestors. The bones of his people were unprotected from the wind and the water. Burningwater thought; unprotected from two indifferent beings.

The beads of sweat hadn't left his chest before he was up and headed to the stairs; naked and cold. Passing through the kitchen to the basement door in the back hall, he grabbed a flashlight and moved down the narrow stairway into the stone-walled cellar. A hard packed dirt floor was five feet from the ceiling beams. There were wide plank shelves set against the four fieldstone walls. Charley Bay moved quickly to the far right corner and set the flashlight to shine on a wooden Clementine crate. He removed the box from the shelf and withdrew polished stone figurines, carved amulets and clay pipes from its center. Placing these objects, in order, in the space left by the crate, he whispered a prayer until only a blue silk cloth liner and one small Obsidian stone remained. Charlie Bay returned to the kitchen, placed the Clementine box on the table and considered the tide.

During high tide, in a southwest wind, the water lapped meekly against the sand and sea grass at the tip of Long Neck. At low tide a right angle formed by beach and dune sand allowed Charlie Bay to walk the border of the western burial ground. He routinely searched the stratified wall for ancestral remains.

This morning's flood tide carried the water above the dune wall and into the sea grass. With this northwest wind the waves would be cutting into the layers of sand that held Casco bones. As the wall melted away, the remnants of his ancestors would poke to the surface. If uncollected, they were in danger of dropping into the river. Charlie Bay had to get to the tip of the island as the water left the wall. But he knew his patience was to be tested for another hour. It was going to take at least that long for the water to recede far enough for him to wade the beach and hunt for bones.

The draft from the back hall that brushed across the skin of his shoulders and thighs reminded Charlie Bay that he was naked. He scanned the kitchen and living room for clothes, a pair of khaki pants left in a heap at the end of the sofa and a navy blue sweatshirt draped over the rocker were enough. With his boots from the back steps and cradling the Clementine crate, he was on his way to the western door. He planned to sit at the water's edge until the moment the tide allowed him onto the beach.

The gray morning light of the horizon left the west mound of Long Neck Island connected to the night. The beams of the pickup headlights reflected off the blades of swaying wet sea grass and dropped into white-capped darkness. Charlie Bay eased the truck to the edge of solid ground. The northwest wind shook and rumbled around the cab. He leaned forward over the steering wheel to check the tide. Straining to see the water level, he knew it was still too soon for the beach. He was angry. He was angry at the moon and angry with himself. The moon he forgave.

Max slept until seven, which was late for him, and woke dehydrated. After drinking most of the cranberry juice left in Sandra's refrigerator, he showered, shaved and felt generally renewed from his travels and professional headaches. He checked his e-mail for the first time in a week; about the norm. Messages on his cell he figured he'd check with coffee. Voice-mail from his office and apartment land lines was another matter. Learning the technical skills required to playback messages from a remote location escaped him. Underlying the block was his belief that to be away from home and office was a reprieve from responsibility, so most of the time he skipped it.

Sitting at Sandra's desk, he found the page of instructions for the day's appointments. At eleven, he was to meet Margaret Garret near Long Neck Island in the parking lot of Golf Land Driving Range; from there it was onto Burningwater. The range was on Rt. 1 and easy to find; Sandra knew Max needed it simple. She also gave him a detailed physical description of Margaret and her expectations for their discussion. Marveling at Sandra's observations, he disregarded the agenda topics but thought Margaret Garret sounded attractive.

Max was early at the driving range and hungry. Wandering over to a near by take-out restaurant, he talked one of the waitresses into grilling him a hot dog before they were supposed to open. He sat on a bench overlooking the empty range, ate and pondered golf. There was time.

From his perspective, golf's greatest asset was as a sport integrated into the lives of either gender at any age. Women and men playing the same sport throughout theirs lives, sometimes even together, was remarkable. His wife Linda liked golf, so from time to time, he succumbed to nine holes that never went well. But a scoreless bucket of balls he considered a relaxing distraction. Max finished the hot dog and wondered when the range opened.

Margaret was uneasy walking up to a stranger with ketchup all over his napkin in an otherwise empty parking lot but Max was her only choice. She didn't hesitate.

"Dr. Sorensen, I'm Margaret Garret. I spoke with Dr Walsh about meeting with you... the reburial of the Casco."

Max stood, grunted a yes as he wiped the corners of his mouth and extended his right hand all in one awkward motion.

"Please, call me Max."

Margaret was uncomfortable with the immediate informality. He was the anthropologist designated to return all of the Casco skeletal material and, in that sense, an ally. But, he was also the representative of the University that withheld the bones of Charlie Bay's ancestors for decades. To Burningwater, he was the enemy and she was cautious. For his part, Max was astounded at the accuracy of Sandra's description. She was a beautiful young woman. Margaret Garret viewed Dr. Max Sorensen as an out of shape contemporary of her father.

"Would you like to talk here for a minute first or do you have something planned?" He gestured toward the bench.

Margaret had a script, a short one and didn't care to sit. Her first goal was to get Dr. Sorensen and Charlie Bay together in order to set a date for the return of the Casco bones. Mediation was foreign territory for her and she planned to keep it simple. She expected to write whatever Charlie Bay needed and assist in a rapid reburial. She was also making it up as she went along.

"Charlie Bay Burningwater is the man that you need to speak with." Margaret had thought about her opening lines, but only her opening lines. "He lives on Long Neck Island. He has no phone and an unpredictable schedule. I thought today…we'd just have to find him. I know the places to look and then…we can go from there."

"Sounds good to me. Do you want to drive and I'll leave my car here?"

Nodding, Margaret walked to the car, "I'll drive."

This somewhat pudgy, graying man, sitting on the passenger side in rumpled khaki pants and faded blue cotton shirt, appeared to be likable. The casualness of his manner was unexpected. Margaret was wondering how he ended up in charge of the repatriation for the University.

"So Margaret, how did you end up with this mission for the Casco and Charlie Bay Burningwater?"

Margaret smiled. "Charlie Bay's a friend...he asked for my help in dealing with the University. I think I'm the only one he knows who went to college. I met with Sandra Walsh and made the request, she connected me to you...Charlie Bay wants the return done now. The reburial of his ancestors is long overdue."

"Oh, so Burningwater and I pick a date."

Boundaries, sequence and relationships now established, in Margaret's mind to be followed and in Max's to be changed.

Driving from Rt 1 down to the shore line on 9, their first stop was to check the fishermen's Co-op for Charlie Bay's pickup. Not far and on the water, it was the most likely place to catch him.

She thought maybe a public space might keep Charlie Bay in check. Burningwater's volatility was a given, Sorensen's was an unknown.

Scanning the parking lot for Charlie Bay's truck, Margaret squinted and felt her heart pound. It wasn't around, no sign of the pickup. She didn't recognize anyone who might know where he was and gave up on the waterfront. Unconcerned about the failure and unaffected by the gray and blustery day, Max enjoyed the Maine coast, enjoyed the smell. He sat in the passenger seat and smiled. Margaret was annoyed. Her next choice was Charlie Bay's home on Long Neck.

The rickety rail ties got Max's attention as they crossed over onto the island. Margaret noticed he let go of the dash once they bounced onto solid ground. He was alert, excited to be on this land of the Casco.

At the crest of the middle knoll, she sighed and mumbled under her breath. Her hope for a calm meeting and date was dwindling, she could see the house to the east, but no truck. He was either at the western door or the liquor store and neither was good. Watching her reverse direction and assuming that Charlie Bay wasn't home, Max wondered where to next. He was relieved when they didn't turn onto the rail tie bridge, but hung onto the dash as they followed tracks across the road-less, high grass of another mound to somewhere.

"There's his truck. He is out here." Margaret satisfied, at least she found him.

Max felt his heart pound. As the gentle rolling hill dropped beneath them, he knew this was the earth that held the Casco bones. It was the ancestral burial ground Sandra harvested so many years ago. He knew giving up the Casco skeletal material wasn't going to be easy.

The meandering footprints in the moist sand that on occasion bumped into the western door were clear and easy to follow. The uniform convexity of the shoreline made it impossible to see to the outermost tip. Without discussing it, they both expected to find him somewhere on the beach.

Walking in step, it wasn't long before Margaret and Max saw Charlie Bay's dark silhouette against the green horizon of the marshland. As they approached, he glanced away from the sand wall and in their direction. Margaret waved her right arm. Charlie Bay saw the motion but did not respond. Returning to his work, he scraped the sandy surface for human remains. The two visitors increased their pace without a word.

Since his April discovery of an ancestor on the sand bar in the Casco River, Charlie Bay frequently patrolled the perimeter of the western door. Once in awhile, he found a few unidentifiable bones and he cared for them as remnants of his people. Burningwater buried all the recovered remains in sacred ground located on the ocean side mound of Long Neck Island. Today, his early morning distress with the wind, the water and the moon proved true. The blue silk liner of the large Clementine crate was covered with bones. The five hours, searching the sand, brought him bone after bone. Each piece of the ancients that spilled from their earth stung him. He was tormented.

Now, with the two beside him, Margaret introduced Max. "Charlie Bay, this is Dr. Sorensen, the representative of the University."

Charlie Bay didn't remove his eyes from the sand or acknowledge Dr. Sorensen. Max leaned forward to greet him with his right hand extended but pulled it back after no response. He felt hostility. Rather than withdraw further Max went academic. Without a word, he focused on the brown-gray remains that contrasted dramatically with their blue silk cradle. He quickly identified some animal bones, probably dog. He also identified a few nondescript fragments, likely human, three prepubescent thoracic vertebrae, definitely human, and a scapula, likely the right shoulder blade of an approximately ten year old individual. Max was excited. If the scapula and vertebrae were from the same individual and if that individual were buried in a traditional flex position, knees to the chest and head tilted forward. And if the curve of the spinal column faced the reshaped northwest wall of the island, the angelic shoulder blade and vertebrae, found by Burningwater, were the outer most portion of a convex spine. Max expected those bones would be the first to erode through the surface, followed by more thoracic vertebrae and a second scapula. From these assumptions he expected the presence of a complete human specimen and that got him talking.

"Could you show me where you found those two bones right there." Trying to be as calm as possible, he leaned closer and pointed into the box held in Charlie Bay's left arm. "I believe they may be components of a complete skeleton, including the crania...that's the skull ...very close to the surface...long bones and all!"

Margaret and Charlie Bay didn't share in his enthusiasm. A stoic Charlie Bay continued to search the sand. Margaret rolled her eyes, mumbled something that ended with "idiot" and fixed a glare toward Max. She was incredulous. The measure of his insensitivity was remarkable. Recognizing that he was overzealous, Max attempted to justify his interest with talk.

"The remains of the child...the one whose shoulder blade you found...can tell us the story of how he or she might have lived...maybe even how they might have died. These bones can talk to us...they can talk to us about the Casco past. If I could see the other bones of the child it might help re...."

Charlie Bay interrupted, "Bones don't talk. They don't tell stories. The bones of my people belong in the earth. Their circle has been broken...their journey broken...they all...all that you possess must be returned now. I won't speak about it any more."

Margaret was astounded at Max's lack of diplomacy. Any sense of professional hierarchy vanished. She saw in an instant, Max Sorenson operating, on his own, with an academic agenda independent of Casco repatriation. He was as difficult and unyielding as Charlie Bay. Finding herself thrust between two stubborn men, she fought to stay on track.

"We need to set a date for the return of all the Casco ancestors. If it's OK with you Charlie Bay...I'll work on that with Dr. Sorensen...you and I can talk...so that you have the final word. OK?"

Charlie Bay didn't respond. To press him further was useless. Right now, the only common ground between the two men was their affinity for the ancestral Casco and the same wrinkled khaki pants. Turning without so much as a glance to Max, she walked back along the shore. Max hesitated for a moment, but followed in sync, one step behind. On their way down the narrow beach he attempted, a number of times, to draw even with her. But, it didn't matter how fast he walked to catch up, she maintained a distance. Earlier, he received the look and now, it was the walk. Max was familiar with both.

On the path through the sea grass back to the truck, he found a yellow range golf ball. He picked it up and put it in his pocket. Margaret Garret started the car and told Max to hold on.

By early afternoon, the wind shifted to the southwest and the rising tide erased all evidence on the beach of the visitors. As the water lapped against Charlie Bay's boots, he found himself inching closer to the location in the sand that brought the pieces of spine and shoulder blade. The words and suspicions of Dr. Sorensen didn't leave him. He was torn. To disturb the bones in the earth was an offense, but to abandon them, let them be washed into the sea, was a violation. With his best recollection, he scraped the spot of his past discovery using the crescent edge of a cohog shell. The enemy was correct. Bone after bone tracked into the wall. The Clementine crate was overflowing. Charlie Bay's uneasiness rose. He knew the skull was coming. He wanted to stop but the tide was surging toward the one bone that remained. Water began to tumble in over the top of his boots. He placed the container in a sheltered section of sea grass above his head and pushed it away from the edge. Leaning against the sand wall, he fought the suction, pulled off his boots and threw them high into the grass. Charlie Bay dug with bare hands. The sand was moist and smelled of salt. The grains packed together under his fingernails spreading the tip of skin from the nail bed. The cold ocean crept to his waist. Time was short.

The small globe Charlie Bay teased free from the earth was encrusted with sand. Holding the human skull with two hands, he gently submerged the bone into the water, washing away enough debris to know it was all there. His eyes filled with tears and his nose ran with clear liquid. Water rushed into the gravesite collapsing the sand above. Cradling the skull and lower jaw in his left arm, he scurried up through the eroded opening to solid ground. Cold and wet, Charlie Bay sat down and used his sweatshirt to clean the face of a child. As the sand fell away from the upper teeth he recognized an unmistakable sign. The edges of the two front incisors were broken at an angle toward the middle of the face. The chips formed the shape of a triangle. Charlie Bay Burningwater knew him. This was his uncle's son; Flat Stone. Charlie Bay wrapped both arms around the skull and pulled it to his chest. He rocked front to back, chanted with soft breaths and remembered.

Flat Stone was in his eleventh year and Charlie Bay was in his nineteenth when an uncle brought his only son back from the city to the Casco homeland. The boy had sores on his skin, his neck was swollen, he was red, drenched in sweat and then he was no more. A grandfather, his uncle and Charlie Bay dug the grave before the ground froze. They listened as his uncle spoke of the heart's pain when a father must bury his son. How was this so? All those years ago, Flat Stone's grave was far from the water. There were others, many others to the northwest; the northwest corner of Long Neck Island, which was no more.

In his mind's eye, Charlie Bay saw seven empty chairs staggered in the circle around him. He looked skyward, cradled the skull of Flat Stone and chanted.

"Uh-kosisco, Uh-kosisco rising above me.
Look down upon a son of the Nations...
call to Earth and Sea that I might be forgiven.
I make this prayer to you Uh-kosisco."

The departure of Margaret and Max at the driving range was business-like; exchanging cell numbers and possible times for contact. She was annoyed and needed a break before connecting with her theatre people. He needed to check out the lab's requirements for supplies and equipment before his return trip to Boston. Their good-bye included a date and positioning for the next encounter. There was no date for repatriation.

Sandra was correct. There was no one around on the South campus. Gerald Wallace's old lab was the last in a row of six corrugated galvanized aluminum Quonset huts along a dead end dirt road. It was an arched tunnel, with few windows and double doors on each end. The paddle lock and hinges on the parking lot side were rusted and the wooden swinging doors were peeling. A second set of doors in the entryway were closed but unlocked. The main room of the building was one long half tube, painted gray with blood red patches of rust splashed at irregular intervals. Dust was everywhere. Max figured Gerry Wallace was the last one to use the lab and smiled. He hit the lights. Makeshift shelves lined both sidewalls to the seven-foot high curve of the roof. The shelves were filled with file-sized boxes of papers and skeletal material. The end of each box was labeled in black marker for their contents. He recognized Sandra's hand writing on the majority of containers.

In the center of the room were three large old oak library reading tables, their surfaces well worn and scratched. On the last table were five file cartons labeled G Wallace. Each box was packed with papers and articles; the cherished documents of a career, a lifetime organized into five containers. The work of Max Sorensen wouldn't fill half a box.

Gerry Wallace died three years ago. Max didn't know until a month after the funeral. Their relationship was professional. They were colleagues and not close. But Max always enjoyed Gerry Wallace's spirit. Despite the thirty-year difference in their ages, the professor's spirit was forever a source of humor and energy for Max. Gerry Wallace called dealing with university administration, warfare and victories, "counting coup"; a reference to the Native American Plains warrior who got close enough to his enemy to touch him, preferably with a slap below the waist. This act demonstrated bravery and skill. In his last contract negotiation with the University in nineteen eighty-nine, Gerry requested and received lab space on campus until the millennium. He chuckled every time he told the story of the administration's neglect to designate, in writing, which millennium. Gerry counted coup. Max found laughter, inspiration and most of all, energy for administrative warfare.

It was Sandra who saved Gerry's research. She heard rumors, not long after his death, that the University, in an attempt to satisfy an ever-expanding need for space, was sending all paper materials from Dr. Wallace's office and lab to the recycling center. Climbing into the dumpster left outside the lab for collection, Sandra retrieved most of the discarded material. She cut her hand in the recovery and later implied multiple OSHA violations at the site. She controlled and occupied the building ever since. Sandra counted coup. Now this marginal surplus building sheltered the writings of Dr. Gerald Wallace and the skeletal remains of the Casco.

Walking around the far end of the laboratory and archive, Max examined the catalog numbers on row after row of boxes marked with the heading, Casco. He dictated a list on his phone's recorder of the material and equipment required for the repatriation inventory until his uncharged battery died. He finished off the list with scavenged sticky notes, stuck them all to his phone's screen, shut off the lights and left for Boston.

Chapter Six

Serving plate after plate piled high with fried clams and French fries, during college summers at the Blue Lobster solidified Margaret's aversion to fried foods. Grilled chicken and spinach salad were routinely her alternative to grease. For Jim Garret the choice was also a usual, regardless of restaurant, time of day or appetite, it was always steak, done medium-well. Jim chose a restaurant as a good location to discuss career paths and family history for safety. He thought raised voices, emotional responses and loss of control were less likely in public and during a meal. But, he also knew, for Margaret, dramatic outbursts in such places were always possible.

Based on their last late night exchange, Jim began on offense. After they ordered, he brought up his first objective. "So Margaret...I know you've thought about it. Would you like me to make a couple of calls to set up the research assistant spot at Fitzgerald and Reynolds? Ah...you know...the firm I sent you all the info on...the Governor's firm...pretty much connected to everyone and everything in state government...I could set it up for the rest of the summer."

If he had waited until the food arrived, there might have been an opportunity to discuss it. But, because of his impatience, her answer without food was direct. She was hungry. "No."

Jim Garret, father, mentor and self-appointed architect of his daughter's career, was affected by her sense of assuredness. He wasn't certain whether the change was in Margaret or in his own ability to recognize it. But it was there and she was clear. On the first point, he conceded.

"OK, OK...so...what are you going to do?"

Surviving Philly, surviving producers, surviving directors, she was hardened enough to know when to tap the edge, "I'm going to workshop the play...*Overturn* in Ogunquit, waitress a few shifts at the "Blue" for some cash and help Charlie Bay Burningwater rebury his ancestors."

"You are going to what!" Jim raised his voice, responded emotionally and lost control. Everyone in their section of the restaurant turned in his direction.

Margaret, knowing that Burningwater was the primary source of aggravation, didn't miss a beat, "That's right...I'm going to keep writing and wait tables." Fortunately for both, their food came. Jim was no longer hungry. Margaret smiled; dove into large chunks of grilled chicken, bacon seasoned spinach and enjoyed the moment.

"Where in the world did that come from...this whole business with Charlie Bay and burying ancestors?" Jim leaned so far toward her, in total disbelief, his tie folded onto his steak. A mushroom stuck to the silk. As he cleaned and repositioned his tie, he slid his plate aside, regained his composure and mumbled about his strategy for a luncheon meeting. After a sigh, he gazed at his daughter who was enjoying her meal and waited for her to explain. He waited awhile, she was thinking about when she could dictate the tie sequence.

"Remember when I told you that I saw Charlie Bay at Casco Point...on the island...during your trip to the Carolinas?"

Now prepared to listen, Jim nodded.

"Well, he asked me then...for help. He said he needed a writer. When the river was dredged...a long time ago...all the work they did uncovered the burial grounds of the Casco Tribe. Graves were exposed...the State University was called to take care of the bones. All the bones they took from the Casco Indian cemetery on the tip of Long Neck were supposed to be returned... maybe thirty-five years ago." She continued to crunch spinach. "But they weren't and Charlie Bay asked for my help to get them back...back to be reburied. We wrote a formal request. I met with the University's representative...an anthropologist...name is Dr. Sorensen... we met yesterday and I'll work with him to get everything returned."

Her casual tone, ability to eat and talk at the same time and her indifference to a professional career plan annoyed him. But, he was a man who built success on the principles of recognizing the positive in each circumstance and developing it to the maximum. He passed on the judgment of the project as wasted time and focused on its potential. Wondering if there were any, Jim asked about a resume builder.

"Is it possible that this could be considered a consulting job or some type of university affiliate position...maybe you could stick it on your resume somewhere?"

Margaret smiled at her father, appreciated his constancy in the struggle to direct career choices and asked for more rolls. He went deeper.

"Why are you doing this?"

"I'm doing this as a favor for a friend and for Molly... because she would have done it." She also came with an agenda. She wanted the story of her aunt.

"Ah, Molly...I never finished did I?"

"No, and I have waited patiently...for me anyway."

Jim acknowledged, but only to himself, that she hadn't pestered him about his half sister. He appreciated it without admission. Tentative, he chose his words.

"Molly was nine years older than me. My first real memories of her were as a sister who had already left home. I didn't know about the half sister part till later. She came back to visit us for a few weeks at a time... during what I found out was between jobs or boyfriends or bouts with the bottle. I believe she truly loved my mother...but even then...looking back on it...I think she was sick. In those years I don't know if she was ever treated. My mother protected me and didn't say much...I guess because of my age. Growing up I never really knew Molly until my mother passed. I was fourteen... as you know I was raised from then on by Aunt Mary and Uncle Kevin...I worked a lot to do my share with that whole crowd in that small house...during those years... Molly roared into my life from time to time... bringing gifts...probably more than she could afford...great gifts. And not just for me...for everyone..." Jim smiled with the recollection. "She always wanted to take me some place...whisked me away to the ocean usually...even in the winter. We'd get plenty of food...all of my favorites ...I ate the whole time. It was great, no responsibilities, no work, just food. Then when I was about seventeen things didn't go too well for any of us. Aunt Mary passed. Uncle Kevin couldn't handle the crowd by himself and he had a new wife within a year...she couldn't handle Kevin or the crowd. So that's when I quit school...got a job at the fish plant... but you've heard this story plenty of times...night school...GED all that."

Margaret nodded, set down her fork and folded her hands on her napkin. She understood every family had two or three key stories, embellished and galvanized into legend; the cannery and night school was one of theirs.

"But also during those couple of years...when all this was going on...Molly came less and less. When she did come, she wasn't well. She was not herself. It was like her spirit had been broken. Then... she didn't come at all. I didn't see her for about two and a half years. I was pretty upset with her for disappearing...for what seemed to me to be a long time. She was the only family I had. Then...just after I started dating your mother she came back. She started visiting now and then with no real explanation of what happened or why. I was very happy to see her, very glad she was back when your mother and I got married, but she wasn't the same. She disappeared from time to time and then she'd come back...same pattern over and over again for years. And later on...since we were doing OK...I'd give her some money to get on her feet...she never asked for it...said that she was keeping track and promised to pay me back. I wasn't keeping track...never expected to be paid back. That's when she started taking care of you. Your brother was too old and wanted no part of a nanny. I guess...I wanted a way to get her more money...I guess...for you to know what I knew in her...the goodness...the caring.... most of all her love...because it meant so much to me."

Margaret watched her father attempt to control his emotions. He was a very stoic man who rarely spoke of his youth and of the feelings he harbored for so long as an adolescent. His eyes watered as he continued.

"But there was a problem. We found out that she couldn't be trusted. Sometimes she didn't take you where she said she did...then she'd bring you home...have the smell of alcohol on her breath...a little glassy eyed...we had to stop. She got gradually worse, especially when she didn't take her medicines. I'd go and see her from time to time while you were in high school without anybody knowing...but eventually even I could see that her illness, depression, required that she be hospitalized. She never came out. When they called and told me she passed....I felt like I let her down. I was ashamed. I told your Mother and that was it." Jim wiped his nose and eyes with the linen napkin.

After giving him a few moments she asked, "Where is she buried?"

"Next to my mother...she never really got to know her own. No matter what...family still has to take care of family the best they can."

They didn't say much to each other in the restaurant parking lot and left in separate cars.

Jr. Walker never sounded better. With a pale blue sky to the east and dark blue river below, Max turned up the volume on Jr. Walker and the All-stars as he crossed the Piscatiqua Bridge into Maine. *Sweet Soul* was the song; Max practiced it thousands of times. Each attempt was a dedicated and impassioned struggle to reproduce the tenor sound of his musical idol. For Max Sorensen, it never happened. He accepted his limitations as a musician and considered the hours of pursuit; sax therapy. His lack of talent and questionable soul notwithstanding, this song seized his emotions, his heart and through the years, never let go. He had Jr. loud on 95 north bound.

It took Max a few days to get organized in Boston. Dealing with his apartment was of no consequence other than laundry. Most of his effort was with research equipment. He chose to leave nothing behind. Max packed a portable x-ray machine, digital x-ray hardware, software and a variety of sensors. The equipment necessary for cone beam radiography he placed on reserve at the University's technology center in case he needed it this summer. Rather than trying to find a system in Maine to run all the photographic capture and 3D imaging software for the temporary lab, he packaged and boxed all the hardware and took backup software from his own lab. And without any hesitation, he loaded up a brand new digital micro video camera and digital video recorder and hoped that no one in his department missed it. He brought his stuff, his Anthropology Department's stuff, his university's stuff and his hope that he might find a reason to need it all.

There were two choices on the rollers of the stainless steel rotisserie cooker, regular and foot-long. Max remembered the store from his last trip. It was a converted gas station tucked away at the end of the Maine State University exit. With Jr. Walker's "Sweet

Soul" still playing in his head, he chose regular and smothered it with mustard and relish. Eating the hot dog, he let his eyes drift around the remodeled building. High above the food shelves and coolers, mounted in a ring around the four walls, was a row of chrome hubcaps. It was fitting to Max, the structure that maintained the big American cars of the sixties and seventies, displayed hubcaps as medals of past performance in the battle lost. At one point in his career, he toyed with the idea of a book on the symbolic aspects of hubcaps in twentieth century American culture. This was just before his separation from Linda and a few months later, even he thought it was a bad idea. For Max however, there would always be beauty in hub caps. But, they had to be chrome.

Now wandering the aisles, he found the soft-serve ice cream counter and its' border of colorful sundaes and toppings. After the hot dog, he felt like dessert but was distracted before he could decide the topping.

There was a bulletin board near the ice cream menu that posted business cards, cars for sale and a one page printed announcement with information for the Casco Nation Census. The Census was scheduled during the third week in July for five consecutive days at a number of listed locations. This was an official notification to all those who wished to be recorded as members of the Casco Tribe and listed on the Tribal Roll. With the letterhead of O'Connor and Napolitano, it appeared to be a legal document, but there was no signature. Max read it twice and considered it out of place for the bulletin board. It struck him as an odd and confusing announcement.

Ethnicity in general confused him. Contemporary America was built of communities of people who, for the most part, believe they were from somewhere else. They were individuals, living in cities and towns across the country, who identified with their ancestral populations. This was ethnic identity defined by belief, not by genes or geography.

In this case, Max knew in order to be a member of the Casco Tribal Nation, the individual must demonstrate one-quarter lineage in the ancestral line. To be listed on the Tribal Roll, they had to be one fourth Casco. But he never understood the requirement. Was it a cultural affiliation? Was it a genetic relationship? Or was it parts, not necessarily equal, of both?

Max thought if he drifted any further a headache was not far off. There was a lot of unpacking to be done. Buying a small banana boat, he left for the final ten minutes of his drive with *Sweet Soul* locked into the replay button. For the remainder of the afternoon, Max unloaded the research equipment into the long room of his summer laboratory. He spent the evening walking the beach.

The task for his first full day was to organize and setup all of the equipment for a functional lab. Conceptually, he wanted to take advantage of the long room and large oak tables. Max envisioned a sequence of recording stations that ended with each specimen packaged for reburial. The easiest part of the setup was to place an examination bin on each tabletop. The exam bin frame was about the size of a door and constructed of two by fours. Max lined the frames with plastic and filled each with about three inches of fine white sand. The examination bins provided a stable location to place and orient the skeletal material for x-rays, photographs and video. With a restless spirit this sequence also allowed Max to move from station to station as his interest dictated. The station sequence included: an unpacking area, the x-ray station, a skeletal analysis bin with digital imaging, a prepackaging skeletal inventory bin and the Casco Collection's final packaging area. Start to finish, Max's stations rambled on for fifty feet straight down the center of the arched building.

On an outside wall, halfway down the room was a desk-sized table Max used for his laptop and printer. In order to test his cell service and WiFi connection, he left a message for Margaret and sent her an email that he was in the lab. To test his wireless printer, he found an Indian Law web-site, located the Passamaquoddy vs. Maine Settlement Act and printed the documents. He glanced at the pages to make sure they were legible but didn't read the text. Scanning the room Max decided enough setup, twirled his wedding ring for a few seconds and went for Casco bones.

From the Casco archive, Max selected a storage carton that contained the human skeletal remains of one individual. Setting the carton next to a sand bin, he lifted a number of light brown long bones from the inside. Plastic bags of additional bones followed, each components of the skeletal system; hands, feet, spinal column, pelvis, ribs. The skull and mandible were the last uncovered and placed the bin. The brown cranium, with empty orbits and a lower jaw set askew, appeared to be surging forward from the sand. Max passed from the practical aspects of the day's setup to the overriding sense of a presence in human existence. The beauty of this specimen made his breath short. This was a treasure. With moist palms, he placed the bones in anatomical order. The result was a male specimen, estimated age of fifty-five, plus or minus five years. For Max, this was spectacular.

Without examining the specimen further, he selected another box from the shelves and unpacked this material at the second sand bin. Again, the bones were in excellent condition. After examination of the pelvis, Max identified the sex as female. Age at death he estimated to be forty years, plus or minus three. There was obvious scaring and remodeling on the skull and bones of the legs. Max noted that both specimens were designated on their box labels as prehistoric; but no dates. Once the female bones were in the exam bin, he was quick to reach for another Casco.

For the third bin, Max selected a specimen from a burial site marked historic. The individual was male with an estimated age of forty-five, plus or minus five years. The thoracic vertebrae showed multiple boney lesions and there appeared to be generalized osteoporosis in locations throughout the skeleton. The world around Max was fading away. It was only the distant rhythmic pounding that brought him back.

"Sorry, how long have you been here? It's not locked, just jammed." Max mumbled into the door as he glanced through the dirty glass at Margaret's back-lit silhouette on the other side. He invited her into the lab and waited for her purpose. Max appreciated Margaret as a woman intent on reburial, all business. He didn't expect repatriation of the Casco to happen as fast as she and Charlie Bay wanted. He finally said, "So what's on your mind?"

"Now that you've had a look at the archive and know what it will take to inventory, I came by to set a date for the reburial ceremony. It needs to be set soon to give Burningwater a straight answer and settle him down a little. He has every right to be impatient and he certainly is angry."

"OK, sure. Come on over to my make-shift desk and we'll take a look at the calendar on my laptop." As they walked down the vaulted room Max probed, "While you are here, could you help me? I have one last thing to setup...help me put the base of this x-ray machine together. It's really a two man job. You know, easy for two...impossible for one." He needed the help and was already stalling on the repatriation date. Margaret wasn't surprised.

The assembly was easy for two. They needed only a few minutes to place the unit in sequence on the skeletal pathway. Margaret was overwhelmed by the examination and inventory process. She had no idea it would require so much equipment and wondered why. Catching her eyes drift to the human remains situated in the bins, Max was ready to shift to the hard sell.

"Could I show you one of these?"

As she moved to a close-up view of human bones, the old Ash Wednesday prayer, "from dust you and to dust you shall return", came to her from an experience long since forgotten. As the words tumbled through her mind, she stared at the gray-brown remains of a human being. This was a foreign experience for her. She needed to dictate, to record these feelings, let the words spill out to be remembered. Before she could get to her thoughts, Dr. Sorensen the educator camouflaged Max the pitchman.

"This specimen is male...about...oh I'd say early to mid fifties at death. He lived in this area prior to European contact...but I don't know the carbon date for this burial site. If there is one, it's in the file on the collection. This skeletal material is a great baseline specimen...complete...in excellent condition and prehistoric. Take a look at this. See how worn the teeth are but with no decay...no European sugar...molasses ...there's an unbelievable amount of wear." Max reached into the sand, removed the intact mandible with a full complement of teeth in the jaw and moved it toward Margaret for a better view. She looked more closely, but didn't reach to touch the bone. Sensing her hesitancy, Max continued. "This fellow...by the look of things...was a marine hunter-gatherer...fish, clams, crabs, small game, deer...any nuts...berries...anything he could find...most of it was probably mixed with sand.

If you look closely at the joints in his arms you can see the difference in the amount of degenerative joint disease between the right and left side...there's quite a bit more on the right than the left...he was probably right handed. He was evidently a hard working individual...at least based on the boney wear and tear...he was a hard worker."

"He was also someone's grandfather... a Casco ancestor... a grandfather waiting to be buried."

Without acknowledging her comment, Max paused. She was driven, possibly an even match, but he had more. He drifted toward the next bin in sequence.

"This specimen is female...also prehistoric." Margaret was drawn to the skeleton and stayed by his side. Max looked for her attention out of the corner of his eye. "Pretty straightforward if you take a look at the pubic bones...she was around forty when she died... also marine hunter-gatherer...but this is interesting." He removed the skull from the bin and rotated it in his hands to the best angle for light. "See in the floor of the orbits that pitted appearance...perforations and up around the eye brows as well...all the bony remodeling on the forehead...these lumps and bumps on a surface that is generally smooth?"

Margaret nodded, uncertain as to what, but she knew she saw something unusual.

"Tertiary Syphilis...the disease was likely present throughout this population."

Margaret's urban world was inundated with information on sexually transmitted diseases; syphilis was on the list as another STD out there linked to bad choices. Margaret wrinkled her forehead.

"Yes, somebody's grandmother with syphilis." Max smiled at Margaret. "Try to put yourself in a different place and time...her time, there was no treatment. The moral code was relative to her community...her lifeway...which is unknown to us. Our codes and creeds didn't exist in her world. As tempting as it is...and I am guilty too...we can't reconstruct lives to judge them...only try to understand them a little better...ultimately with the hope of getting perspective on our own." He paused and gave her a chance to collect her thoughts.

The ongoing, everyday struggle not to observe human history from an ethnocentric viewpoint was so engrained in Max that his casual and non-judgmental tone regarding both Margaret and the specimen left her taken aback. She forced herself to refocus on a date for burial. Max refused to let up.

"Now here's another interesting..."

"Max we need to set..."

Sensing the opportunity was about to be lost, Max interrupted with his pitch's finale. He picked up the skull of the historic specimen.

"Take a look at the increase in the pathology of the jaws... all these abscesses...perforations in the upper jaw. The assumption is that with a dietary change, presumably more refined sugars, their health changed for the worst... look at this." Max pointed to the holes in bone. "It's hard to know whether it hurt or not. The response to pain is so culturally mediated...it's something we'll probably never know...but changes in diet did have an impact."

This time, as he held the bone toward Margaret, she touched the top of the skull. It was cold. Exchanging the skull for a vertebra, Max kept going.

"Tuberculosis was present in North America prior to contact...but it was population density dependent. So that meant that before the Europeans arrived...it only showed up in individuals who lived in close permanent quarters...horticulturists...you know farmers...sedentary peoples. The skeletal evidence for TB is a lesion that looks a lot like this one on the thoracic vertebrae. Chances are this fellow didn't catch TB while living as a Casco. He might have moved to town...worked in a mill or a fish processing plant...got sick and came home to die. A tough life for people, the ones who left and tried to fit into a different world...the Euro-American world...it was tough."

Margaret found the depth of Max's sensitivity and compassion incongruous. How was it possible for him to have such empathy toward the Casco plight? And at the same time, he was so insensitive toward Burningwater and the repatriation of Casco people. Margaret pressed him back.

"If he came home to die...shouldn't he be buried with his people?"

"By the looks of things he's going to get there. The question is when? I'd like just a little more time with the collection than it takes for a simple inventory and repackaging." Before she responded, he continued with his rationale. "You can tell in a heartbeat that this is an absolutely spectacular collection, a treasure. There is so much more to be learned. So here is what I thought...

By the way Margaret, what do you do anyway?"

"I'm a writer...a..."

"Ah writing...not one of my strengths...so you've got plenty of time and flexibility. Perfect!"

"Not really...I already have a project for the summer...two projects...plus Charlie Bay."

"But, no deadlines?"

"Self imposed and we have to set one for this."

"A writer with discipline...also not one of my strong points... what do you think of this idea? And in it there'll be lots of time for you to write.

I thought with some help...I was hoping you...with all this equipment...we could digitally record an examination of each specimen as it is inventoried and prepared for reburial...right here...right down this whole assembly line...radiographs...video...all of it. In a short time, we can archive the entire collection as a digital record for researchers and students to study long after we're all dead and buried. There are funds available... you'd get paid as a research assistant."

It was hardly a truthful offer, but Max did have Sandra's credit card, she would have a title and he was desperate. Unable to speak, Margaret was astonished.

"I'll need to round up three or four components of the collection at other universities and museums...that's going to take some time. Before they arrive...if we work together...I bet we could have what's here digitally archived. Together, we can be as fast as I could be just doing the inventory by myself...what do you say?"

His proposal of a digital archive as part of the inventory was suspected when she saw the recording equipment. She figured he was up to something. The offer to be paid as an assistant was a surprise and absurd. Margaret was quickly coming to realize that Max Sorensen operated on his own repatriation agenda, not Sandra Walsh's. She couldn't turn him loose in the lab with a date and expect the reburial to get done as scheduled. He was slippery, scattered and needed to be watched. As a way to complete the inventory more quickly and with consistency, it was a good idea. She did have flexibility and she could still write every morning. Anything that was going to speed up the reburial and keep an eye on Max was a good idea, good for Charlie Bay.

"It wasn't what I had in mind for the summer...but as long as Charlie Bay says that it's OK...I'll help you to prepare the Casco...but no pay.

Dr Sorensen, let's get this straight...to postpone the reburial for more research projects...as far as Charlie Bay is concerned not possible...absolutely not...so whatever else you have in mind is not going to happen.

Dr. Walsh knows about this plan?"

Max looked guilty. Lines of authority were something her father taught well.

The phone in Sandra Walsh's living room rang the programmed four times before the caller came over the speaker. Max made no attempt to get up from the winged-back chair to answer. He knew who it was. Holding his sax, he remained still and listened for the message.

"It's me and I know you're there Max... pick up. I left a message on your cell which was useless. Come on Max...pick up. We have to talk about this incredibly ridiculous stall that you're trying to build into the Casco repatriation. I know you're listening to me...in my living room...probably with your sax...trying to play the same song as ever...with a stack of your old Bette Davis movies."

"Barbara Stanwyck," Max whispered as he waited for her to call him a jackass. He touched the reed to his lips and wasn't disappointed.

Under stress Max's mind meandered to familiar places. It was December of 1977 when he first heard Jr. Walker's recording of *Sweet Soul*. On his way home after a paleopathology conference at Michigan State an unpredicted lake effect snowstorm stuck him in a bar at Detroit airport for three hours with ten dollars and a jukebox full of old Motown. By accident, he punched in the flip side of his first choice: the All Stars' version of *Come See About Me* and three minutes of *Sweet Soul* later his world was never the same.

Through the years other tenor sax players like Boots Randolph and Illinois Jacquet inspired Max, but none like Jr. Walker. For him, *Sweet Soul* was a personal anthem that took him to places otherwise impossible to travel. Sandra was correct on two counts: he was with his sax playing *Sweet Soul* and it was a stall. He had no choice but to pursue both and getting the stall to work was a problem.

During situations like these, when he was drawn into circumstances he thought he understood but didn't, he missed Linda's jolt of clarity. It was her ability to assess and order chaos, usually chaos he created, that he found so attractive. He loved his wife; he loved her clarity. Their last good kiss was on a Monday afternoon four Junes ago. He knew, the moment it ended.

The initial six months of separation was the most difficult. Alone for the first time, he had a constant longing for balance. He missed hearing the other side. Now, he was accustomed to being alone, almost desiring it. He was afraid of disruption. Rationalizing the solitude as a necessity, at least at this stage of his life, he tried to convince himself he needed it to produce; to produce something scholarly, something of quality and value to his profession. Even from Max's perspective results were mixed.

From the very beginning, it was not easy for him to produce. Years ago, during the writing phase of his dissertation research, he was up most of one night, alone at the kitchen table, writing and rewriting a small, two page section of the first chapter. Frustrated and insecure, he pushed through hour after hour of dissatisfaction with his work until he finally achieved what he thought was reasonable. When asked by Linda at sunrise to care for the boys, he fell asleep. She threw the two precious pages, along with his electric typewriter off the front porch, into the picturesque center quad of the graduate housing apartments. At the top of her lungs, she accompanied the thrust with the phrase, "this is not a dissertation, this, is just masturbation". To this day, he swore that she received spousal applause from other graduate couples. For at least a year after the event, Max's greatest fear was that the only productive aspect of his research was its association with that nightmarish phrase and its catchy potential to become a bumper sticker.

Sitting in the darkness, interrupted by Barbara Stanwyck's voice and the flicker of a black and white film, alone with his wants and desires for the Casco, the strife continued.

The land line rang for a second time, Max didn't move.

"Max, it's me and this time you had better pick up. Put down the beer and the cheese spread and whatever other high sodium products you have to comfort you in this chaos you're creating and pick up."

Max stood, walked to the machine and muted the voice. He decided to see Burningwater in the morning.

Chapter Seven

The files of papers, names and numbers contained every document and bit of information, some in hard copy, some scanned, concerning the Casco excavation except the one Max wanted. After searching through the stacks and doc folders twice, he decided that for some inexplicable reason, the compulsively thorough Dr. Walsh forgot something. Whether the oversight was intentional or not didn't matter. He needed a copy of the Casco agreement. He needed burial ground excavation details: who signed what, where and when for the removal of bones. Despite the early morning hour, Max worked online applications and email requests. Before nine and after five, when dealing with Federal and State bureaucracies, web pages and e-forms had their advantages. Without speaking to a single human being, he requested from the Bureau of Indian Affairs, the State Historical Commission and the State Archeologist's Office all of the transaction records and Tribal Council agreements regarding the Casco excavation. Sitting back in the desk chair, he looked at his notes, thought about his completed requests and wondered if any information was ever going to show up.

The strategy for his backup plan was a simple one; find out who, on the Tribal Council, signed the release for the excavation, convince one of the members to support the continued research on the Casco Collection and enlist their assistance in overturning or at least postponing Burningwater's request. However, in order to stall Sandra on the other end, he first wanted to get Charlie Bay's permission for an examination of the collection to go along with the reburial inventory. Even with Margaret's help, the process would last long enough to find a Casco ally. He thought this tack had a chance.

Deciding to speak with Charlie Bay was one thing, finding him was another. He retraced Margaret's search path with no luck. As a last resort, he elected to park at the fishermen's Co-op and ask anyone who bothered to listen where he might locate Burningwater; still no luck. Max observed that most lobstermen spoke a few well-chosen words and gave little information. With each inquiry and to his amazement, he usually gave more than he got. Figuring that he had outsider, tourist or maybe even anthropologist written all over him, Max explored the one remaining possibility. He headed on foot up the river shoreline toward the anchorage's only boatyard.

Small wooden rowboats, scattered in a palate of colors against the white sand, lined the narrow river beach. Each boat had an anchor line that stretched up into the green dunes. Max hopped and stepped over the taught ropes as he walked west along the leeward side of the river. Two hundred yards beyond the skiffs, he reached three long, parallel and barn red boathouses. The air was humid, the sand was soft and sweat beaded across his forehead. He was wet and winded. To catch his breath he sat on a launching railway that extended from a bay door into the river. He felt his heart pound much faster than the pounding hammers. Collectively, the boathouses echoed with the sounds of boat building and repair.

Looking into the shed from the bright sunlit riverfront made identifying anyone working inside impossible. Max was unable to see anything but shadows. He gathered himself, walked past the waterfront railways, around the far building and searched for landside access. On the west corner, a ladder led from the beach to a large open-air work dock. As he climbed to the top, Max peered at eye level onto the platform's surface. Gray weathered two by sixes were rough and worn. Missing or rotting planks had been repaired in a patchwork of plywood caps. A few bait barrels stood on the surface along with two stacks of lobster traps. There were no railings on the waterside edges. With a ten-foot tide, from some locations, it was a twelve-foot drop. Max didn't look down. He looked straight ahead and beside a wooden dory, he found Charlie Bay Burningwater.

Charlie Bay was poised next to the overturned boat holding a crank hand drill. The wood bit at its tip was only inches from the faded red dory bottom. Charlie Bay didn't move. He didn't push the drill bit forward into the hull or pull it back to look up as Max rustled his way onto the dock. Charlie Bay Burningwater was too busy praying for forgiveness.

The boat stretching out in front of Charlie Bay was the Alton built dory he fished from for almost sixty years. He and Earl Alton built the boat to row. It was never meant to hold an outboard motor. But for the past two years Charlie Bay was not strong enough to row in open ocean and for the past two years his boat never touched the water. Expecting to get over this backache or that arm pain and expecting at this stage in his life, to get stronger rather than weaker, Charlie Bay was postponing the inevitable. He hated outboard motors. He hated gasoline. And, he hated the thought of cutting a hole in the bottom of his boat for an outboard well in order to use both. The wind, the tide and time overtook his strength, but not his loyalty to the principles of his boat building master.

At seventeen, with a hard body and adolescent drives, Charlie Bay knew about sex. Earl Alton taught him about women, Scotch whiskey and wooden boat building; especially boat building. A master craftsman with an appreciation for voluptuous women and fine Scotch, Earl Alton had lived his whole life next to the boat shop on the tidal flats of the Casco River. What he knew about fishing and boat building he learned from his father and his father's father. For some unknown reason, during the last year of his life, he chose to teach a lot of what he knew about boat building to Charlie Bay Burningwater.

It was a strange apprenticeship to those who drifted into Alton's boat shop for a seat by the wood stove. Earl rarely spoke a word to young Burningwater, he worked and they were always together; the young man's eyes glued to his every move. The result was Charlie Bay's Bank dory, maybe Earl's one hundredth and last; for Charlie Bay, his first and only. Earl told his pupil that a man's dory was the same as his wife, to stick with her in good times and bad and only have one. Earl expected the dory to last longer than both of them, wives and all.

Earl Alton's boat shop was the last building on the dead-end road that followed the Casco riverbank west from the fishermen's Co-op. Parked alongside the peeling white shop was a rusting yellow school bus, with no engine and no seats. It was always filled with long lengths of white pine. Next to the bus was a make shift wood-fired boiler constructed from an oil tank. It was used for bending oak frames and steaming knees. There was no sign. Folks in search of a dory were told to just look for the bus and the boiler at the end of the road. The doors to the two-car garage sized building were never locked. If someone came by and borrowed a tool while Earl was on the water, he knew what was gone and generally had a good idea who took it. In the fifty-eight years of building boats only a few tools were lost and none were stolen.

Only two power tools: a band saw and a table saw out fitted the shop. An electric drill and Earl's big firm hand never met. There was an assortment of hammers, planes, chisels and screwdrivers but the hatchet and jackknife were Earl's favorites. The plans for each boat were in his head and he rarely drew a line.

Most of the tools in Alton's shop were kept in row after row of different sized fruit boxes. The boxes lined four shelves on each wall of the building's interior. There wasn't a draw or cabinet in the room but every tool had its place. For years, Earl collected the solid wooden crates left by the traveling Fruit Man. Every Thursday, during the summer; the Fruit Man cleaned his truck and deposited the best boxes under a light pole at the fish pier. From time to time, Earl left him a bucket of clams. Charlie Bay continued picking up the crates after Earl Alton died and did so until the Fruit Man died. Clementines were his favorite.

The Bank dory that Earl and Charlie Bay built was nineteen feet, five inches in overall length. On the white pine bottom, the five planks ran stem to stern. In each piece chosen for the dory, the grain held the line and Charlie Bay gradually understood in the daily scouring of the wood piles an unspoken principle of Earl's life; the board showed the builder. Each plank in the lapstrake hull told them where it belonged. Earl Alton listened, Charlie Bay learned and for almost sixty years their work served Burningwater well.

Thanks to Max Sorensen the planked bottom was going to remain intact a little longer. Looking for any excuse not to cross cut the dory's hull for an outboard motor well, even if it came from an enemy, Charlie Bay stopped praying to Earl for forgiveness. He set the drill on the dock.

Max approached Charlie Bay and saw the uneasiness in his face. Charlie Bay was upset. This was not a good time, this was the fisherman's domain and the self-absorbed Dr. Sorensen refused to acknowledge it all.

"Hi, remember me, Max Sorensen, from the other day, with Margaret, on the beach?"

Charlie Bay didn't answer or turn toward him. He dropped his eyes and mumbled, "damn".

"This your boat?"

Charlie Bay nodded yes.

"It's a Bank dory isn't it? Built in Nova Scotia or some place in Massachusetts, Amesbury maybe?"

Max was showing off. Charlie Bay was surprised but he had no intention of crediting Max's familiarity with wooden boats. The Mystic Seaport Museum Marine Bookstore was on Max's regular rounds. He read a lot, had no woodworking or carpentry skills and consistently wrestled with any tool, nails or screws. Blood was the usual result. Charlie Bay looked at Max's callous-free hands and pride got the better of him.

"Built here."

"Did you build it?"

"Some...an Alton Dory, his last one." Charlie Bay was searching for the upper hand. "So it is a Pipeboat for the dream journey."

He succeeded.

"A Pipeboat for the dream journey?"

Charlie Bay again nodded but this time with one singular dip of his chin and didn't say a word. Max wondered if he were about to enter an area in which he had limited experience. It was the dance between the ethnographer, the trained participant observer and the informant, the local knowledge willing to divulge cultural traditions. Was it about to unfold? Or, was Burningwater teasing him? With very little to lose, Max took the chance.

"What makes this a Pipeboat?" There was no answer. "Who goes on this dream journey?"

After pursing his lips and squinting, Charlie Bay answered, "The Pipeboat People."

"Where do they go?"

"The spirit world."

"And you need a Pipeboat to do that?"

"It helps." Charlie Bay hadn't enjoyed himself this much with an outsider in quite awhile.

"Is it because it was the builder's last boat before he died and he was as close as he would ever get before crossing over into the spirit world? Is it what makes this a Pipeboat?"

Removing his pipe and tobacco pouch from his breast pocket and then pinching a small amount of tobacco, Burningwater made an offering to the four directions and to the earth and sky. Max felt his heart rate increase and the blood pound through his neck.

"Among the Nation, there are those who, even though they are of this world, live also in the spirit world. But because they live in both worlds, they need a means to travel between them. For those among the Pipeboat People, the journey must be made in Pipeboats."

In the lee of the boat shed, the smoke from Charlie Bay's pipe drifted skyward as his eyes stayed on Max. Why was he here?

" Is this a Casco Pipeboat and you are the Pipeboat People?"

Max caught himself, considered the moment as a rusty old anthropologist duped by a shrewd Casco and got back to his purpose.

"I have a request."

Burningwater shifted to the hull of the overturned dory and clenched the pipe stem tighter in his teeth.

"I would like to have your permission for some additional documentation of the Casco Collection. I'd like to record their examination as we do the inventory for reburial. I have it set up so it won't take any longer." Max didn't wait for a response. "Those bones have a tremendous story to tell about the way your people lived years ago; before and after the Europeans arrived here. The bones can talk to us and tell a lot about lives, diseases, deaths, about how people worked, what they did and what they ate. What do you say? Can I have your..."

Charlie Bay interrupted him with a hard edge to his voice. "I told you before, bones don't talk. They don't tell stories. They don't tell anything. They have nothing to say. They must be put in order; in their proper place...in the earth. It has to be done so that the spirits of my people can take their rightful place...make their journey. Removing them from the burial ground has broken the pathway...their journey has stopped. The bones are a part of my people...they're connected to their spirits."

"But Burningwater it's a great chance to learn. Chances to learn come in spurts with glimpses of our past that we had no idea about before. Most of the past has just been built over or plowed under...just lost and forgotten...no connection to us. We are great at saving the moments in a sculpture or a painting but we are awful at understanding the people. Bones tell us things...just like the tools that your people made...the wood they carved or the boats they built. We can learn an awful lot about them, your ancestors...your past. By understanding what happened...hopefully...we can get a better handle on where to go for the future. And here...right here with your people, is an unbelievable opportunity to do just that...to get a glimpse...a chance to know the past of the Casco...improve your future...all our futures by not making the same mistakes...by not repeating the same injustices."

"Time is not a straight line."

"What...what do you mean?"

"You're talking about the past and the future as dots on a line...we stand between them. You say my ancestors are the past...you will help me understand my future. The past is yesterday...the past is today...the past is tomorrow. I already am my future."

For a second Max understood, until his stubbornness, his education or his inability to surrender blocked the insight. He was confused. "I don't understand."

"Time is a circle...time isn't a line...time is a circle." Seeing Max remained lost, Charlie Bay's patience was fading, "My ancestors are yesterday and they're tomorrow. They're with me today. But some aren't going to continue on the journey of the Pipeboat People because their bones are in boxes on a shelf instead of in the earth. Don't you see that they must be reburied? They must be in the earth!"

In his anger and frustration, Burningwater came very close to grabbing Max Sorensen by the throat.

Recognizing the threat, Max strengthened his voice, "Those bones will be recorded as we do the inventory for burial. They will all be reburied. I just need your permission to have them a little longer. No one is trying to keep them... so much can be gained. To bury all that information away...so much will be lost...lost forever!" Leaning over the dory hull, Max was also tempted to go for the throat.

"You don't want your history lost. I don't want the spirit of my people lost. If bones are not buried...spirits are lost forever." Charlie Bay leaned in, inches from Max's face. "Spirits are lost forever unless...unless we act in their favor...unless I act in their favor." His voice trailed off. He lowered his head and their conversation was over.

Max realized that the loud and angry voices of the argument resulted in a headache for him and a crowd of friends for Burningwater. Five fishermen drifted into view behind Charlie Bay; young, strong and disturbed by Max's presence on the dock.

No one spoke. Looking at the six men bound together by the ocean, Max realized how different his world was from a lobsterman's life on the water. Their weathered faces and strong arms reflected lives dedicated to harvesting the sea. Max knew he was being threatened without being in danger. It was time to leave.

On his second step backward, in a casual attempt at a dignified exit, he tripped on a plywood patch, lost his balance only to regain it at the dock's edge. Even with his clumsiness, Max didn't remove his eyes from Burningwater. He was holding to the hope that he might receive a nod or a glance; just some slight indication for an extension, nothing. Charlie Bay's eyes never left the red bottom of the dory.

Half way down the ladder, Max finally looked to the sand and found an incoming tide, water to the second rung and not a speck of riverbank beach clear to the fishermen's co-op. He wondered which was more humiliating, the water or the return. He decided the water was not only more embarrassing but colder and climbed back onto the dock. Shaking his head at Max's reappearance, Charlie Bay mumbled, "damn".

The fisherman closest to the road pointed in the direction of the Co-op. Max followed without a word. He kept his hands tucked in his pockets and meandered to his car, all the while, reviewing his options.

The sound was recognizable but not the song. As she came closer to the open outer doors, the tenor sax was amplified by the laboratory's metal arched roof. Slipping through the second doorway, Margaret searched the long tunnel of music for a source. Her eyes found a shadow tucked among the stacks of cardboard boxes that held the remains of the Casco. The dark form was swaying to the music. Unnoticed, she moved closer. As she watched Max playing, she saw practice. At the song's end, she was silent. He stared at the skeletal specimen displayed on the exam table. It was as if he was waiting for a response.

"Do you think they heard you?"

Identifying the voice, "Margaret, come on over." He motioned with his sax for her to sit on a nearby lab stool. "That was *Sweet Soul* by Jr. Walker and the All Stars, or as close as I can come to Jr. Walker, which today wasn't very close." Max smiled. Margaret was unresponsive. "You have no idea who Jr. Walker is...do you?"

"None"

"Motown...the late sixties...a sound like nobody else on the planet...Jr. Walker? Here's the way that it's supposed to sound. Jr.'s dead but his music lives on...

digitally re-mastered, zeroes and ones, ones and zeros or whatever... you know numbers...numbers into the future."

Withdrawing a plastic CD case from a small canvas bag of supplies, he loaded a disk into his laptop and clicked play. Watching him, with his eyes closed, hang on every note and connected to some other place, she wondered if he had beer for lunch.

"I don't expect this song to do for you what it does for me...that's not fair to you or to Jr. Walker." He spoke softly, the song faded. "But the amazing thing is...when I first heard that song...it was an analog recording. You know on a record...a forty-five. It was the B side on vinyl. Then I had it in my record collection...you know... albums with liner notes and photographs. One of a kind album covers you could hold in your hands...big jackets you could read liner notes...over and over while you listened...vinyl."

"I know vinyl, Dean Martin."

Max froze for a second trying to figure out the Dean Martin reference and couldn't. "So you know it's a recording technology that wore out, scratched, broke, melted or just plain deteriorated with time.

This...I downloaded myself and burned the disc...not bad...huh?

But Margaret...what you and I can do here...with all this stuff that we have...ah, now that's a very different story, we can record and document the whole Casco Collection digitally...in theory...hopefully in practice, this is a method of archiving that won't let the data wear out...keeps it in zeroes and ones indefinitely. And to me, that seems to be a pretty remarkable thing when you think about it. Of course, if I think about it too long... well..."

Max was beginning to ramble and loose her, but the wonderment and enthusiasm with which he approached what he describe to her as; routine documentation and inventory, was genuine.

"What do you mean Max? I'm a little lost. I thought this was standard procedure...maybe it's not."

"It is...it is...in my book it is."

Gazing at the specimen nestled into the sand of the examination bin, Max continued to reflect aloud, "It's unbelievable really...the chronology of my life and my professional life...how it courses the transition from an analog world to a digital world. For you...it's only been numbers...ordinary...everyday life...for Burningwater it's never been numbers...never been quantified. I'm some where in between...a liminal being...in a quiet cultural and global revolution that's almost incomprehensible. Thinking about it...before you came I ended up having to take some sax therapy.

I got very excited at the possibility of creating a site on the internet that would make available all these data of the Casco specimens we're going to document... make ...accessible to anyone for research, comparative studies, to just look, to stimulate interest...the works. We could just put it out there...what you and I are going to record... for the world to see. But then I panicked...felt like a jerk. I got the blues."

Puzzled, she raised her eyebrows and shoulders.

"In the latter part of the nineteenth century, as the so called Indian Wars were drawing to a close...the U.S. Surgeon General ordered the military...some of the Civil War generals, you know the famous ones, to have their soldiers collect Native American heads and an occasional complete skeleton. The rationale was two fold: one, to measure cranial capacity for some state of the art supposedly scientific racial comparison which verified the intellectual supremacy of Euro-Americans and two, display aboriginal skeletons in museums for anyone who desired...to see...study or simply experience the soon to be extinct Indian. If I were to put the Casco Collection on a Website...digitize the whole thing...put it out there in cyberspace...am I any different...other than a century or so older? Am I just creating a digital museum with the same ethnocentric ignorance and arrogance five generations later?" Max paused, now considering the question. "Troubling questions...huh...all in the name of science and cultural understanding...possibly not such a great idea from another lost academic...so...I got the blues...went to an old friend...Jr. Walker and suddenly...you're standing here."

The lab was still. Amid the dust, the boxes and the bones sat a man overflowing with incongruity. At one moment he was charging relentlessly toward the ideals of accessible knowledge on the internet for the greater good and in the next he was questioning the narrow local cultural context of the greater good. Fortunately, for Margaret to clarify the repatriation and for the oncoming pain in Max's head, his ability to grasp, ponder and hold an expanded reality was short-lived.

"There's one other thing I should tell you. I went to see Burningwater this morning...to ask for permission to..."

"I know. I already heard."

Max was surprised at the rate information traveled. "For a group of people who don't say much...a few words spread awfully fast."

"Even to me."

"And you still came?"

"I came because we had an agreement. I understood that I was the one to talk with Charlie Bay so we could avoid what happened the other day on the beach. Charlie Bay is a very angry Indian and with good reason. I agreed to meet with Dr Walsh and at her request to work with you. I did this because of an old friendship and because of someone I care about. Charlie Bay needs protection from you and people in the University system like you. He needs my help to get back the bones of his people as fast as possible. He doesn't want to talk with you any more. He just wants the bones back and he expects me to deal with you as the school's representative to do it. Now...is that the way it's going to work...or not?"

Margaret was flush. She knew he was scheming. Max was sheepish.

"Ya, that'll work."

She wanted more.

"So what was so important that you had to see him...so important...that you couldn't discuss with me? What are you up to? What do you want to do?"

"What I want to do? OK. I'll tell you what's on my mind. This lab is set up to document, record and inventory all the material before repatriation. What we are going to do...starting today...is digitize the whole thing...on DVD, radiographs, microvideo images...the works. Together we can do it as part of the inventory and ...it's not going to take any additional time. And that's going to be a great archive..."

Margaret interrupted, "...but it's not enough is it Max...what else do you want?"

Max twirled his wedding ring. "Do you see those boxes stacked against the far wall...marked DNA?"

"Yes...the three smaller ones."

"There are a couple of techniques...that have been used successfully for a while now...they're being refined all the time. Anyway, they allow the extraction of DNA from ancient bone. It's really not all that complicated but we would have to consult a DNA lab...follow their protocols. I have a friend...a colleague of mine in Pittsburgh, who's in the field and he could work with us. There is a standard for harvesting uncontaminated samples from each specimen and sending it to a lab for whatever is the current state of the art analysis. Collecting the samples from the Casco bone would be our job...those boxes contain the necessary materials...all the stuff to harvest and ship the bone."

"No Max...absolutely not...no more research!"

"But Margaret, it's not research. It's harvesting DNA! The key is archiving the DNA...stuff you could store...pull as new techniques come along. This could go on for centuries!   Now...that's got some research potential...stuff you could store and pull for centuries!"

Max unclipped his sax from the strap around his neck and set it on the exam table.

"The other thing is...there's the chance to compare ancient DNA with living people...particular groups. You'd be able to tell if people...are...who they say they are.

But, the whole thing, it takes time and that's why I went to Burningwater this morning. It takes some time."

The ring of the land line phone interrupted Max's academic ramblings.   Standing close to the desk, Margaret reached for the receiver. But Max, with his arms outstretched and palms pressing toward her, tried to stop the pickup.

"No, don't! I know who it is! I don't want to talk..."

Margaret also knew who it was and she did want him to talk.

"I've already gotten three e-mails from her today. I shut off my...I know what she's going to tell me. Just take the message." Max started to walk away as Margaret picked up.

"Hello", she shook her head no in his direction, hit the speaker phone button before he got too far and gave him the look. "It's for you. Dr. Walsh."

"...of course it is." he mumbled as he walked to his sax, clipped it to the strap and held it for protection. "Sandra? What a surprise."

Margaret rolled her eyes, dropped her head and sat on the stool next to the phone.

"Max you jackass...you're acting like an idiot. I don't get it Max. Why does the bumbling jackass show up when I need perfection? Where is your head? Don't tell me I already know." There was a pause.

"So...having gotten that off your chest...what's on your mind Sandra..." He winced and a few more idiots and jackasses followed. Margaret liked this woman.

"Now listen carefully Max...I don't want any other research projects with the Casco. I don't want you dragging your feet while you try backup plan after backup plan to postpone the repatriation...most of all...I don't want any incidents like this morning. If this type of confrontation ever got to the press...the University would take a public relations beating. It's an absolutely no win situation. It would be a disaster. Do you hear me Max... a disaster! I want the reburial to go smoothly and quickly...remember...no incidents. Do you understand me Max? Am I clear enough...even for you?"

"Clear as a bell...Sandra...clear as a bell." He was giving in to Sandra's orders but Margaret suspected by the look in his eyes that he wasn't giving up.

"Good. Now do it. Just do whatever it takes to repatriate the collection. You can turn your cell back on." were Sandra Walsh's final words.

Shutting off the speakerphone, Margaret looked at Max as he spoke.

"You set me up for that call."

"You saw Charlie Bay this morning without me."

He smiled. "Tunnel vision can be discourteous."

Although, still unsure about Max Sorensen, Margaret was sure about Dr. Walsh. His response and readiness to move forward needed to be pushed. "Can we get to work on the repatriation?"

"Sure...I guess now's the time." Tucking one hand in his pocket and holding his sax with the other, Max swayed his way to the first inventory station humming, *Sweet Soul*.

Chapter Eight

Even in an unfamiliar community, Max possessed the ability to find what he always claimed was the best bakery in town. About two miles from the beach he discovered a small, storefront bakery tucked into a private residence. A stout woman in a baker's apron served hot blueberry muffins in the morning and pie by the slice in the late afternoon. He was a daily sunrise and a sometime end of the day customer.

The scent of fresh blueberry muffins filled his car only seconds after opening the bag. He ate one before starting the engine and saved the rest for the cemetery. It was over three weeks ago Max first noticed the small classic New England burial plot. The site was located just off a secondary road and occupied less than an acre. High grass surrounded stained, gray granite markers. There were no miniature American flags stuck next to headstones, no plastic baskets of flowers and no visitors. For almost a month, a neglected cemetery of tilted headstones and un-mowed lawn caught his eye and his curiosity.

Finally arranging the schedule with Margaret to free a morning, he was anxious to investigate this Euro-American record. The inscriptions on the first tier of headstones didn't disappoint him. Most of the markers listed mid to late seventeenth century birth and death dates. As was a common tradition of the era, spouse, children and parents were recorded on the same stone. By the dates, Max knew these individuals, buried in rows of orderly plots, were contemporaries to many of the specimens in the Casco Collection. The gravestone inscriptions indicated that most of the people were of Western European descent. The markers gave a written record of their existence in time and space as well as described their relationship in a family. Each stone connected the individuals to a lineage, a lineage of North American families, potentially traceable through town and Baptismal records to living ancestors.

For Max, at times such as these, it all seemed so remarkable. He was in a laboratory on the coast of Maine, attempting to reconstruct the unwritten record of a people who occupied the same earth as their European counterparts. The Casco, who also had mothers and fathers, brothers and sisters, sons and daughters; all remained unknown. And again as a scientist, he was pushing forward, in a different part of the world than the Nile Valley, to trudge his way through physical morphology. Attempting to compare and contrast the lumps and bumps on bones, he sought an understanding of the Casco people. He sought to know the Casco lifeway, a lifeway all but extinct. According to Sandra there was only one known lineal descendant left on Casco land. The remnant of the Casco people was Charlie Bay Burningwater and he was the obstacle.

Finding a large fieldstone at the border of the burial ground, Max sat on the hillside facing the July morning sun. The evaporating dew left the scent of tall grass and the bag at his side the aroma of fresh blueberry muffins. His thoughts drifted around the traditional pathway of recreating a lineage; the family tree. Reconstructing from bones and words, assigning names and numbers, Max usually built a tree or a bush or some ascending schematic to objectify generations of life. But with the Casco, his mind had shifted to a component of available technology, a method that resolved the morphological reconstructions of the past one hundred and fifty years with microbiology. It was ancient DNA. For the last six weeks, bathed in the allure of Casco bones, Max was unable to let the prospect of ancient DNA go. Seated in the warm sun among the markers of passed lives, he ate two more blueberry muffins and twirled his wedding ring.

Despite the majesty of handling human skeletal material, even the most remarkable encounters, with repetition, were now routine for Margaret. But the reverence and dignity with which she approached the repatriation inventory never waned, a fact that wasn't lost on Max. To him, she was a novice assistant with remarkable instinct and sensitivities. Her work, over the past weeks had settled into a rhythm of performance and responsibility.

For her part, Margaret wondered if Max, without her help, was capable of completing the job. She respected his expertise and tolerated his occasional lack of focus but in the back of her mind, she always felt he was on to another project. However, between the extraordinary experience and her almost daily opportunity to inform Charlie Bay of the progress, she considered her place in the reburial process fortunate. It also allowed her time to write. She finished the re-write of *Overturn* and thought it was better, not where she wanted, but better. The first draft of *Shadowcatchers* was done, the ending surprising her. Her dictation files were organized and thanks to Max, she dove into Motown, mainly the Temptations and the Four Tops. All in all, this time around Maine seemed to agree with her.

Left alone in Professor Wallace's building for the first time during the repatriation inventory; she enjoyed the quiet and the solitude. Over the past month and a half, she and Max documented, catalogued and prepared for reburial all but eight of the entire Casco Collection. Those remaining specimens were on loan to a Native

American research project underway at a small college in eastern Connecticut. For the up-coming weekend, Max planned to attend the Glastonbury Lacrosse Tournament, in an area coincidentally close to the school. Arrangements were made for him to pick up the material on the following Monday morning. Their inclusion into the collection was set for Tuesday.

Because more cargo space was needed for transport than was available in Max's Volvo, Margaret offered and he accepted her family's SUV for the trip. The exchange of car for truck was planned for later this morning. But the switch was complicated by Jim Garret's need to tow a newly purchased twenty-three foot, fiberglass power boat from the dealership to his office. The center console model with a two hundred horsepower outboard engine, loaded with extras was headed to her father's parking lot for temporary storage. Expecting Max back from the cemetery around eleven to go for the swap, Margaret used the time to organize the boxes of Casco bones for their trip to the new burial ground on Long Neck Island.

The number of individuals in the Casco Collection was well over one hundred. In order to facilitate handling and moving the skeletal material at the final station, complete specimens, juveniles and partial remains were placed in large foot-locker sized cardboard boxes and labeled on the outside. Fragments, small bones, loose teeth and unidentified bone, all of which were associated with ID numbers, were placed in small brown paper bags or wrapped in unprinted newspaper and packed in the cartons alongside the skull and larger bones. The end result was seventeen boxes whose contents varied in combinations of age, sex and skeletal components.

Two weeks ago, before making the final decision on the packaging, Margaret wanted to first check with Burningwater. She brought him to the laboratory for his approval of the way his ancestors were to be returned to the Island. When they arrived at the parking spot adjacent to the lab's entryway, Charlie Bay took one look at the building and refused to leave the truck. He told Margaret to handle the job in whatever way she saw fit. He didn't speak to her for the next four days and never gave a word of explanation.

As she stacked the boxes by the far door, Margaret thought about the incident. She was still uncertain why he came to oversee the preparations, but never came inside to view the bones. Placing the last box near the doorway, her thoughts were interrupted by clatter at the opposite end of the building. She looked over to see Max banging his way through what was now a familiar and noisy entrance.

"Did you move this?" Max asked, as if startled by a small table and trash barrel that he bumped routinely. Margaret shook her head no.

"Want some blueberry muffins?" an offer which he made daily and which daily, she refused.

"No thanks. How was the cemetery?" This was a question, odd for anyone but Max Sorensen. She was beginning to enjoy his eccentricities.

"It was terrific; just a spectacularly beautiful and interesting plot. Thanks. I appreciated the time to make the visit." His enthusiasm was genuine. In his mind, they were co-workers, the Casco bones were common ground and he was free to express pleasure in studying the dead even to a playwright. Placing the bag on the desk next to a bag from the day before, he walked to the far end of the building and to the piled boxes of the Casco. Extending both arms to the stack, as if to hold them up just a little longer, he mumbled, "Damn...I hate to see you go."

"But, go they must Max."

He heard her and raised his shoulders and eyebrows in submission. Margaret thought this gesture a bit much.

Testing him, "Max...tell me again what you wanted to do with the equipment over there. The stuff we never opened." She pointed to the containers labeled DNA.

"Ah, remarkable that you should ask...chasing that thought occupied the majority of my morning."

"And what did you think?"

"After all this time together and you're still asking me open-ended questions...you are a courageous woman." With a broad grin and without any hint of manipulation or desperation, he gestured for her to sit down; this was going to take awhile. "You know if you go through the anthropology literature...there is an underlying trend...kind of a theme to the whole thing. With questions both answered and unanswered...there always has been this nagging issue of origin. Here we are...humans...struggling through our existence...with relative success...increasing population numbers. And we have this drive to try and figure it all out...to understand where it all came from...our humanness...what makes us human...why being human works."

Other than picking up the SUV, her work for the day was done. Max certainly wasn't and she wondered how long this rambling was going to last. They were scheduled to drive in his car to her father's office to make the switch for the truck by noon. She saw the appointment as an escape deadline.

"So...those of us dealing with the physical... human bones...we try to reconstruct the trail...bit by bit... the best we can with what technologies are available to us along the way. We create this latest and greatest taxonomy...the latest family tree. Then we argue, discuss and debate. We rethink, retest and discuss and debate all over again. But we have done it...for the most part...with morphology...shapes of bone...bits and pieces of this or that, measurements, images...for a hundred fifty or two hundred years...essentially the same way...through comparative anatomy."

Recognizing a look in Margaret's eyes as similar to one in his wife's and sons' eyes just before they found any excuse to leave the kitchen table during a lengthy, tedious discourse, Max focused his thoughts.

"OK. OK, more to the point. North America with European contact is a terrific model for change. We have five hundred years of wave after wave of cultural intercourse...with society after society altered irrevocably as Europeans...then Euro-Americans...African Americans all expanded into already occupied environments. What the hell happened? The historic record paints the European perspective...with all its ethnocentric biases. Later...that same historic record gives us the American perspective...with manifest destiny and a justification to exterminate aboriginal peoples. The oral record of Native Americans only begins to balance the inaccuracies and enormous voids in the written record... but it's oral... so sparse. And the physical material fills in a little more about Native American death...diseases ...populations. But how many people were living on the east coast of North America when the Europeans arrived? Three million? Four million...or more? What happened to them all...their descendants? Where are those who remain?

There are three federally recognized Tribes in Maine: the Penobscot, the Passemaquody and the Casco. Where are the rest of the vibrant and growing communities that inhabited this territory in the sixteenth century? Obviously...disease, warfare...politics took their toll...what about assimilation and relocation in the eighteenth, nineteenth and twentieth centuries? Where did they go?

Ancient DNA." Max spoke as if released.

Margaret knew this was coming, was surprised at how he got to it and had no idea where he was going.

"Ancient DNA. Not back to DNA again Max."

"Ancient DNA, I can't stop thinking about it. We've been trying to accomplish with morphology...with ethnography and all the rest of it...something that may be best answered at an intracellular level. I think we'll be able to reconstruct the trail genetically. I don't know much about the methods, but the prospect of such a huge leap forward is driving me nuts. I haven't been this excited about an idea in years. You know Margaret...I've always been a little obsessive...

"...a little?"

"...this is a frontier almost beyond comprehension and the Casco can be right smack in the forefront.

Here's what we do. We take ancient DNA samples from the Casco Collection as a pristine and distinct Native American Nation...say thirteenth and fourteenth century radiocarbon dates which we already have...the DNA guys identify genetic markers specific for the sample...which I think they can do. Then...follow the amplified marker through time to the living Casco of this latest July census. It's beautiful. These boxes of bones are a genetic gold mine. We can trace the relocation and assimilation of the Casco with microbiology and overlay the results with a known cultural history. Spectacular."

"They aren't just boxes of bones, Max. They are Charlie Bay Burningwater's ancestors."

"I know. I know. Don't you see...that's the beauty of it!"

Margaret dropped her head and glanced at her watch. "I can't believe that you're back onto ancient DNA."

The ride to pick up the vehicle was in silence. The annoying smile on Max's face intensified as they pulled into the parking lot and her father's boat came into view.

"Wow Margaret, take a look at that...your father means business."

Still upset about his scheme to skirt the issue of outright compliance with the Casco reburial, she didn't answer.

"I'd just like to use the men's room inside and I'll meet you back here when you get the keys. I gotta take a close look at this boat. That design and hull shape is one of my favorites...beautiful "Pointer" lines like those...that Downeast sheer...even in fiberglass is an art form."

The childlike quality of excitement and the appreciation of esthetic elegance in a boat, as yet another distraction, left her even more frustrated. Max followed one step behind Margaret on the walk into the lobby of the six-story contemporary office building and they parted without a word.

Jim Garret's suite of enterprises occupied the entire sixth floor. One of his real estate companies owned the building, but there was no mention of his name or promotion of his businesses anywhere. The street number, twelve fifty which stood on the lawn in stainless steel and JSG and Associates on the Directory for the top floor were the only public forms of identification for his corporations.

Familiar with security and catching an elevator, Margaret was out of sight as Max, out of place and underdressed, headed across a polished marble floor for the information desk and directions.

"Hi, ah could you direct me..." Max was distracted by a group of three women and one man passing by the counter whose physical appearance was dominated by what he perceived as extremely well defined Native American morphological characteristics.

"Direct you to the Casco Tribal Role registration in the main reception room?"

"Ah...no...to the men's room." He remembered that this was the week in July for the Casco census, didn't listen to the directions and wandered to the rest room on his own wondering why the census registration was here.

Expecting the secretary to have the keys at her desk, Margaret wasn't planning to see her father and was surprised to be led into his private conference room. Jim Garret was alone in the large beige chamber and hunched over a stack of collated folders.

"Margaret! Come on in. I'm just getting ready for a presentation this afternoon. Good to see you up here... doesn't happen often."

Jim extended his left arm to direct Margaret's eyes to the center of the oval shaped conference table and a glass encased model of one more of her father's hotel and resort complexes. She nodded and smiled.

"I can see that you are taken by the project." He grinned, knowing that his daughter had little interest in his work.

"Well, you know I am but...to me they all kind of look the same."

"Yes they do but, this one is different. For one thing it's bigger. You see that...."

"I see...it looks great... I hope it goes through and it's like always...very successful." Margaret smiled at her father.

"All right, all right, enough...here are the keys. Where is the anthropologist? Sanderson? I wanted to meet him." He set the keys on the table.

"Sorensen, Max Sorensen. He's out looking at your boat."

"Sorensen huh, well I was close."

Both drifted toward the wall of windows and observed Max bobbing and weaving his way around the boat and trailer.

"Curious guy."

"Dad, as you would say, just the tip of the iceberg" letting her exasperation show in tone.

"So, how's it going with him? Are you ready to finish up the project?"

"Ya, I think that we're doing OK. We have the remaining portion of the Casco Collection that Max is supposed to pick up this weekend with the truck...that should be inventoried with everything ready to go by the middle of next week...but now he's rambling on about some ancient DNA archiving and DNA screens of living Casco tribal members...who knows the exact timetable. He is one idea after the next...it's endless with him."

"Ancient DNA? Where did that come from? I thought that this was a University reburial for Burningwater."

"It still is, but Dr. Sorensen seems to get distracted with additional research pretty easily. I don't think it's ..."

Their conversation was interrupted by the voice of Jim Garret's secretary on the speakerphone informing him that one of his attorneys, Sam Mitchel had arrived.

"Thanks. Send him right in." Taking that as her cue to leave, Margaret picked up the keys. "Wait a second; I'd like you to meet Sam, a nice guy...bright, bright attorney. Stay just a couple of minutes."

Sensing a political connection or a law firm employment connection but not a social connection, she stayed and expected some of her father's networking in the opposite direction of theatre.

"Sam, come on in. I'd like you to meet my daughter... Margaret."

Sam Mitchel was a head taller than Jim Garret. He had shiny jet-black hair that was combed straight back and met in a wave just above his starched collar. His stomach was flat and he had a great tan. After spending most of the summer with a rumpled academic dressed in solid T-shirts, khaki pants and sandals, a silk shirt and tie, tailored suit and Italian leather shoes were captivating. Whether it was Sandra Walsh or Sam Mitchel, Margaret recognized and was attracted to the energy of powerful people. Jim Garret looked for her instinctive response. Margaret looked for a wedding ring.

"Margaret was just telling me about her reburial project. Fill Sam in...on a little of your work with this skeletal collection and about this ancient DNA."

"Sounds fascinating...I'd like to hear about it."

"Well, it's the repatriation of a Native American skeletal collection housed at the University. I've been working with an anthropologist from Boston. We're about ready to rebury the Casco Collection but now...with Max Sorensen...he's the anthropologist, there's some talk about DNA from bone and archiving it to trace Casco genes in other collections, maybe even living people. "

"That's amazing work. Can you really do that?"

"If he has the time to collect the Casco DNA, and from what he has said...once the samples are archived...it seems that you can.

I'd just like to get the bones back in the ground... but he wants to get the DNA before the reburial...hold it in an archive...make it available for later research."

Jim was proud of his daughter even if this wasn't his plan for her summer. Knowing full well the look, Margaret was embarrassed and wanted to leave.

"I really should go, nice to meet you..." Uncertain whether to call him, Sam or Mr. Mitchel, she let her sentence tail off and turned to her father. "Thanks."

"See you later Margaret. Oh, you were down a quart of oil in the truck. So I filled it and left a spare in the back."

Margaret was gone. Despite his desire to support and sponsor his daughter, even in the simplest ways, he still wrestled with the principle that sometimes the most mundane things between a father and daughter are better left unsaid. He wished that he never mentioned the oil.

Checking to make sure that his Jr. Walker CD sat in the consol tray was the last thing Max did before a long trip. He was excited; two days of lacrosse and even better two days with his son Paul. The lab work through July with Margaret was productive but long. He was ready for a break, lacrosse and family was a good one.

The past two years of following his son's collegiate athletic career provided Max a positive direction in his sometimes disconnected personal life. Sports brought he and Paul together. It gave them the chance to talk. The evolution of sport's conversation between father and now adult child reminded Max of the growth in the relationship with his father. He was beginning to see with his son, how he once was, the attitude change, the tolerance and the affection. As *Sweet Soul* played, he was happy, looking ahead.

The moment Max walked through the gate onto the early morning athletic fields, his concerns with the Casco drifted away. For the next forty-eight hours, he was going to immerse himself in lacrosse competition and the endurance of college athletes, all without leaving the bleacher seats. There were thirty-six teams, three divisions, a game an hour, on six fields from eight in the morning until five at night. The tailgate food was sausage with peppers and the grill opened at nine.

Max viewed events such as these as pay back to a father, sometime coach and always chauffeur to games, tournaments and practices for two boys during a decade of youth sports. He had Paul's schedule and his own love for a game he never played. Once again, he was the participant observer.

The sidelines to each fresh cut field were bordered by competitors; this time of the morning, young men of few words. They carried equipment bags packed with sticks, pads, helmets, spare shafts and T-shirts. There were more college, company and association logos than Max knew or could track. Interspersed among the players, were young women, fewer in number, most with coffee and most in conversation. Other support for the tournament came from a small collection of mid-fifties parents carrying coolers and lawn chairs; fathers reliving their own reconstructed athletic past and mothers clinging to an adult son's ever dwindling athletic future.

And with all this stuff was an aspect of the game that always caught Max's attention, the technology. Titanium shafts, injected molded helmets, custom pads and shoes for every surface; all of it seemed far from the hand-carved wooden sticks and rawhide pockets of only a generation ago.

The photo of a purification ritual with members of the Iroquois League, the players dipping their wooden sticks into a sacred brook for spiritual power, surfaced in Max's mind. He looked at titanium and thought of wood. He wondered what was lost. Were the players still connected to the spirits of the game? The question reminded him of the moment he tried to define the spirit of lacrosse for his son. Max sat in the sunshine, remembered it like it was yesterday.

It was over six years ago, during Paul's sophomore year in high school. The team's lacrosse season was off to a slow start, dropping their first four games. After the fourth loss, on a rainy day and a muddy field, Max sat in the car with his frustrated son, both soaked to the bone. Cold and wet, he imparted what little knowledge he had of the game. In humble tone, he affirmed that lacrosse was physical, intellectual, social and emotional, and all played their part in wins and loses. But the game was also spiritual. Lacrosse was a sport that benefited from the spirits of those who played in the past, generation upon generation. He explained to his son, it was time for him to tap into the experience and skill of those who came before, to connect with the legends. Without questioning his timing, Max lifted the short sleeve of the school uniform to expose a portion of Paul's shoulder pad. He took a pen from his briefcase and drew the Native American symbol for a Thunderbird on the fabric. As he pulled the sleeve back over the pad he remembered whispering, "to play on the field with the spirit of the Thunderbird."

Max recalled listening to his son sigh and seeing him roll his eyes toward a foggy window. But the next game, Max watched with pride as Paul scored four goals in their first victory. The high school team ended their season that year fifteen and five with a regional tournament championship. Young Sorensen was the

MVP. Max and Paul never spoke a word about the conversation that day in the car or the symbol of the Thunderbird. As far as Max knew, his son didn't touch the image or change shoulder pads but he never had the courage to look.

After enjoying the first game, despite a loss, Max had an hour before the second. He found a seat on a small sunlit six-tier bleacher beside one of the playing fields, removed his shirt and basked in the warmth of a mid morning temperature serge. The current game was between two clubs from Baltimore, apparently well known to one another. Their fans and friends remained on the player's sideline opposite the bleachers. They mingled among the coolers, equipment and substitutes. Two or three kept yelling nicknames and inside jokes to laughter from players of both teams. Max assumed these guys were older, maybe much older. The "Has Been Farewell Tour" on their shirts was a give-away. The four or five people who sat with Max on the bleachers disappeared at half-time and he was joined by a beautiful strawberry blond wearing shorts and a tight T-shirt. By her side, at the end of a polypropylene leash was an Alaskan Husky. As she sat near Max, both watched the dog crawl under the stands for shade. Once again, feeling closer to thirty than seventy, he sucked in his stomach and struck up a conversation about something authentic and at this stage of his life, sincere; the weather.

"Great day for the tournament..."

The woman smiled and nodded. Age, physical condition, athletic ability and lacrosse skills aside, he was connected to this event. He was invigorated by the atmosphere and without any intention of letting the moment go; regardless of how incongruent, he kept going, "Ya...just a perfect day for it. Do you get to many games?"

"No, not really...this is new to me. I've been dating one of the guys with the green shirts for just a little while...don't know much about the game."

Relationships and boundaries established Max had time, plenty of energy and most important an audience.

"Lacrosse is a Native American game."

Her hazel eyes expressed surprise and interest. That was all he needed.

"Ya, the game was played by many of the Nations up and down the east coast of North America; probably with the Iroquois and the Cherokee the most well known. Often times...disputes were settled by Lacrosse games ...that's why it is sometimes called the "Little Brother of War". It was played on huge fields...maybe a mile long... sometimes games lasted into the night...with many, many players running around under a full moon...playing in the moon shadows."

Now Max was surprised. She seemed genuinely interested in the historic background and her response was an invitation to carry on.

"For tribes the game also had a spiritual side... games between tribal members were often played as part of bigger rituals...seasonal celebrations. There were all kinds of pre and post game ceremonies and rites to empower and protect the players. Along with that, of course, was the game's tie to the culture's mythology, some great origin myths."

"Origin myths...? What do you mean?"

"Well...I don't mean origin myth in the sense of human beings but more like stories that you heard as a kid...tales and legends of how things came to be; plants and animals; you know..."

She understood and smiled. He took a quick breath knowing that half time in a one-hour game was short.

"My favorite of the lacrosse myths is "How the Bat Got It's Wings." He didn't wait for another signal. He intended to get this story in before they started the second half. "You see...it seems that on a particular day...the four legged animals with teeth were challenged to a lacrosse game by the flying animals without teeth. They were all set to play, when this scrawny little four-legged animal came over to the birds...to the leaders of the birds like the hawk, the eagle and the Thunderbird ...said that the four-legged animals didn't want him. They said that he's too small...too weak...can't run fast enough...can't see well; all the usual reasons to be cut from a team. So the flying animals had a discussion... they asked the bear and the wolf if they could take this castoff for their team...the bear and the wolf laughed and agreed that the flying animals could have the weak scrawny little four-legged being. So the birds adopted him. Now...the Thunderbird decided that since they had adopted this animal, who calls himself a bat, they must enable him to fly.

In order to achieve this, the hawk hooked some of the bat's skin from his stomach to the bat's front claws and tried to get him to fly. It doesn't work. There is not enough wing. So...some other birds...especially good at building nests...took some hide from the sacred drum used to announce the game and sewed it to the bat's wings for strength and speed. The bat flew...although somewhat erratically at first.

As the game progressed, he didn't play much because it was a very close game. And when the sun went down...both teams were boasting of their superiority but it remained undecided well into the darkness...into shadows of the full moon."

Max saw the players beginning to warm up. The referees were at mid field. He figured that he had about twenty seconds to finish. "It was then...because of exhaustion for so many of the players and the darkness ...the eagle put the bat into the game. Amazing! It was remarkable. The bat darted and flew in and out of the moon shadows...caught the ball in his teeth and scored the winning goal. And that is how the bat got his wings."

Both were laughing, Max's arms were waving, the Husky woke up and the second half was uneventful. At the end of the game, the dog and the strawberry blond ran onto the field to be greeted by a rugged and sweaty defenseman, each with a kiss. The Husky was first. As the couple walked across the open field, the young woman turned and waved to Max. Delighted, he smiled and waved back but she had already looked away, tugged by a wandering Husky and the broad arm of number thirty-four. Max flashed to Margaret, thinking she was maybe three or four years older than the strawberry blond. Then he thought how both were young enough to be his daughters.

A great day followed. At its end, after a tailgate dinner with son and friends, Max returned to his hotel alone in search of a Barbara Stanwyck movie on cable and looked forward to starting it all over again in the morning.

When Max saw their silhouettes, facing one another, framed by the counter tops and hoods of the Microbiology Lab, he thought that they were twins. Startled, he froze in the doorway and then set the Anthropology keys on the closest counter.

"Don't worry he's my brother. And no, we're not twins. Most people do a double take."

"Sorry I thought you were ...ah...I didn't want to disturb your work." Max thought about a clone joke but passed.

"No trouble...find everything you needed...it's Max right?"

"Yes, I did. It was all organized and waiting for me."

"David's organized...I'll get him his keys when he's back from holiday...I'm Ryan Decker."

"Max Sorensen...here's all the signed paperwork."

"My brother Alan... also a microbiologist...but not here...Pittsburgh...unlike me...he's into DNA. I was just showing him one of my projects...trying to broaden his perspective."

Max perked up, "Oh really...that's great...Pittsburgh? Hmm...interesting...ever work with Cliff Patterson and any ancient DNA?"

"Yes some...he's a departmental colleague of mine. Why, do you know Cliff...better still do you have any ancient DNA?"

"Yes and possibly."

"What have you got?"

Max eased his way into the room and extended his hand, "Max Sorensen."

"Alan Decker."

"It's a Native American collection...archived, radiocarbon dated...I've been wondering about a specific protocol for harvesting a DNA sample."

With knowledge and his brother irritated, Alan Decker was interested. "Well, the biggest problem with archived collections is contamination."

Max sensed this individual could be a good source of technical information and pursued him. Ryan, bored, drifted off to an adjacent section of the lab.

"So, what would I use...a core from long bones...drill a hole and then go into the shaft and scrape around?" Max was probing.

"You could. How are the teeth?"

"The teeth? They're OK...why?"

"The methods to analyze ancient DNA are growing and changing all the time. The key is how, and where to collect a sample.

You need a sterile, dedicated environment. You know...sterile gloves...filtered air...UV light...the works and the best place to get the material is the inside of the teeth...the hollow part...the nerve chamber. It's a great site to harvest." Alan Decker also enjoyed an audience.

"The teeth...how do you get to it?" As the discussion continued, Max began to twirl his wedding ring.

"It's not too difficult...under a hood...you take a sterile surgical mallet and chisel...split the molar teeth in half and curette out as much material as you can into a sterile, labeled, 5ml polycarbonate tube with a good twist tight cap and send it to us.

Some anthropologists have told me...the good thing about the technique is...when they get good at breaking teeth in just the right way...they can glue them back together...no one can ever tell they harvested the stuff.

I'm telling you...the methods and technologies for analysis are only going to get better. The future looks remarkable...it's truly unbelievable what we're going to be able to do. The hard part is getting hold of good ancient samples...even if it's just to archive."

Neither brother understood the few disjointed mumbles of Dr Sorensen, but both caught the word, Casco. Max remained where he enjoyed it most, un-tethered.

Chapter Nine

The Casco seated in a circle around Charlie Bay were silent. Some eyes fixed to his, others stared away. Like before, Charlie Bay faced the Ancient One and didn't back down. He stared into the eyes of his ancestor, drawn to this man. Burningwater poured over his features.

The Ancient One's shoulder length white hair was parted in the middle. It fell in an arc that followed the downward curves of his brow, his eyes and his lips. The Ancient One's arms were folded across his chest and pressed a large bird's wing to his left shoulder.

Charlie Bay let his eyes drift to the woman seated inches from the wing's tip. A blue scarf covered her forehead. A red woven blanket sheathed the curves of her body. Her beauty had hold of his heart. The sorrow in her eyes made Charlie Bay uneasy.

A grandfather sat alongside the sad eyed woman. The old man's weathered brow was shielded by a felt hat, a dried starfish pinned to the front. His hair was bundled at the ears by shreds of a cotton kerchief. The two streams of gray slid down the back of his shoulders and clung to his faded navy jacket. The grandfather's eyes were tired and glazed. His lids puffed.

One by one, as always, Charlie Bay met his ancestors. He met them eye to eye with strength and an edge of arrogance. He held firm that his choice was the right one. But again, it was the empty metal chairs staggered between the Casco that shattered his defiance. The vacancies haunted him. They were seats of the missing, spirits whose dream journey had been halted. Each empty chair pressed his obligation to act in their favor.

Charlie Bay tried to retell his side of the story but he had no air.

For Margaret, there was nothing like the smell of a southwest breeze bouncing off an incoming tide on a sunny July afternoon. As they turned to walk along the south side of Burningwater's home, the ocean wind hit them both dead on. Margaret smiled and let the wind blow back her hair. In the moment, the same wind carried a raspy gasp and a single choking cough.

"Did you hear that...sounds like death!" Max spoke Margaret's thought. He was first up the stairs to the porch, "Are you OK?"

As Charlie Bay nodded, Max froze. Margaret bumped his shoulder and knocked him out of the doorway as she rushed to kneel next to Burningwater.

Max didn't understand, "Where are his clothes...what's going on?"

Grabbing a small quilt from the back of the couch, Margaret covered Charlie Bay from the waist down. Max stared at the scarred skin of the fisherman's chest and stomach. Regaining his breath, Charlie Bay pointed toward Max, "In on the floor...next to the sofa." He sighed and rolled onto his back. "I got hot sleeping in there...moved out here."

"Would you get his clothes Max?"

Max entered the house without taking his eyes off Charlie Bay's scars. "Sure."

Margaret turned to Charlie Bay, "You're OK, right?"

"Fine...ya fine." He cleared his throat.

Returning with his clothes, Max handed them to Margaret who, in turn, handed pants to Charlie Bay. Without any concern for modesty or hint of embarrassment, Charlie Bay stood naked before the two of them and began to dress. Unsteady in his attempt to step into his work khakis, Margaret reached toward him and held his elbow. He entered a foot into each leg and pulled up his pants. Burningwater thought underwear was useless. Max studied his scars.

After he dressed, Charlie Bay sat back on the wicker couch and looked to Margaret.

"We thought you were choking. It sounded like you couldn't get enough air. It frightened us...the sound I mean..."

She leaned back against the rail of the porch. Max sat in Charlie Bay's rocker, received a look from Charlie Bay that went unnoticed by Max. Turning back to Margaret, who observed both, Burningwater chose his words carefully.

"I can't get breath in the dream."

Margaret unsure, led with a question, "Was it a bad dream...like a nightmare?" She was hesitant and surprised that Charlie Bay volunteered any information about something so personal. It was unusual.

"It's a spirit dream that I've had for many years...over and over. I can't breathe in the dream...I'm like the others. I wake up trying hard to get air...get air to speak...but I can't...I have no wind...no air."

"Oh, you mean a recurring dream..." Max interrupted. Margaret interrupted him with a look that indicated it was better if he didn't speak. Max understood.

"Who else is in the dream...who are the others?" Margaret wanted more of the dream.

"My ancestors are in the spirit dream. The Ancient One and many of my people stuck in the same place. There are empty chairs, spirits waiting for the bones. The bones taken from the western door, they are waiting for them to be found and returned. I believe it's their bones, those ancestors in the dream. Their bones must be returned. Their spirits will be freed. We must act in their favor and rebury them all.

The missing bones halt the spirit journey. As I told you once before Sorensen, it's spirits, lost forever unless we act in their favor."

Max looked to the floor. Margaret stayed on Charlie Bay.

"The dream also holds me because of things that I did...my choice. My spirit is also captured until the bones are returned, until the bones are buried. I will wait no more...the empty chairs...I can wait no more."

Max, now back on Charlie Bay, was finding it difficult to be quiet. A glance from Margaret had kept him silent. Thinking that he had done well in his sensitivity to Margaret's signs and signals, Max asked, "What empty chairs...where did the empty chairs come from? What do they mean?"

"Max please." The empty chairs also confused Margaret.

"I believe that they're the ones lost...bones lost... spirits lost...my people unaccounted for in this world and in...."

Charlie Bay saw by the looks on their faces that he said enough, maybe too much. He took a deep breath, slapped his knees with both hands and changed direction. "Come on, I've finished the burial site. I'll show you where we'll bury my ancestors tomorrow morning!"

And with that stunning declaration, he stood up and hustled barefoot down the front steps. Dumbfounded by his pronouncement for the time of reburial and his abrupt recovery, Margaret and Max were left on the porch staring at one another.

"Tomorrow morning? We can't do it tomorrow morning...it's too soon!" Max grumbling, "We're not ready...it's too soon. Margaret come on...talk to him...tell him we're not ready."

The panic in Max's voice drew a smile, "We are ready Max...everything is done."

Walking about twenty yards behind Charlie Bay and headed west past the blueberry patch, Max was a step behind Margaret and winded.

"Come on Margaret...his recurring dream about some empty chairs can't dictate the repatriation of the material. That's crazy! We can't do that! There's got to be some order to the whole thing. It's going to take a little time to get it organized."

"Like what? Everything is boxed...we bring it over in the morning. Why not? It's done."

Max was desperate, "Sandra! Sandra's not here. She wanted to be here."

"Do you really think that it matters to Burningwater whether Sandra Walsh is present at the reburial? Anyway...if she really wanted to be here...we could call her and she could catch the red eye tonight.

Come on Max...why stall any longer? What are you really after? What do you want?"

"I want enough time to break open some teeth and archive the DNA. That's what I want! That's all I want! It'll just take a day or so!"

They walked to the top of a small rise that overlooked the two western mounds of Long Neck Island. Across the crest of the hill a trench, approximately five feet deep, four feet wide and thirty feet long, ran from north to south with a sloping entryway on each end. Charlie Bay stood on the opposite side of the burial pit, within the sound of their voices.

Max was, by the exasperation on his face and the tone of his voice, at the end of his attempts to buy time. "You know I can get a lawyer and tie this up for a few days...then I'll drop whatever legal tactic works before the press can make a big deal out of it. Come on I just need a few days to break a few teeth that's all!"

Both walked to the edge of the trench on its eastern side. Startled by its size, they looked down into the final resting place of the Casco Collection. Across the trough was Charlie Bay Burningwater who heard every word.

"No bones shall be broken...no bones of my people shall ever be burned or broken." He spoke with a vengeance neither had seen. Margaret thought of burned or broken bones in "Heartache of the Hunter". She held her eyes to Charlie Bay's trying to tell him everything was going to be alright. Max lowered his head.

Thinking that the driving range was a good place to release some of his frustrations with a minimal risk of injury, he drove directly from the island to a large bucket of yellow golf balls. Attempting to hit a golf ball as hard as possible without keeping score or chasing after it was supposed to be soothing. Maybe it was for those who were good at it. Max wasn't and his anger remained. Time after time, he watched the yellow range ball bounce and skid across the ground in front of him. The longest rolled just past the seventy-five yard marker. He wondered if he was ever going to hit one in the air and if he was ever going to get more time with the Casco. Both thoughts fueled his erratic bursts. Max was enraged by knowledge lost.

After the last ball skidded off, he was spent. He sat on a bench with the empty wire bucket hooked to the end of a titanium driver and rattled them both between his legs. Looking due east across the range, the sand landfill and the tidal marsh, he squinted to make out the three small knolls of Burningwater's home. It was one far away green bump against a blue ocean horizon. From this perspective, the landfill and the marsh comprised a huge flat area and a tremendous amount of territory. Recalling the view from the rail tie bridge toward the south and west, it seemed that there were only two ways to access this enormous tract of land. One was narrow, rickety wood and marginally negotiable and the other was staying straight after the three hundred yard marker on the range. This spot opened onto the whole place.

As the wire bucket spun from the head of the club to rest under the bench, Max lost control of the driver and lost his train of thought. Groping around in high grass for the wire handle, he found another yellow range ball and wondered if Burningwater ever returned to that first site. The site where, almost two months ago, he swore there was a complete skeleton to match the shoulder blade nestled into the silk liner of the old man's collection box. First impressions were difficult to overcome. He considered in the moment why his lack of diplomatic skill was such a nagging constant and he wondered where the range ended and the Casco Reservation began.

Finally meandering to the equipment return counter, he heard the high volume mid-afternoon summer traffic. The seafood stand was busy, the bait and tackle shop, a convenience store and the golf all had a number of cars in the combined strip parking lot. Addressing a long faced man surrounded by buckets of golf balls, Max killed time and curiosity. He placed his driver on the counter and asked for information.

"Here you go. Say...ah...who owns this place?"

The man shrugged his bony shoulders. "I don't know."

"Well, who signs your checks?"

"My boss...but he doesn't own it...he just manages all these buildings."

"All of these buildings...is he around...your boss?"

"He's home...he's the boss." The lower third of his face grew horizontally into a smile as he took the club.

"Does your boss have an office or a card...so I could call him?"

It took a minute, but after shuffling through an under the counter draw jammed with papers, in no apparent order, the attendant produced a business card.

"Great...thanks a lot." Max glanced at the card, put it in his pocket and walked to the take-out restaurant for a hot dog.

The problem was one that Margaret feared as a necessity from the moment she met Dr. Max Sorensen and one, she hoped was avoidable. Charlie Bay Burningwater needed an attorney. It was up to her to find one. Her choice to handle the repatriation of the Casco without a lawyer made it difficult to find one last minute. She had two resources; some casual attorney friends that her consulting firm used from time to time and her father. After a few calls, it was apparent finding someone familiar with Maine law in Philadelphia was a dead end. She knew her father was not.

Late afternoon was a reasonable time to catch him between private meetings and evening functions. Calling ahead for a time in a crowded schedule was usually ineffective. Just showing up unannounced and sitting strategically between offices, a few moments of his time was never refused. Besides, instinct told her to ask for his help required meeting face to face.

Entering the inner suite of offices through an unmarked side door, she announced to her father's executive assistant that if possible, she hoped to catch him for just a few moments. Cordial as always, his assistant, blond hair and dark roots, informed Margaret that his current meeting was about to end. She signaled with the tilt of her head that a seat on the sofa across from a small conference room was the best chance to intercept him on a tight schedule. Margaret sat and waited, trying not to listen.

"Congressman Bob Shaw please. This is Sharon Williamson from Jim Garret's office confirming the Congressman's flight tomorrow morning from Washington into Portland and the car to meet him. Sure, I'll hold...hello, Congressman Shaw...Jim's looking forward to tomorrow...I'm just checking to confirm...wonderful.

Anything you need let me know...it's a good-sized boat...you'll just be in the river but you could take one if you wanted. The patches are good too...there really shouldn't be any waves...well...don't eat a big breakfast." Sharon rolled her eyes in Margaret's direction. Both women smiled. "It'll be a pleasure having you here tomorrow...goodbye."

Without a second's hesitation, she hit speed dial for another number and changed screens. "Congressman Gundermun, please."

Recognizing the names but wanting no part of politics, Margaret was hearing the Temptations' *Ain't to Proud to Beg*, the chorus playing in her head, until her father burst from the conference room with four other pin striped men in tow.

"Hey, Margaret...this is a surprise. What's up... everything OK?"

"Ya...everything's fine. I realize you're busy but I want to check with you about something...maybe a couple of minutes...that's all it'll take."

"Sure, I have a second. Come on back in here. Go on ahead...I'll be right there."

Jim Garret and his daughter slipped into the vacated conference room and Margaret came right to the point.

"Max Sorensen is talking about getting a lawyer to tie up the reburial for a while so that he can do some additional DNA archiving with the Casco...you know the DNA stuff I told you about before. Charlie Bay might need a lawyer to deal with it and I...I didn't get anywhere with my contacts in Philadelphia...so I need your help for a name."

Her last sentence was key and Jim Garret responded in kind. Leaning back through the door and holding his hand in the air to pause their conversation, "Sharon, grab Sam before he leaves...have him come in here...would you, please."

To Margaret's amazement he didn't turn and re-evaluate her summer. Pensively, he waited for his colleague.

"He'll be right in," were his first words and after a moment, he ventured his position. "Margaret, this could turn out to be a hurricane. I'll get you the name of a good attorney who knows Maine antiquities law...then as much as I'd like to help...I'm going to have to step back. This is all yours...you're on your own."

"That's all I'm asking. Thanks."

"Ah...Sam great. You remember my daughter, Margaret." Both smiled at one another as Jim kept talking with increased abruptness. "Well...it seems that there might be a problem over the reburial of the bones...

the bones of the Casco...the project that Margaret told us about the other day.   And...Dr. Sandersen...on the University side...wants to stall a bit to do some DNA studies...with Casco DNA...a Casco DNA archive. So...Margaret needs the name of someone to aid in expediting the reburial...who's out there?"

"Hum...Vince Simmons...in Augusta...has worked on and off with the Historical Society and some antiquities issues..."

"Perfect...he's perfect. Sharon!" once again leaning out the door, "...see if Vince Simmons is around for the next couple of days...it might be necessary to get in touch with him. She'll give you the numbers Margaret. Sam and I have to run." He didn't kiss her goodbye and left in a hurry with Sam hustling to remain at his side.

This time, the search for Burningwater was simple. Expecting to find him working on the burial site for tomorrow's ceremony, Margaret returned to the island late afternoon and found Charlie Bay's truck between the blueberry patch and the open grave. Following the sounds of low, rhythmic chanting, she walked down the narrow path to the work dock and fishing shack. Hovered over a galvanized wash pail, Burningwater was singing in an unfamiliar language and stirring a long wooden shaft into a bucket of bright red.   Draped over the nearby lobster traps and hung from the roof, along with any other spot that supported fabric, were royal blue strips of material drying in a light southwest wind. He stopped chanting.

"Don't worry...it's not the blood of Sorensen."

Margaret smiled. She wondered what he was doing.

"These are traditional Casco colors. The silk is from parachutes my Uncle Robert brought back from war."

"Parachutes?"

"Silk parachutes. For years, I used the nylon lines from the chutes to knit heads for my gear."

"Knit heads?" She was lost and dangling.

"Ah...went to college...became a writer. There're things college doesn't teach and writers should know. There're many things universities don't understand."

Margaret nodded and Charlie Bay taught. "Heads are the woven net of a lobster trap...look over there at that one. The lobster crawls up the head...falls in...can't get out for awhile...that's if it's knit right." Charlie Bay smiled. He was happy. "I saved the silk...been saving it for years. The bones will all be wrapped in silk of traditional colors...I'll do it first thing in the morning... soon as you bring all of the bones over here."

"We packaged everything in biodegradable paper and cardboard boxes and tried to return the material with some dignity and respect." Anxious, tired and defensive about her inventory efforts, she wished that she never uttered the word, "material". Charlie Bay bristled. If he was happy, he wasn't anymore.

"Margaret...respect is not calling the bones of my ancestors...material...specimens. It's not taking them from the ground and putting them on shelves in universities...sending them all over the place to be touched...touched and broken. That's not respect, it is desecration.

The bones are a part my people...people which I helped bury...grandmothers and grandfathers...Flathead, Flathead's father, Bass Catcher, Gull and Gull's mother, my Uncle Two Moons, my Uncle Hollis...my Uncle Robert of the silk parachutes and Bat Player... even...Bat Player." Charlie Bay's voice trailed off in anger and hurt.

Margaret was embarrassed but not confused. She must prepare him for the worst. She worried about his volatility.

"Charlie Bay there's a chance that there may be a problem...having the reburial ceremony tomorrow. Max may try to put it off for a few days...with some legal stalling. I know it's not good news but we are prepared ...it won't last long...if it happens at all. It's going to be all right...there will be a reburial."

Charlie Bay stopped stirring the silk in the watery red die. Turning slowly toward Margaret he was stern. "Margaret...you're a good woman...you've a gift...you write. You've done a good job...you've done all I asked. But, I told you today...I can wait no more...it will be tomorrow." Once again mixing the cloth, he began to chant ending their conversation and Margaret thought her role in the reburial.

The lights were on in Gerry Wallace's laboratory. Margaret anticipated that Max would have trouble staying away from the Casco Collection archive. As she passed through the entryway's unlocked door, light reflected off Max's sax and caught her eye. It was lying on the near corner of the first exam table, the only object on the oak surface. Everything else was gone; the sand bin, the digital x-ray materials, all of it gone. Her eyes darted to successive tables, each a bare wooden slab with only an occasional dust outline of its function as a station. He was packed; just about everything was packed. Only the portable x-ray machine remained standing. The makeshift desk, with the exception of some stacks of someone else's' mail, was empty. The hardware was sealed into three boxes on the floor next to the travel cases of the digital video and recording equipment. The frames of the sand exam bins were stacked against the outside wall. As she walked beside the tables, the echo of her footsteps was more pronounced. The arched building's function was reduced. She thought it was over. Seeing Max's smiling face bounce from behind the cartons containing the Casco, she knew otherwise.

"Margaret! Nice timing. I need your help taking apart the x-ray. Can you give me a hand...hey, this same thing happened once before, a couple of months ago, didn't it?"

"Ya...it did. Sure I'll help Max...but...tell me why you look so happy...what are you up to?"

"Up to...me? Come on Margaret, what makes you say that?"

"I've seen that look before...you're not going to let it go are you?"

Smiling, as a man coming to terms with his own obsessiveness and shrugging his shoulders in submission to his compulsions, he playfully answered, "Would you expect anything less? Help me take this thing apart and I'll show you what I've set up".

After their time together, Max, truly did not view Margaret's position as for or against his academic pursuits. He simply enjoyed her presence. She was bright and beautiful. For Margaret, on each occasion she appreciated him as an insightful anthropologist, his unilateral research pursuits reminded her that he was still an enemy of the Casco.

"So what do you think of this." Max beamed and pointed after they finished with the x-ray.

She knew what it was and wanted to hear what he had in mind, "What is it?"

"It's a portable hood with air filter and UV light. Isn't it great? I talked a guy in the Micro Building into letting us borrow it for a couple of days...maybe an opportunity will present itself."

"Us?" Margaret scanned a small table set next to the hood and saw all of the material and equipment to collect DNA samples. "Max you are exhausting!"

The words were haunting. Max went for his wedding ring but stopped.

The echoing tweet of the phone left Margaret grunting in disgust as she hit speaker, "It's for you."

The voice was a familiar one.

"Max, it's me. I thought I asked you to keep your cell on."

"Sandra. How are you doing...bad reception here."

"I'm headed to the airport in Seattle...I'm on a red eye tonight...I'll be there first thing in the morning. I want to be there for the reburial ceremony. So...stall if you have to...just until I get there."

Thinking that now was as good a time as any, Max pursued the inevitable, "Sandra, I was hoping that maybe we could stall things even for just a few more days...I've got a great project all set to go...I'm anxious to go over it with you as soon as you get here. I think that you'll be excited by it."

Margaret saw this coming. Sandra's voice exploded through the speaker phone, "Excited by it! I'm already excited by it! Don't you even think about any more projects...you just wait for me...all I want you to do Max, is wait for me...understand...don't be a jackass...wait for me."

"OK...we'll talk when you get here."

"We certainly will. Is Margaret there? Margaret can you hear me?"

"Yes...I'm here."

"Margaret...as far as I'm concerned you are a Saint. You lasted two months with this man. You my dear...you are a Saint. The gates of heaven will open for you. I'll see you both in the morning."

Neither spoke. Max sighed, raised his eyebrows and pursed his lips. It was time for both to go. Margaret walked with him to the doorway. Max shut off the lights and eased the door shut behind them.

Chapter Ten

The first early morning words spoken from Max
Sorensen's dry mouth were coarse and loud. "What do
you mean...they're gone! Well ya...I came back to get my
sax...they were there...they can't be gone...I saw them. I'll
be right over...don't touch a thing."

Crashing through the entry doors to the lab and
knocking the trash barrel out of his way indicated to
Margaret, Max was upset. But she still thought somehow,
in some way, he was responsible.

"Take a look...there're gone...just the Casco nothing
else. What happened to them?"

"I don't know. Why are you asking me?" His eyes
darted around the corner of the room which twelve hours

ago sheltered the nineteen trunk-sized cardboard containers of the Collection.

Margaret didn't go for the innocent look. "Well, you're a logical choice."

"Logical choice? I...ah...I'm not the logical...ah.. well ya...I mean I think I know why you'd think that but, I didn't take them. Burningwater...he's the logical choice. He had more reasons...I didn't do it. He did it." Max appeared to be dumbfounded. First, the collection was gone and second, she was accusing him of theft. "Look, it must have been Burningwater. He probably got two or three of those young fishermen...they came over late last night...took the Casco...took the burial into his own hands. Who else would? It was them. Did you call anyone?"

"No, just you...I was dropped off. My father has the truck for the boat. I haven't been over to the island or anywhere else...I haven't seen anyone or talked to anyone but you."

Max was still scanning the floor, for what, he had no idea. But, because of his confusion, his nervous energy dictated he do something. Unable to determine whether he was listening or distracted, she moved to block his path.

"What are you doing?"

Without lifting his eyes he answered, "I'm looking for clues."

Margaret was confrontational, "Clues...what clues? Someone pried open the rusty lock on this door...came in...took only the Casco...left and closed the door behind them. Police Max...the police look for clues. We need to find Burningwater...because it was either you or Charlie Bay...nobody else would want these bones. I vote for you."

"The lock...I didn't see that. You're right, but let's not call the police till we check with Burningwater. I don't want this to become an incident...especially if we can resolve it ourselves."

"An incident...it's already an incident. Dr. Walsh is going to be here in an hour or so and by that time it will be larceny ......probably with University Police...Max it's more than an incident."

Despite his concern, she suspected that Max whisked the Casco off to a rented storage unit somewhere and planned to accomplish whatever he needed for DNA in the next two or three days. Then, before things got too far out of control, the Collection would reappear. She knew him well enough and believed this strange man was more than capable of such a strange plan.

"Oh, Sandra...I forgot about her...bad timing."

"Let's get going...we have to tell Charlie Bay. You can worry about Dr. Walsh later."

The burial site on Long Neck was unchanged. Yesterday's footprints in the sandy windblown soil were the only evidence of activity. There was no sign of Charlie Bay. There was no sign of the Casco. Margaret walked from the crest of the hill to Charlie Bay's fishing shack on the work dock. In silence and one step behind,

Max followed without a word. Strips of red and blue silk were piled on two benches and weighted with bricks. The stained maroon bucket sat in the center of the platform surrounded by splashes of the traditional Casco colors. There was a quiet rustle of the oaks and poplars in a midmorning ocean breeze. The air was salty, no Charlie Bay.

As usual, curiosity was suppressed only so long for Max Sorensen, "What is this place...what's all this cloth?"

"It's where Burningwater builds his lobster traps and the silk is for the bones of his ancestors. He's planning to wrap them in it...you know...in bundles. It's parachute silk...dyed the traditional Casco colors."

"Parachute silk?" Max was lost.

Margaret was back to the car.

As they approached the tip of the western burial ground, there was no truck, no Charlie Bay. Max pulled the Volvo cautiously to the edge of the grass and both peered into the flat green water of a near high tide. To their left, on the southern branch of the Casco River, a large white center console was powering past them.

"It's my father...my father's boat, remember?"

"Ya, nice boat. He sure has a crowd on there...some in suits 'n ties...what's he do anyway?" They watched the boat pass without getting out of the car.

"He's in real estate...used to be retail...now's recreational developments...golf resorts...you know, those kind of things. There must be some big deal going on...those suits are on Congressmen...I overheard the travel plans yesterday."

"Congressmen...U.S. Congressmen?" Max shook his head. "Hmm...I wonder..."

Margaret was sorry she brought it up, "Come on let's check the fish pier."

Never rowing beyond the mouth of the river for almost three years was intolerable for Charlie Bay. Making up his mind in early July that he wasn't going to miss this season's late summer run of soft-shell lobsters, he mustered the courage two weeks ago to cut the outboard well into the hull of his Alton built, Bank dory. He was unable to get over it. Each day, at around high water, he made the trek to the fisherman's Co-op where the dory was anchored in the shallows. Resetting the hook from time to time, he picked spots with just enough depth for most of the tide to swell the new seams without letting the boat sink. The joint leaked less each day, but each day Charlie Bay was there, bucket in hand, dressing and tending the wound. Any thoughts of strapping his brand new, two-year-old twenty-five horsepower Johnson motor to the dory were painful. Still feeling he was strong enough to row surged from his heart with each pail of water and his back ached more with each bend.

As Max and Margaret drove into the Co-op, the SUV with Jim Garret's tandem boat trailer stretched across the parking lot.

"I see why your dad needed the truck. He thinks big...that's one long rig."

Margaret spotted Burningwater's pickup and paid no attention to Max. "Charlie Bay's here...his skiff's still in the dunes!"

"Good...now we'll find out what really happened."

Max's air of confident innocence didn't surprise Margaret. But she realized that her impatience wasn't so much to identify the guilty party, as it was to resolve the whole thing; to bury the Casco and move back to her apartment in Philadelphia. She wanted to push *Overturn* and re-work her third play. She was ready to leave Maine, enough was enough.

Max parked next to Charlie Bay's truck and they walked a short beach to wet sand. The dory was moored in three feet of water about ten yards to the lee of the fish pier. Sitting on the gunnel of the dory's inland side, Charlie Bay watched the two of them as they approached. He was suspicious. Margaret waved him into shore. Watching Burningwater gracefully skull the dory closer, silhouetted behind him, she saw the center console Pointer docking at the fish pier float. She rolled her eyes and dropped her head.

"Oh great...now all we need is to have Sandra Walsh show up yelling jackass. Max...I'll talk...try to stay in control...there's my father and the Congressmen out there at the dock."

Max squinted toward the float and a small group of people unloading from the outboard. "Look I gotta find out what happened to..."

"Max please. Just give me a chance to ask him... don't accuse him of anything."

Climbing out of the dory when it scraped the sand and wading in his boots the few feet toward Margaret and the shore, Charlie Bay's eyes did not leave hers.

"Charlie Bay we have to talk...there's a problem."

He didn't respond and stopped in shallow water.

"The Collection...ah...the bones of your ancestors are missing. They were not in the lab this morning when we went to pick them...they're gone."

Max moved into the water, face to face with Charlie Bay; sandals soaked and long khaki pants splashed to the knees. Raising his right hand and pointing at Charlie Bay's chest with his index finger, Max shouted, "Did you take them? You took them because you didn't believe that we would bring them over here this morning...didn't you...you took them. Who else would want those bones but you...you stole them right out from under us because... you don't trust us."

He was impulsive. He was passionate. And before he took another breath, he was drenched. In one lightening quick swoop, Charlie Bay Burningwater took down Dr. Max Sorensen to roll and groan in the sandy water at Margaret's feet. Her first instinct was to let them drown. She was angry. She reached into the churning water and grabbed whoever and whatever brushed against her out-stretched hands. As she turned her face from the spray and the flailing limbs, she saw her father jogging along the pier. His head was turned toward the commotion and he was accelerating. Knowing things were now going to get worse before they got better, she leaned into the twisting, entangled men and yelled, "That's it...stop! I've had it with both of you"

Wobbling and stumbling to their feet, they were again face to face. This time, Margaret stepped between the two winded men and pushed Max to one side, "That's it Max. Don't say another word." Her father interrupted her as he ran down onto the beach and stopped next to the disorientated Max Sorensen.

"Hey, what's going on...Margaret, are you OK?"

"I'm fine...fine." Margaret's glare was now on the dripping wet face of Charlie Bay Burningwater.

Charlie Bay let his eyes drift from Max to Margaret to Jim Garret. His stare was returned. A few seconds later Charlie Bay turned back to Margaret and announced, "I'm going home." With his boots full of water, his pants sagging to expose a portion of scarred bare skin and his head high, he sloshed his way to the dory, climbed in and made ready to row across the harbor for Long Neck Island. No one spoke as he left. Max was exhausted and unable to speak even if he wanted to, which he didn't. He realized that once again, he said too much.

The silence was broken by a request from Jim, "Margaret, since it looks like this is all settled, can you come over here with me a minute?"

Without acknowledging Max, the two turned and walked up the narrow river beach to the parking lot. Max dragged his wet body to a nearby skiff and sat on the bow in an attempt to regain his strength. He watched the graying form of Charlie Bay and the dory glide through the harbor until out of sight. He watched Margaret meet the Congressmen and other guests. After what Max perceived as small talk, she marched to Charlie Bay's truck, climbed in the driver's side and without so much as a glance in his direction, she drove away. Max wondered if Sandra were home.

"Well, what happened to you? Did you fall in the ocean somewhere?" was Sandra Walsh's boisterous greeting through the screen door as Max climbed the back steps.

"I had help."

"Why in the world do you look so forlorn?"

Max hesitated, knew no alternative and looked up toward the ceiling as he spoke, "The Casco Collection is gone." Then, cold and wet, he waited.

"Gone?"

"Missing...stolen...gone...from the lab last night." Max tried to look innocent.

"But, how could that be?" She whispered the words as she leaned against the kitchen counter.

"I don't know what happened...someone broke in through the back door...pried it open. They just took the Casco...nothing else...no equipment...nothing...just the Casco." Max mumbled as he glanced around the room to avoid her eyes.

As fast as she seemed to lose energy with the news, she regained her vigor, "Come on Max you're coming with me. Didn't I say no incidents... didn't I? I want to see the lab and I want the whole story...then, we're going to see Burningwater. Come on."

"But I'm all wet."

"Yes you are and consider that the least of your problems."

During the drive to Gerry Wallace's lab, to the best of his abilities and with a genuine attempt at objectivity, Max recounted the most recent episode in the Casco saga. At the end however; he did interject his innocence and his conclusion that Burningwater was the culprit.

The hollow steel shell echoed with Sandra's labored breathing and Max's wet leather sandals. Looking for any excuse to be as far away from his mentor as possible, he stopped at the desk as Sandra kept walking toward the Casco end of the building. He checked and shuffled unopened mail as apparently more important.

"Time to check your mail Max...looks like once every week or two wouldn't hurt. I'm going down here to have a look."

Max wanted nothing more than a hot shower, dry clothes and to be alone. It was too early for a beer, cheese spread and a Barbara Stanwyck movie. Instead, he chose the mail and a seat on a stool in the middle of the room. Examining the return addresses, he discarded the junk mail and sorted until he identified the long awaited response from the State Historical and Antiquities Office.

The cover letter was a short, simple form message with two enclosures. The first was a copy of the authorization for the skeletal excavation of the Long Neck Island site signed by a State official, Sandra, as the representative of the University and in clean block letters, the only signature of the Casco Tribal Council; Charlie Bay Burningwater. Just one signature for the Tribal Council; Max was puzzled.

The second document, un-requested, but involving the Casco, was a land transaction. Charlie Bay also signed this document as the sole member of the Tribal Council. On the record, the Casco agreed to a renewable ninety-nine year lease for all of the occupiable land at the western end of the reservation. The deal was made with only one individual; Seal Swimmer. This struck Max as a casual arrangement with no specific boundaries. But it was an intriguing contract. It was dated over a year before the dredging, the excavations and the huge land fill. The lease entitled Seal Swimmer to essentially all of the buildable land adjacent to Rt. 1...whatever parcel size that might become.

As he sat re-reading the two documents, he was interrupted by his cell.

"I got it...see cell phone on and ringing", he called to Sandra and followed with a whisper to himself, "...at least it can't be you."

Sandra was immersed in investigation and didn't look up.

"Hello", the caller's voice was unknown to Max. The questions were startling but he answered without hesitation. "Yes, I do...I agree to do that...I'm sure Burningwater would...ya, I'm sure...after dark, Pier Twenty-two...by water...I'll be there. How did you get this...?" He closed his phone.

"Sandra, you're not going to believe this. Come on, come on, hustle! We've gotta tell Margaret...we're going to get them back. Hopefully tonight...just have to round up a boat. Let's go...I'm driving."

It was difficult for Sandra to decide which was more disturbing; the odd requirements of repossessing the Casco Collection or Max driving across the rail tie bridge onto Long Neck Island. Neither of her concerns mattered to Max, he just wanted to find Charlie Bay and Margaret. As he suspected, they were at the reburial site and were not disturbed as he skidded to a halt next to the open grave. Max popped from the driver's seat baring a broad smile and hurried his way around the car straight to Charlie Bay. Fearing another confrontation, Margaret grabbed Charlie Bay's arm as they came to their feet.

"It's OK...it's all right Margaret. He didn't take the bones...he didn't do it."

"What do you mean...how do you know he didn't take them?" She let go of his arm.

"You can learn a lot about a man when you wrestle him in the River." Charlie Bay smiled.

Max stopped in front Charlie Bay with such a genuine grin even Margaret almost smiled.

"What is going on Max...why do you look so happy?" As she spoke, she wondered if her words were interrupting an awkward embrace between the two men but, considered it out of character for both. Margaret was the only one uneasy with the silence. "Well... what's going on?"

"Just a little while ago...at the lab...I got a call. I don't know who it was...but if we want the Casco back we can pick them up tonight...after dark at Pier Twenty-two on the Portland waterfront. It has to be by water...so we'll need a boat. The only condition is that they have to be in the ground tomorrow. I said we would. They aren't lost...we're going to get them back!" The excitement and joy in Max's voice matched his expression. "So...we need a boat."

"I suppose I could get the center console...which would work...it's in the water." Margaret wondered to herself about the idea and decided to leave her father out of this.

Max had another choice. "I was thinking...maybe...based on the nature of the mission...ah...this required a Pipeboat...in a sense...this is now a part of the dream journey. You do have a motor for the Pipeboat...what do you think Burningwater...can we take the Pipeboat?"

"I have a motor...brand new. I need gasoline. Gasoline...hmm...you...me and gasoline..." Charlie Bay's voice tailed off in a chuckle.

Max joined him and Margaret still wondered what was going on.

"Who called...you have no idea who it was?"

"No he didn't give his name...the number was restricted."

From inside the car came a muffled voice, "I pass...
you three are on your own...only you Max...no one but
you...I sure can pick'em."

"I'll get you two by boat...at the fish pier...about a
half hour before sunset..."

Max interrupted, "Sunset...what time is sunset?"

Pointing skyward, Charlie Bay shook his head,
"Look to the west and watch...university Americans. I've
a lot to do." He glanced into the burial trough and left
without looking in Dr. Walsh's direction.

Margaret looked to Max, "Sunset's around eight...I'll
meet you at the dock at seven-thirty. Who do you think
was on the phone, any ...?"

Max shrugged his shoulders. "I'll see you tonight at
seven-thirty...I gotta get a shower."

A rule, generally understood by all and routinely
enforced by the Harbormaster, was the five-knot/no wake
zone of the Casco River anchorage. For the few
lobstermen tending to some late day chores, it was an odd
sight. To the recreational boaters settling in for the night,
it was an annoying disturbance. But, for the bass
fishermen enjoying the flat calm of an evening lull and
dotting the harbor in their small aluminum boats and
kayaks, it was terrifying. As if from nowhere, came a
roaring rumbling wooden wedge, with the bow raised so
high from the water that a wall of foam crested amidship
on the red bottomed hull. Waves from the wake rolled
through the moorings tumbling and rocking everything in

their path. The tranquil river harbor was set into complete disarray by a clam digger with an outboard, and who, despite his best efforts, was unable to see what floated in front of him. The motorized dory's inability to plane through the water, lower the bow and afford at least some visibility, combined with Charlie Bay's frozen grip on a wide open throttle, left the placid anchorage in watery chaos. The dock was in one direction, the Pipe boat, at full speed, was headed in another. Margaret and Max were left to stand on the fish pier float in disbelief as Burningwater zigzagged his way through the boats and moorings, never hitting anything but coming close to everything.

"Do you think he's going to be able to bring it into the dock?" Margaret was using concern as a mask for amazement.

"This is going to be an adventure. Looks like Sandra made a good choice." Max grinned. "He'll be alright...let's give him a little time."

As Max spoke, Charlie Bay buzzed within fifteen feet of the dock sending everyone on the float to their knees and cutting most of the fishing lines running from the pier. This sent catcalls from anyone within ear shot of Charlie Bay. His look was brief, but Max thought that he saw a twinkle in Charlie Bay's eyes as he flashed before the sunset crowd of fishermen.

"He'll be OK...don't worry. He just needs to get close...cut off the engine...he can row or drift in. We just need to get to him before these fishermen do." Max was chuckling as he helped Margaret to her feet.

"It's really not funny...well...maybe it is...look at him go." She smiled and shook her head.

On his next pass, Charlie Bay was headed straight for the float; still at full speed. Seconds before he was to ram the dock and after everyone nearby except Max and Margaret ran for safety, the outboard engine stopped and the dory rolled to the float on the crest of its' own wake. Fending off the bow, Max signaled for Margaret to climb into the boat as he tumbled in over the gunnel behind her. After the less than graceful boarding, Max was left seated on a wet and slippery floor to stare aft at the silhouette of a man poised against the red sunset sky.

Charlie Bay stood indifferently to the presence of his two passengers. Burningwater caressed the inside of the Pipeboat hull and softly chanted a prayer. Neither Margaret nor Max moved until he was finished.

Finally, Max said, "We should go."

Without hesitating, Charlie Bay pulled the starter cord, held the throttle at wide open and sent Margaret and Max lunging backwards, groping for something solid to grab.

Once he found some stability, Max leaned toward Burningwater and shouted, "You don't always have to run at full speed...there's half throttle you know...she may ride better." Taking Charlie Bay's lack of response as an opportunity, Max reached for the outboard tiller, grabbed the rigid hand and twisted the throttle to slow the motor.

The salty old fisherman grinned, "...wondered how that worked."

In the newfound calm and quiet, Max pointed to the words indicating various speeds and gears on the side of the throttle without any knowledge of Charlie Bay's illiteracy. Burningwater nodded politely and grinned, this time at Margaret.

At the slower speed, they took a moment to organize and center themselves for the journey. Margaret sat on the bow seat and faced forward; a familiar spot, with her legs nestled among the orange lifejackets. Max sat amidships and faced the stern as if to aid in navigation, but without any idea of where they were going. Charlie Bay stood forward of the well and the cove seat, white knuckled and as far from the gas tank as possible. Passing the bell buoy at the entrance of the Casco River channel, three motionless figures headed seaward.

As Charlie Bay turned northeast to round the rocky peninsula of Casco Point, both Max and Margaret were captivated by the contrasting view of the brilliant western sky and the dark shadowed edge of the shoreline evergreens. The State Park forest trees melted into the black rolling swells of open ocean and set the foundation of their inland horizon in darkness. They watched the watery world around them fall into night.

To alleviate his concerns with dusk and the cold merciless appearance of the sea, Max moved closer to Charlie Bay and asked, "Where are we headed?"

"Right now...Spain." Charlie Bay answered without a change in expression. "Move up toward the bow with Margaret...so we can go faster. I'm going through this gut at Seal Rock...run up along the shore northeast...'til we hit the next bay...from there...we head inland."

Passing closer to the ledge than the coastline and once again at full throttle, Charlie Bay piloted the dory through most of the lobster buoys and over a few as they cut Seal Rock. The higher portions of the ledge formed a black crescent-shaped stone mass intermittently protruding from the swells and surrounding a large pool of kelp swaying on the surface. Seal pups, skirmishing around the rock and seaweed, paused to watch the boat and passengers intrude. Max was hanging on as if for his life. The seals caught Margaret.

"Charlie Bay...seals!"

Focused on the waters ahead, Burningwater didn't alter his stare or share her excitement.

"Seal Swimmer...hey...Seal Swimmer...look there they are!" Margaret yelled again.

Seeing that Charlie Bay was unresponsive, Max took the opportunity to divert his fear of traveling on the open ocean at night. "I think he has seen seals out here before." He waited for the look. He wasn't disappointed. "What did you call him...Seal Swimmer?"

"Ya, Charlie Bay used to be called Seal Swimmer... before the fire...when they changed his name. Look... there's two more."

"Seal Swimmer," mused Max, as he recalled the lease contract between the Casco and Seal Swimmer. He was puzzled by the possibilities until the surges of much larger ground swells rekindled his anxiety. Seal Rock quickly faded into the distance. The sunset sky turned to the black of a moonless night as the dark waves rose and fell beneath him.

The Pipeboat's course traversed the crests of the rollers and slid into their watery valleys. With each upward thrust of the waves, Max felt his gut push into the base of his throat and his frame compress. As the craft fell off and rolled into the following trough, his split second relief was overtaken by a weightless descent until another rising wave began the cycle again.

Over and over, as they progressed into the night, the rolling continued. The endless rhythm was finally broken when Max vomited two cheese dogs and diet Coke over the starboard rail. Resting his chin on the gunnel and spitting the lingering bitter contents of his mouth into an indifferent sea, he turned to Burningwater, "I really didn't need the nitrites anyway...don't worry...I'll be alright...I'm fine."

As the vomiting resumed and Margaret, her hand on Max's back, gazed at their skipper with big dark, apologetic eyes. Charlie Bay shook his head and looked skyward. He wondered how his relationship with the eternal world of spirit beings came to be linked with a seasick university American and big-eyed writer. Returning her stare, he nodded in assurance and turning seaward, he nodded into the darkness.

Chapter Eleven

Charlie Bay slid the dory alongside the rafted trawlers docked on Pier Twenty-two. In the darkness he found a small landing float on the inland side. Max and Margaret were surprised at how fast he had learned to handle the outboard motor in tight places. As they stepped onto the float, eight-foot wharf pilings surrounded them in a forest of moist black columns, visible only one tier deep and echoing lapping waves. The dark and damp place was unwelcoming to two of the three trespassers.

"You know I almost went to work here once...right here on this fish pier. Couldn't do it for some reason...I don't know...work in a fish plant. I stayed on the Island. Most that did come here to work...never came back. If I remember right...there's a shed door and an office at the end of the dock. Now I remember...I couldn't fill out the papers." Charlie Bay looked at Margaret and laughed but not about the job application. He was going to bring the Casco home.

Without speaking, they climbed the dock ramp and walked to the water end of the pier. There was a dim security lamp at the peak of a warehouse roof. It cast a gray hue over the front entrance and the dock. The door was a six-foot plywood panel set in a large sliding shed door. The shed door was locked but the inset panel door was wedged open. Pulling it toward him, Max stepped back and they all peered inside.

"Where's the office?" Max raised his eyebrows at Charlie Bay.

"Well...it was here. They must have moved it. There's some light over in that direction...further down. It's probably there...let's go." Charlie Bay's voice was a notch higher than usual.

Max hedged, "I don't know...I got the call. Whoever this is...they're expecting me. I don't want anything to go wrong...Sandra wouldn't forgive me. Why don't you two wait here...as soon as everything is set...I'll get you...we'll get the Casco together."

"But..." Margaret broke in and Max responded.

"Please...do me this favor. Let me go talk with who ever this is...I'll come back." Max began walking toward the light alone.

Margaret turned to Charlie Bay, "I'm not going to let him go down there alone...are you?"

"Ugh, ugh." Charlie Bay shook his head no. Margaret started after Max.

Holding her arm, Charlie Bay whispered, "Wait... give him a minute and we'll follow. I don't want anything to go wrong either."

After he passed from sight, the couple crept to cover, hiding in the shadows, but close enough to hear the noise give Max away.

Knocking over two stacked empty polyethylene bait barrels was easy for Max, catching them as they rolled in different directions was not. As he stopped one, the other came to rest at the foot of a man who stepped in from the darkness.

"Quite an entrance," a voice came from the cavernous warehouse.

"Yours too." Max was not amused but he was intimidated.

"Dr. Sanderson...I'm Jim Garret," were the words that came in a businesslike manner along with an extended right hand.

"Sorensen...Max Sorensen," Max corrected firmly in tone and grip, no longer intimidated.

"Sorensen...I'm sorry. I'm usually pretty good at names...sorry." Jim was upset with himself at the discourtesy and embarrassed. His sincerity was Max's first impression as both men picked up their barrels. "Come on over to the office here...so we can talk."

"My father...what's he doing here!" Margaret started to stand up until Charlie Bay restrained her.

"It's best we just listen."

Margaret stood for a few seconds thinking about it and slid back to cover.

Switching on two desk lamps to light up an office which was nothing more than a few chairs, file cabinets and a small refrigerator in an otherwise enormous storage space, Jim offered Max a seat.

"Not the way I remembered it," mumbled Charlie Bay.

"Well...the world around Long Neck does change." She was angry with her father but Charlie Bay was closer. "What is he doing here?"

Walking toward the refrigerator with a coffee maker on top, "Would you like coffee...something to drink?" Jim tugged at the artificial wood grain door as if by habit, but never looked inside.

Max was surprised by the invitation and felt for some unknown reason they were about to settle into conversation. "Ah...do you have ginger ale?"

"Ginger ale?" Jim was baffled, who asks for ginger ale?

"It was a tough ride over here...it's been awhile since I've been on rolling seas...you know..." Max patted his stomach.

"How about a Diet Coke?"

"Diet Coke...sure. Why did you steal the Casco Collection?"

The question and Max's directness didn't disrupt Jim Garret. The need for small talk was over.

"You can't steal something that already belongs to you." His affect was flat, matter of fact and passionless.

"Seal Swimmer...you're Seal Swimmer." The lineage fell into place in Max's mind; a son, in Native American tradition, named after his father.

Jim Garret nodded a deliberate yes. "Named after he became Bay Burningwater."

"You are Burningwater's son," Max whispered, as he grasped the relationships and their implications. "The bones are your people."

Jim Garret spoke clearly. "By blood."

Margaret's knees buckled. She sat back onto the bottom of an overturned work skiff. "He's your...that means I'm..." Her words were in short quick breaths; words buying time to understand.

With his mouth grinning broadly, with his eyes twinkling and rolling open the palms of his weathered hands, Charlie Bay looked to Margaret, "So my granddaughter...you too dove three times in the waves and surfaced as a harbor seal."

Margaret whispered, "You are my grandfather."

Sitting in an office chair directly across from Max, Jim Garret clarified the conditions of the Casco's return. "You agreed on the phone that the bones would be buried tomorrow...no more studies...no more research...no DNA."

In their phone conversation, Max didn't recall the stipulation of no further study and no DNA. To the best of his recollection, it was never mentioned. He was hesitant. One last time, he was waffling, still unable to accept the commitment to rebury.

Anxious to resolve the issue, Jim ended, once and for all, any more research on the Casco.

"Right now, the bones are set to be run through the fish waste processor first thing in the morning. They're going to be broken, crushed and end up dumped into the Gulf Stream five miles out. You want them...they are to be buried in Reservation ground tomorrow morning."

The thought of crushed and broken made Max cringe. "You went to all the trouble of taking them...you've got'em. Why ...?"

"Some overzealous colleagues arranged to have them removed from the lab and I..."

"But why?" Max was frustrated, "Why do that?"

Max was asking why they were stolen. Jim answered why he was offering their return.

"I had seen rage in him before. The damage it caused our family...my mother's suffering...it was all so aimless. But today on the beach with you...I saw his rage ...experienced his fire." Jim paused as if amazed by the insight. "For better or worse...the fire is in the hunt for those bones...despite it all...my lack of understanding of his ways...his life and everything he has done...I owe him. I have to act in his favor. You want them or not?"

"Yes, ya of course I do...I'll take them. But why did you take'm in the first place?"

Margaret leaned toward an opening in their camouflage and whispered, "Ya, and I want to know why you never told me..." Charlie Bay cut her off abruptly with a firm hand over her mouth and a restraining hug.

He said into her ear. "Be patient granddaughter. On this night...he's doing all he can...there'll be a time."

Margaret relaxed into his arms, knowing from experience that her father's ability to divulge family history came in bits and pieces.

"Why we took them? The DNA stuff panicked us a little."

Max looked at Jim and decided to give it one more try. "You know I could do cone beam radiography... create a 3-D file of the skull...reconstruct it in resin with laser polymerization...no bone whatsoever, no DN..."

"No. The deal is...you choose...crush or bury?'

"We bury." Max let go.

Both men acknowledged a deal, Jim extended his hand, the tension in his body gone.

Max remained seated, shook and looked back to the floor. Suddenly slapping his knees, arching his back and looking up into the darkness, Max repeated the reason, "Ah...the DNA stuff! You mean, one of my less than sound research ideas...that's been driving me crazy... along with everyone around me...panicked you. The DNA."

It all came together for Max; the marsh landfill acreage off Rt. 1, the resort development project and the Congressmen.

"Casino. A Casco Casino. You're building a Casco Casino! That's it...it's gambling!" Max burst into uproarious laughter. "Ah...you're unbelievable. You are recreating a Casco gene pool from who knows where. Because there's no one left...so you're reconstructing it... a new genetic Nation with an old name." Feeling the blood pound through his heart, Max was off and running. For a fragile ego, anticipating the confirmation that he had figured it all out was energizing. "All I am...with those bones...archived Casco DNA...a Casco genetic profile...potentially accessible to any one...I'm just someone holding the information to mess it all up!"

"Well...it might. We are rebuilding the Casco Nation with folks who believe that they are Casco. Genetically who knows?" In a conciliatory fashion, with a raised brow and tilted head, Jim acknowledged Max's assessment. "Down the road...with confusing information spun by the wrong hands...it could be a big problem. There're already plenty of problems ahead..."

"Problems...ah...one's got to be the Settlement Act. Didn't the Penobscot and the Passamaquady try to pursue gambling on their reservations awhile ago and lose in the State or Federal Courts?"

"I see you know some Indian Law...they did end up with Bingo but to the point...the Casco weren't part of the Settlement Act and in the deal with the State of Maine...they were passed over...an insignificant piece of the whole thing. There was no land claim made by the Casco Nation. They were and still are just a Tribe shunted aside and left to die...back then just a handful of members who really didn't matter... "

"Ah...so you are the mysterious force behind the approval for the Casco of federal recognition...how'd you do that?"

"We went through the Bureau of Indian Affairs...not the courts. Once the Passammaquady and Penobscot set the precedent and established federal recognition for the eastern tribes...as long as we didn't make any trouble...like land claim lawsuits...we didn't have any trouble. The Casco people have been living on that land for who knows how long before the Europeans showed up. There just haven't been a lot of them out there lately. But that really didn't matter with the B.I.A. ...based on the evidence of occupation...they went right ahead and granted federal recognition without state regulation."

Max smiled, "So the Casco are a federally recognized tribe and therefore with Congressional specification under the Indian Gaming Act...very eligible for casino gambling."

"Could be a two hundred million dollar a year industry."

"So, your first problem is extinction...that's why the tribal roles. Who's out there that claims tribal affiliation...who thinks they're Casco?"

"We got twenty-three people with no vested interest...no idea of what's going on...who believe that they are Casco. The records are terrible. Only five have a slight chance to demonstrate...with birth records...the required one-quarter lineal descendantcy for federal tribal membership. If we go to oral lineage reconstruction with the others...we're weak...maybe we have eighteen who claim to be Casco by one story or another. If you add all that to unsatisfactory DNA comparisons between known Casco bones...and who we have as living Casco...and there's no DNA matches...the project dies in Congress as a scam...extinction wins. Now...we have people who believe they are Casco...good honest people...with DNA it's too risky...extinction will not win again."

Jim considered the integrity of those who signed the Tribal Role. "You know...these people...with absolutely no knowledge of anything to gain...these folks have said, "I'm Casco." They believe it." Pausing, Jim looked at the floor, "And then there's Burningwater, who is Casco body and soul....who has always believed."

Max saw Charlie Bay as a genetic problem.

"What are you going to do about him? He's the living DNA remnant of the Casco Nation."

"The irony is that he's not listed on the current tribal role...the one true Casco...besides...someone would have to find him first...by now you know that's not easy...in today's world he doesn't exist."

"He got you started with the land on Rt. 1 didn't he...I saw the contract."

"Ah huh...land from guilt. With that land I crossed over...nineteen years old and with leverage on the other side. I started with miniature golf...built it myself working third shift right here at this fish pier...a summer later...it became the driving range and a clam shack. Then it became the landfill...with that landfill came capital...a lot of capital. That changed everything...it was on and on from there. I was in a different world. I was no longer Casco."

Charlie Bay lowered his head and once again was compelled to recall how, in a moment from which to mark time, he released a son and enslaved a Nation.

Still fuming at her father, Margaret missed Charlie Bay's torment. "Why is he telling Max all this? This is more stuff I knew nothing about..." Her voice tailed off with the desire to know.

"Max is not a threat to your father. He's a teacher...not a businessman. With our ancestors in Reservation ground...your father knows that none of this can be used against him by others. My son has a warrior's way of thinking...he attacks and he protects. He is a harpoon and a harbor."

Testing Jim for more of the story, "He was the only one left on the Tribal Council wasn't he? He could do whatever he wanted. There was no one else."

Jim nodded acknowledging Max's grasp of the circumstances, "The death in his generation was unbearable, not just dead bodies...relatives...friends... there were plenty of those...but, it was a death of spirit... individuals and community. Alcohol sucked it out of some people...my sister Molly...Burningwater...'til they all but disappeared. Looking back on it, I think he saw what was coming. There was absolutely nothing he, or anyone else, could do to change it...the ancestral ways of being were slowly and sometimes quickly exterminated. He was the end of the line. I've often thought that he saw my energy to build as an alternative to booze and depression...an alternative that he didn't have. I needed land...which he did have. Ha...it was so lousy nobody else wanted it until they needed a place to dump all the sand." Jim paused. "He gave me the only thing he could give and I took from him the only thing I could take."

"So you have all this Casco Reservation land...you control the access and from what I can see...there's an awful lot of land out there."

"...over four hundred acres suitable for development."

"And now you're rebuilding the Casco Tribal role and Casco Tribal Council from scratch...Congress specifies the sovereign nation status of the Casco so it's within the structure of the Indian gaming regulations... what about the State?"

"You're pretty good at this...looking for a job?"

"Oh no, it's the design...constructing the whole thing...the long odds."

"Well...the next step is to enter negotiations with the State. Imagine it...a handful of rag-tag Casco as a sovereign Nation...on equal ground with the State of Maine." Both chuckle at the incongruity of the image. "Basically the negotiations are to discuss the State's share of the revenues. Maine has no regulatory power over the Casco as a federal tribe...there are no restrictions against Casino gaming...there's no ban anywhere on the books because the Casco aren't a part of the Settlement Act. Since there's no State regulation or tax on the gaming...Maine is not going to get anything. We can leave them out and antagonize everyone or we can give the State a share up front. If the pot's sweet enough in profit-sharing...there should be a relatively smooth and quiet agreement before the anti-gambling forces or anybody else gets vocal."

"Who's doing all this...handling the money?"

"Casco Casino Board of Directors."

"You?"

"Oh no...not me."

"But you picked every member of the Board didn't you."

Jim smiled and skirted the question, "They're all good, bright and honest people...experienced in the right areas. And they're all dedicated to the mission of the project."

"The mission of the project...what's the mission of the project...besides making tons of money?"

Nursing one Diet Coke, Max knew this was a chance to hear more of the Casco story. In an attempt to keep the conversation going, he was just about to ask for another one, when Jim kept going.

"Besides making lots of money...adoption of abandoned and lost souls."

Max was stunned, "What?"

"To assimilate orphaned Native Americans who identify with the Casco Nation. You know...to do with the revenues exactly what the spirit of the Indian Gaming Regulatory Act intended...create opportunities for healthcare, housing, education, childcare, job training...to support all of it...college...graduate school...seed money for Native American businesses. You know the law...the whole thing...redistribution of wealth. We will adopt and educate by creating sound economic resources...rebuild a Nation...hopefully within a generation."

"You're going to have people showing up from everywhere."

"I hope so...but Dr Sorensen...this is not a quick get rich entitlement plan filled with cars, big houses and flat screen TVs. The key is the education of a Nation...developing its identity...its skills and talents. People hear Indian gambling casino and they think money in their pocket. The greatest value of the project isn't in doling out cash...but in elevating the knowledge base of the Casco tribal members...give people the chance to become builders...educators...business owners or whatever else...all within Casco culture. Money is not the end...the mission is to build and sustain a Casco ethnic identity with individuals who actively contribute to the strength of a diverse American culture!"

Jim took a breath, calmed himself and came back to Max. "It's education Dr Sorensen...education."

Overcome with the irony of Jim Garret's passion, Max was unable to respond. His life's work was espoused by a businessman with a clarity and conviction dormant in his own being for too long. A humbled Max Sorensen asked for another Diet Coke.

"Could I have another one of these?"

Jim handed Max the cold drink and continued, "You are right...assimilation of various tribes and beliefs is difficult...but ignorance is the enemy...victory is collective."

It was apparent to Max that from Jim Garret's perspective, regeneration of native peoples required, at least initially, unification and education. The elevation of Native American cultures was to be found in ethnic solidarity and educational opportunity. There was not a lot for Max to say. He whispered, "It's a noble endeavor."

Having no desire for compliments, Jim returned Max to the pragmatic. "Just because you are doing what you believe is a good work...hopefully for the betterment of many...it doesn't mean that it will turn out alright. That's why I'm so adamant that those bones are not a part of any DNA research or an accessible data base. This is just one step in a very long sequence."

Stepping this far into one man's vision of the Casco future and with really nothing to lose, Max asked his last key question without antagonism. "What's in it for you...why do all this? You're not on the Casco Role or on the Board of Directors...you've separated and distanced yourself from the Casco...what do you get out of the enormous effort?"

"It's pretty straightforward. I get to design, develop and build...then I step away...let somebody else manage and operate it...a casino is like nothing else...it's an extreme environment designed to captivate...transport people into a world that suspends their everyday reality ...constructs a new reality...one that's dedicated to the redistribution of wealth. They lose and we gain... gambling to redistribute wealth...it's a Native American tradition."

Leaning forward in a straight-backed chair toward Max, with hands outstretched as if poised to shake his own excitement into a docile academic body, he spoke, charged with energy.

"There are no hotels on the marsh, just the Casco Casino with all kinds of terrific restaurants...any type of food you want...big and small entertainment pavilions for marquee names. The first building phase is a quarter million square feet of earth-tone single story domed modules interconnected with loops of an indoor tube system...to connect players to every gaming location in the entire Casino. The monorail transportation...from a string of hotels and parking on the periphery will take people across the highway...through the woods and out to a Native American gambling village removed from the rest of the world in time and space...take them into another place to spend money and be entertained."

"But how...no bank today is going to loan money for reservation development because technically the Federal Government owns and will always hold title to the land?

Ah...but you own all that land around the western periphery...where the hotels will go...don't you? That's how you can raise the money to build the casino. Otherwise no private investors are going to put up that much cash for a building on a federal reservation where they can't hold a mortgage. But banks will take a mortgage on the hotels off the reservation land and reduce their risk for the casino.

It's going to take a lot of cash...you must be going to leverage everything you have." Max shook his head.

Jim smiled, but again didn't answer the questions. "There's a four hundred room, five star hotel planned for the hill on that northwest corner that will overlook everything. Max...this is a five hundred million-dollar deal designed for expansions over the next twenty years. It's a very conservative step-by-step approach... see why we panicked...it's got to go step-by-step."

Max hesitated and for some reason flashed to Linda, "Tell me something...do you drive your wife crazy with these ideas...I mean all these incredibly big ideas...don't they upset her?"

"What?" Jim was unable to make the connection.

"You know these enormous plans...all the big ideas...one after another...don't they drive your wife nuts?"

By the look on his face Jim knew that Max was now struggling with an issue different than Casco bones or Casino plans. Jim saw only turmoil. He did the best he could to answer.

"Ya they did...at first...but now I never discuss them. I just show her when sections of a project are done. Then we talk about what's coming next...usually just the next step."

"When parts are done...nothing about the whole thing?" Max considered this. "I don't know if I could do that...keep quiet about it...I think that I'm a leaper...onto the next couple of steps right away...can't stay with it to the finish." Max's head ached.

Sensing Max was done, Jim stood, walked to his side placed his hand on a shoulder and asked, "Hey, you alright?"

Max didn't answer.

Both men knew the Casco Casino story was safe. It was given and received in the spirit of the Casco reburial. It was entombed in Max and on this, he knew silence.

"Remember the job at hand Max...get the bones and bury them on Reservation ground in the morning. Come on...let's get going."

Lifting his head, Max nodded and came to his feet. Their eyes met.

Jim mumbled, "I'd like to tell Margaret about this...about everything myself," both as something to say and to verify a secure exchange.

For Max, it was never an issue, "Sure...of course." He smiled at the thought of Jim dealing with Margaret. "You have my word."

Shutting off one of the lights, Jim gave Max the information for the retrieval of the Casco Collection.

"Did you tie up at the work float on this pier?"

"Ya."

"As you came to the float, you passed some rafted trawlers. The last one...outboard...at the end of the dock is called the RITA MARIE. In the main hold are the boxes of bones. The hatch is unlocked and you can load from the water. I'll take care of security...no one will bother you. It should take you less than a half-hour.

You're on your own...good bye Dr Sorensen." Jim shook Max's hand and disappeared into an unlit corridor.

With his eyes still adjusting to the darkness, Max was startled as Margaret and Charlie Bay stepped forward from their cover. "Whoa...were you two there to catch that?"

"We pretty much heard all of it...although there was some of your mumbling I didn't get..." Margaret confirmed, "...but most of it."

"I've had enough...it's between you and your father... you and your son...I'm staying out of it...I don't want to rehash that conversation, OK?" He looked at Margaret and glanced at Charlie Bay as they all nodded in agreement. "Now let's get the Casco...take them back to the island."

The deck of the trawler was moist and cold. To Max and Margaret the smell of fish was overpowering. Charlie Bay took the hold, Margaret carried the boxes to the gunnel and Max stacked the cartons in the dory. They worked without speaking. Before they left the trawler's side, Charlie Bay restacked all of the Casco containers. Max wasn't offended.

The trip back to Long Neck was a slow one. The size of their fragile cargo and the darkness made speed secondary to safe return. Having mastered the throttle, Charlie Bay stood and looked over the packed dory as if each box were a lobster trap and he was making the traditional August reset of his gear closer to shore.

Margaret was cradled in the bow, facing aft and dozing amid swells and bones of her people. Again, Max sat amidships, but this time facing forward, each arm outstretched to his side, stabilizing the load. The breeze of the night air erased his headache and the roll of the sea relaxed him near sleep. Charlie Bay, unlit pipe clenched in his teeth, stood at the helm and watched the dark water as the midnight southwest wind began to stir the crests of the ground swells into small splashes of foam. Occasionally glancing under the extended arms of Max Sorenson at the placid face of his granddaughter, Charlie Bay Burningwater whispered a prayer of thanksgiving. For two of the early morning hours, the Pipeboat of the dream journey made its way homeward.

Chapter Twelve

It didn't take long for Max's wrinkled khakis to be wet above the knees. Even in daytime he knew the Maine water was often unbearably cold, a few hours from first light, it was worse. His feet were numb and his body chilled. But that didn't stop him from the evenly paced task of handing the containers of the Casco Collection on shore to Margaret. With the Pipeboat anchored in the sandy shallows as close to Charlie Bay's work dock as the outgoing tide allowed, Max waded from the dory's side to the water's edge. From there Margaret stacked the remains of her people up on the dry sand. She didn't say a word.

On shore, Burningwater began to organize his preparation for the reburial of the Casco bones. Lighting two old kerosene railroad lamps and placing each on a pole at opposite corners of the platform, he set up a worktable between them in enough light to overcome the early morning darkness. The red and blue parachute silk, tobacco in a sealed tin and a Clementine crate lined with obsidian, he brought from the fishing shack. Laying strips of the cloth, tobacco and the stones at one end of the table, Charlie Bay called to Margaret for the first container long before Max completed unloading even the port side of the Pipeboat. Margaret carried the cardboard box, which she labeled and packed just a week ago, from the sand, up the two steps onto the work dock. She set the carton on the table in front of him. His eyes sparkled in the reflected light of the lanterns. Remaining still, Margaret watched as Charlie Bay unpacked the first box, carefully setting the packaged long bones of an ancestor on the tabletop. He removed the unprinted newspaper and exposed the contents. Pausing for a moment to view the skeletal remnant of a member of the Casco Nation, Charlie Bay then ran his hand across the light brown shaft of along bone.

He spoke with relief. "They haven't been burned or broken."

Margaret saw a man approaching peace. She saw her grandfather fulfilling his obligation. And only she heard the splash.

"Whoa...that's cold!" Came the muffled voice followed by a second splash. "It's OK...nothing got wet...except me."

Margaret turned as both she and Charlie Bay, now aware of the splashing, peered out in the dory's direction onto the black water.

"Are you alright?" Margaret was concerned more for the Casco containers than Max.

"Ya, ya I'm alright. I just stepped in a hole filled with quicksand and lost my balance. But the box didn't get wet...just my..." His voice tailed off but returned louder, "So I'm wide awake now."

Acknowledging the adventure with Max Sorensen was a constant in the reburial process; Charlie Bay rolled his eyes and shook his head.

Redirecting his focus to Margaret, "I need you to take my truck...go onshore and call Bud Walker before sunrise...before they'd be heading out on the water. Let him know the burial will be mid-morning...here on the Island...over by the blueberry patch...he'll know who to tell. Then call anyone else you want to come."

His lack of specification with "call anyone you want" made her uncertain about her father. Did he want him there or not? She hesitated. The moment passed.

"After you get the rest of our ancestors up here... there's some driftwood kindling and split oak on the inland side of the shack...you know...same as always. You can build a fire at the hearth site for the Wet One. Be sure you light it."

Margaret smiled. Recalling the feeling of Molly wrapped next to her; tucked together in one blanket, warming the soles of their feet at the hearth site and curled beside a fire built by the Storyteller, she nodded yes. His phrase "our ancestors" surfaced, she lingered in front of him and nodded again.

Moaning and groaning through the transfer of the Casco from the Pipeboat to the work dock provided Max an opportunity to express his wet discomfort. With placement on the platform of the last carton, Charlie Bay signaled Margaret, by a tilt of his head, in the direction of the firewood.

"She'll build a fire. There's some dry pants in the shack. They should fit. They're not mine." The comparative belly size, by Charlie Bay of his own wirery build to the midriff bulge of Max Sorensen, was enough to get a laugh from Margaret.

Recognizing he deserved it and appreciative of the chance to get warm and dry, he stopped fussing. "You wouldn't have a beer in there too...would you?"

"Might."

Heading into the doorway of the fishing shack, Max whispered to himself, but loud enough for both to hear, "Charlie Bay...you're a man after my own heart."

A short time later, Max reappeared before a newly lit fire wearing navy work pants and holding his wet khakis, a wool blanket and a quart bottle of beer. The twist off cap was in place but a small light line of foam indicated about a third of the beer was already gone. Kneeling by the fire and adding wood, Margaret watched the sparks from the kindling rise to just above her head and disappear. She relaxed as her cheeks collected the warmth and her breath drew in the pine scented air.

"Ah, this will do my bones a world of good," was the grateful response as Max spread the blanket near the flame in a spot with lateral views of Charlie Bay on one side and the Pipeboat on the other.

"I'm going to make some calls and get a change of clothes. Need anything...you want a ride somewhere?"

"No I'm fine. I'd like to stay here." Max looked out onto the water. "Don't worry...I won't disturb him...I'd just like to stick around until they're in the ground. Really...I'm done."

This time, Margaret believed him, "OK."

"Oh...be sure to let Sandra know." He exhaled a deep breath. "That was close...I almost forgot her."

"I didn't."

Max expected the look he often received from Margaret concerning his mentor, but it never came. Tired, Margaret walked across the work dock. Passing slowly but leaving Charlie Bay undisturbed among Casco bones, she found the path back to the house. When she reached the crest of the hill between the new burial ground and the truck, Margaret looked to the east. A line of stars cut the horizon sky from the water's edge to the streaking dark clouds overhead. It was going to be a good day to rebury and she considered her father.

Settling in with a lifejacket for a pillow, the blanket and beer, Max watched Charlie Bay bundle the bones in silk from the corner of his eye. The fire leaped and snapped at his toes. As his belly warmed and the muscles of his legs, bathed in heat, began to loosen, he spoke with no expectation of conversation.

"I wonder if he's going to make it happen? It is truly amazing you know...what he's trying to do. What a dreamer...your son...what a dreamer. But it's a noble call...educating a Nation.

I've two sons. Two sons...one's just come back from Japan...James...he's an engineer...been working on an elevator that goes horizontally and vertically. You know...like this." Max demonstrated with his right hand by holding the bottle of beer, first dragging it across the ground and then raising it to his mouth. After taking a large swig he continued. "A horizontal and vertical elevator...great idea...Jimmy lives in San Diego now...not sure what he's working on...

My other son...Paul is still in school...college...he's a lacrosse player...you know...the old Native American game." Max assumed that his sarcasm wasn't going to elicit a response and continued rambling. "That kid can run like the wind...especially with some huge defenseman chasing him...he runs like a bat out of hell... just like a bat...dashing and darting all over the place... you should see him fly. Once...when things weren't going so well for him...I wanted to write the Eastern Cherokee word for bat...I think it's..."tlaniwa"...or something close to that. I wanted to write it on his shoulder pads for the spirit of the bat to guide him...to pass on skills and cunning...just before I wrote it...even I thought it was too much...so...I drew a Thunderbird instead...just something...anything to get him in touch with the spirits." Max's voice faded as he drew near sleep. "I wanted to get him in touch with the spirits of the game...spirits who played the game before."

Charlie Bay spoke without lifting his head or interrupting his work. "To evoke the spirit of the Bat or the Thunderbird is a serious matter...the power of the spirits can not be taken lightly."

Max was startled. He didn't think that Charlie Bay was listening. Sitting up and turning toward him, he had an edge, "Yes it is serious...it wasn't taken lightly."

Without acknowledging Max in any way, Charlie Bay continued to bundle bones. After a long silence and seeing that it wasn't going to be discussed any further, Max slid back down against the lifejacket to get the last word.

"It wasn't taken lightly...I appreciate them to be very effective spirits...the kid's been playing great ever since." Annoyed that his understanding was challenged, a tired Max Sorensen folded his arms across his chest, closed his eyes and fell asleep.

The coals were still warm but the sand under Max's heels took on an early morning damp chill with the loss of flame and a low sun. He woke with pain in his back and the immediate thoughts of an aging body and poor judgment. With increased awareness of his surroundings, he shifted to a concern for Burningwater. Checking the dory, he saw the empty Pipeboat resting at anchor. He looked toward the work-dock and saw the open cartons of silk bundled bones awaiting the final episode in their journey. But, he didn't see Charlie Bay. He rose to his feet and he surveyed the platform corner to corner. Tucked in among the lobster traps, he caught the crown of matted white hair on top of the fisherman's tilted head. It appeared to Max, that the keeper of the dead, who sat limp among the traps, was exhausted and asleep. Easing his bare feet across the platform and working his way through the maze of containers that blanketed the weathered surface, he moved next to Charlie Bay. Max was startled; Burningwater's eyes were wide open and fixed to his lap. Charlie Bay didn't move. In his large strong hands, he cradled the gray brown skull of a child. Max froze.

With watery red swollen lids and rhythmically clenching the muscles in his taught jaw, Charlie Bay Burningwater turned his head toward Dr Sorensen and spoke with piercing clarity.

"They're not all here."

"What?" Max knelt down next to Charlie Bay, their faces only inches apart.

"They're not all here."

"What do you mean they are not all here? I checked the inventories three or four times. I marked off every specimen and recorded it. Charlie Bay...I counted the boxes at the trawler and when we unloaded...there were nineteen both times. They're here...it's all of them." Max was tender.

"No."

"How could you know that...how could you possibly know...did you dream?   Did you have the dream again...the spirit dream...with the empty chairs...?"

"I didn't sleep. I didn't have the dream this night."

"How could you know who's here and who isn't?"

Charlie Bay hesitated, as if afraid to say the words. Then, he spoke without doubt. "It was the bones...the bones told me. They talked to me...told me that they're not all here."

"But bones can't..." Max was set to argue, his own words stung him. He withdrew and admitted from his experience "the bones told him", it was true. The bones told truth. "OK...it's OK...I understand...the bones told you."

Watching Charlie Bay's hands begin to tremble, Max spoke softly, "It's OK...Charlie Bay...it's OK." He placed his right arm around Burningwater's shoulders and his left; he gently set atop Charlie Bay's hand and the child's skull. He pressed his forehead against the white stubble of a leathery cheek and whispered, "I know the bones told you...they're not all here."

"The spirit journey for the missing ones has been halted...I haven't been forgiven." Charlie Bay ended with a whisper, barely audible to Max.

"Uh-kosisco, Uh-kosisco rising above me,
look down upon a Casco son...
Uh-kosisco, call to Earth and Sea
that I might be forgiven."

Sitting on the deck and leaning against some nearby lobster traps, Max did his best to respond with kindness and to comfort a man in anguish. "Ah, forgiveness...that's a tough one...forgiving yourself...even tougher. Chances are Charlie Bay you are forgiven...even if you can't forgive yourself...maybe someone else needs to lead the way..." Max points skyward, "...praying for forgiveness...I always figured praying was a good thing...trouble is...I'm no good at it...it's beyond you and me...you're headed right..." Max's voice trailed off in this small burst of affection. It was all he had.

"I must persevere...I must hunt until all the bones are returned...I must persevere."

"Persevere...ah...another tough one. I'd pray for that one too...perseverance...by far...not one of my strengths...can't help there either." Max shook his head and reached over to touch Charlie Bay, this time on the knee. "Charlie Bay...look...you can only do what you can do...so today...today you rebury the Casco."

Neither man moved. Max felt his heart pound. Charlie Bay continued to stare at the skull until his chest expanded and air whistled through his nose.

Looking toward Max he rose to his feet, straight, determined. "Today I will."

Directing the reburial, Charlie Bay assigned Margaret, Bud Walker and five other fishermen roles in the procession of the Casco bones from the work dock to the burial site. Showered, refreshed and wearing a sleeveless, dark blue cotton summer dress, Margaret had Bud Walker staring as she processed beside Burningwater. Still holding the child's skull in one hand, Charlie Bay carried the tobacco tin in the other and set the pace. In both arms, Margaret held a large bundle of red silk wrapped bones. The six fishermen followed her; each baring an open carton of prepared Casco ancestors. Unassigned, Max gathered his damp clothes and followed off to one side and behind. He was unable to take his eyes off the group as they approached the mass grave. The lobstermen, dressed in work pants and t-shirts were led by Bud Walker. They marched out of step but in single file to the edge of the burial site. As if well rehearsed, each placed the containers next to the western side of the trough in a row, removed the contents and gently placed the bundled bones at the edge of the grave. They made two more trips back and forth to the work dock for the remainder of the Casco. Without being asked, Max collected the empty cartons. In several trips, he neatly placed them in the bed of Burningwater's pickup and stood apart from the lobstermen.

A small number of visitors arrived as Charlie Bay worked the western border of the grave and made final preparations for the placement of the remains. Those present included Dr. Sandra Walsh, two other members of the Anthropology Department, a photographer from the local newspaper and the wife of T.J. Toomey, one of the fishermen. Jim Garret was not among them. Annoyed with the presence of a photographer, Charlie Bay stated bluntly, no pictures, but allowing him to stay.

He asked the largest of the six lobstermen, Paul Flarety, a burly man with huge tan forearms covered in a brush of blonde hair to stand next to the man with the camera. Upon her arrival, Sandra acknowledged Max with a smile and a shake of her head at his motley appearance. She embraced Margaret and they engaged in quiet, private conversation.

Without introduction, Charlie Bay moved to a spot beside Max at the southern entrance of the burial trough. He sprinkled some tobacco in the four directions and to the sky and earth, eased his way into the grave and began to systematically place the bundled bones on the dirt floor. Appreciating that the reburial was underway, the participants moved alongside the remains of the Casco. Each bundle was arranged with the skull facing west and the long bones extending in an east-west orientation. As he approached the center of the trough, Charlie Bay signaled with a wave of his hand. Walker and Toomey began to cover the bundles in the pit with sandy soil. No ones eyes left the trough but Burningwater's as he continued the rhythmic deposition of his ancestors. Situating the child's skull next to the last bundle, Charlie Bay finished the repatriation. He first invited Margaret and then the others to shovel dirt over the final section of bones. As they threw sand onto the Casco, tears overcame Margaret and Sandra, but for different reasons. Max remained standing at the grave's southern end, with his hands clasped just below his waist, twirling his wedding ring. Charlie Bay Burningwater moved to the northern border of the fresh soil to stand opposite Max

Sorensen. With his lips moving inaudibly, he made a last tobacco offering in the reburial.

Sandra leaned and whispered into Margaret's ear. "Is that it? Do you think it's over?"

"I'm not sure, but I think so." Margaret caught Charlie Bay's glance as he signaled for the guests, the ceremony was over.

Stepping forward next to Burningwater, Margaret smiled, "My grandfather and I wish to thank you for coming...it means a lot to have you here...thank you for your help. We have blueberry muffins and coffee on the front porch of the house for those of you who are hungry. Everyone is welcome."

Charlie Bay was startled by the open invitation for food, "We do?"

"Yes. I brought them back this morning from the best bakery in town...you can't send these people away without feeding them something. I also have gifts for Bud and the men as a sign of our appreciation"

"You do...where did you get those?"

"I shop...gifts I've saved. Remember I'm a child of retail...collecting good gifts for the right time...it's tradition."

"It is?" Charlie Bay was lost and surrendered. "OK...well...I never planned on that either but OK. You take them up...I'll be along in a bit."

As the small group drifted in quiet conversation toward the house, Max and Charlie Bay were left standing alone at opposite ends of the gravesite; bones of the Casco buried between them. Max watched Bud

Walker hustle to Margaret's side as the sun attached to the skin of her bare arms. She did have great shoulders. He saw Sandra's face express relief and quiet joy. He was happy for her. Then, he turned his attention to Burningwater.

Staring at the salty fisherman, Max felt a newfound sense of similarity, somehow, in some ways, they were alike. The two of them shared a continuous search for bones. There was common ground in their hunt, granted, to different ends but a hunt with the same intensity and reverence none the less. They were connected to something. Max couldn't pinpoint it. Maybe it was a link to the dream journey of the Pipeboat People, a journey with an intuitive attraction for both of them. Or maybe it was just the bones. Whatever the source of the union, as Max studied the weathered and worn face of Charlie Bay Burningwater, he saw a kindred spirit.

As Charlie Bay looked back at Dr. Max Sorensen, he saw a tormented soul with a strange job.

After the moment's unspoken exchange, Max waved good bye to Burningwater without a word or expectation. He walked away slowly at first, then picking up speed to catch Sandra and Margaret before the house and the food. Halfway to the small meandering cluster, he glanced over his shoulder and caught sight of Charlie Bay standing motionless on the burial grounds. Burningwater was alone, silhouetted against the billowing white clouds and the blue late morning summer sky. He was a solitary figure, once again, among his people. The singular, framed image of the man was burned into Max. It was an image he would remember.

"Hey Sandra...wait up...excuse me for a second." Pulling Sandra aside, "Did we get them all...did we give them all back?"

"Max...what are you talking about...what do you mean?"

"The bones...did we give them all back...all of them?"

"Well ya...sure we did. If you gave him everyone on my master list...we gave them all back. You did... didn't you...check them off the list?"

"Of course...I double checked it a couple of times."

"Then why ask?"

"Burningwater says they're not all here...some of the bones are still missing."

Sandra hesitated, "Oh....but how could he...."

"Is there any possibility that there are still some out there...that someone else took some material from the site. Were any other University people...other anthropologists around?" A sense of frustration was seeping through his voice with the thought of lost Casco.

"Max...it was almost forty years ago. There were people crawling all over the tip of this Island...with no particular direction other than to beat the clock. I don't know...maybe it's possible. But they're sure not mine."

"But possible."

"Ya."

It was a revelation about the excavation that Max never entertained; other collectors. His head ached and it was time for him to go. "Ah, I'm going back to your place...pack my stuff...maybe get on the road today. I'll see you later."

Nodding, Sandra left unconcerned as Margaret approached Max carrying coffee and a blueberry muffin.

With his eyebrows and shoulders raised, Max asked, "Your father?"

"Charity golf tournament...he flew out last night. I never saw him."

"Ahhh...golf." Max drifted off.

"Max you look a little lost...are you OK?"

"Ya...I'm OK. Maybe it's just time for me to go... time for me to head home. I'll catch a ride back to the Co-op with one of the lobstermen...get my car. I better get going...thanks Margaret. I'll see you...sometime I hope." Uneasily gesturing in the direction of some parked pickups and a lobsterman's lone departure, Max leaned forward, kissed Margaret on the cheek and took the muffin but not the coffee.

"Max...here is something to remember us by." Reaching into her dress pocket, Margaret removed a CD in a clear plastic case. "It's a recording of the Storyteller's...my favorite. I couldn't put it on your phone or your iPod because you don't...I made the disc for you."

Flipping the case over nervously with one hand, Max saw the words "Heartache of the Hunter" neatly written on the label side. He smiled but didn't speak.

"It's important to me...I thought you might enjoy it."

"Thanks."

Watching him hitch up his borrowed pants and hobble his way toward the trucks, she whispered, "Good-bye Max."

Packing was not difficult or long. The lab equipment and supplies were already boxed. His clothes were either in the clean or the dirty pile, stuffed in two kitchen trash bags and all into a duffle bag. Papers, journals and CD files were stacked into one of Sandra's file cartons. Still undecided, the most effort and energy of the packing went into the question of whether or not to leave. For some unknown reason, leaving was not easy.

Max set aside his sax, packed his limited Barbara Stanwyck video collection and put on his bathing suit. The heat from the early afternoon sun was cooled by a strong salty southwest wind. Standing on a kitchen chair in the exact spot of the backyard to see the ocean, he checked the tide and the surf each trip to the car. He was restless, anxious and exhausted. Two grilled hot dogs and a beer failed to soothe his uneasiness. Finally, sitting outside in a sun-drenched corner of Sandra's home, wearing only a generic blue swim suit, he retreated to Jr. Walker and sax therapy. The past twenty-four hours melted away.

After over an hour of intermittently playing *Sweet Soul* and wrestling with the power of a solitary Charlie Bay Burningwater standing on the crest of the burial site, Max was jolted by an unseen neighbor. With a voice enjoyed by gruff men, Max was told, "Hey, either play a different song or quit playing!"

This was followed by a woman's reprimand, "Gil, we're on vacation. You're supposed to relax. Now, let the kid practice."

"It's not a kid. It's an old guy in navy boxers and he keeps playing the same damn song over...over and over again...how crazy is that?"

Undaunted, the shirtless tenor soloist stood on the chair, hit a few high notes and checked the surf. The waves were perfect.

The water was much warmer than at the time of his early morning tumble. With an incoming tide, onshore breeze and sunshine, Max stood ankle deep and figured the water was about sixty-five degrees. But it wasn't the tolerably cold water, it was the surf that renewed his spirit and energized a tired body. Age and degenerative joint disease were now irrelevant. These were by far, the best waves of the summer. Max knew it was instinct, ability and endurance that defined a capacity for body surfing. With child-like joy and the belief that he possessed a fair amount of all three, he tiptoed into the breakers.

Max had no recollection when the experience of riding waves with his Aunt Pearl passed from an adventure to a passion. He simply acknowledged that he loved it and was forever grateful to "Pearl the Curl" for teaching him to body surf.

Aunt Pearl LaPierre dragged a young Max Sorensen up and down the southern Maine coast, stood him in freezing water waste deep and taught him to wait for the perfect wave. She also taught him not to be surprised if the perfect wave took him to the bottom. She told him again and again, don't fight it. Let it take you down and when the wave lets go, push up off the sand. She started every day in the surf with "...remember, let it take you down...wave lets go...push up." He considered Pearl and repeated her words.

Once Max had waded to surf above his knees, he dove into the first rolling layer of water. Wet and happy, he studied the waves. Through years of body surfing, Max knew Maine waves usually came in sets of three. In his judgment, the second wave was the best ride. Size and curl were important but the key was break point. Now in waist high water, he watched as three and four footers crashed to shelves of rushing white foam. Max eased deeper for the exact spot to catch, not the first break, but the full thrust of collapsing arc. At the precise moment, on a perfect wave, Max left his feet, buried his head between out-stretched arms and lunged forward along with the rumbling layer of ocean. The ride in was spectacular. Out of breath and in water only inches deep, he struggled to his feet, tugged at his sagging suit and ran back to do it all again. Max stayed in the water so long that his body fatigued but not his uneasiness.

As he balanced on a wobbly grate in Sandra's outdoor shower, Max let the spray beat against his neck and run down his back until all the hot water was gone. He finished packing his car, wrote Sandra a brief note of thanks and headed back to Boston. In place of *Sweet Soul*, he listened to "Heartache of the Hunter", again and again.

Chapter Thirteen

The Casco seated at the circle around him were silent. Some eyes fixed to his, others stared away. He faced the Ancient One and stared back into the eyes of his ancestor. He was drawn to this man and poured over his features.

The Ancient One's shoulder length white hair was parted in the middle. It fell in an arc that followed the downward curves of his brow, his eyes and his lips. The expression was sealed into his face. The Ancient One's arms were folded across his chest and pressed a large bird's wing to his left shoulder.

He let his eyes drift to the woman seated inches from the wing's tip. A dark blue scarf covered her forehead. A red woven blanket sheathed the curves of her body. Her beauty had hold of his heart. The sorrow in her eyes made him uneasy.

A grandfather sat alongside the sad eyed woman. The old man's weathered brow was shielded by a brown felt hat with a dried starfish pinned to the front. His hair was bundled at the ears by shreds of a blue cotton kerchief. The two streams of gray slid down the back of his shoulders and clung to his faded navy jacket. The grandfather's eyes were tired and glazed. His lids puffed.

Next to the grandfather was an empty metal chair skewed to the outside of the arch. Dust masked its color. Beside the empty chair was a young woman with pitted skin. A crescent scar marked her right cheek and a bird amulet hung around her neck. Her head tilted forward and her eyes were sheltered from view by dark disheveled hair. A child, swaddled in sealskin, stretched across her lap.

One by one, he met his ancestors. He met them eye to eye with strength and an edge of arrogance. He held firm that his past choice was the right one. But the seven empty metal chairs staggered between his ancestors shattered his defiance. The vacancies haunted him. They were seats of the missing, spirits whose dream journey had been halted. Each empty chair pressed his obligation to act in favor of the missing.

He tried to speak but he had no air.

Choking and unable to breathe, Max woke up. He gasped raw and wheezing gulps of air. Max lurched forward and took a deep breath. As his lungs filled, he fell back onto the damp sheets, glanced into the darkness and panicked. For a few seconds, Max had no idea where he was. Eyes darting side to side, he brought the room into focus.

"What the hell...?"

The similarity of inexpensive highway hotels was a comfort for him as he stood and walked toward the bathroom. Remembering that this was Baltimore and the Fall Lacrosse Tournament, he groped for the two switch light panel on the entryway wall. With the glow of a dim bureau lamp and the bathroom overhead, Max made out the room in faded brick red and beige, sparse with cheap generic furniture. In short shuffle steps, he went back to sit on the edge of the bed. Beads of sweat ran from under his chin, over his chest and collected on the rolls of his stomach. He was breathing heavily as he whispered again, "What was that?"

This trip was planned in the summer during his stay in Maine. It included two days before the weekend lacrosse games with friends in D.C. and a visit to the Smithsonian for research. He was scheduled to leave Boston on Wednesday morning, spend Thursday and Friday in the Capitol and make the quick trip to Baltimore early on Saturday for round one of the tournament.

His first day in Washington, the plans fell apart. By chance, he stumbled on to an exhibit of late nineteenth and early twentieth century Native American portraits by Edward S. Curtis. Fortunately for Max, old friends were forgiving as the rest of the world, for forty-eight hours, disappeared. The black and white Native American photographs were stunning images, full of physical form; morphology, what he enjoyed most, the lumps and bumps of bone.

After tearing himself away from the Curtis exhibit in D.C. late on Friday afternoon, his first day of lacrosse in Baltimore was terrific. The mild mid-October sunshine was a welcome relief from the cold and damp New England autumn. Saturday was a perfect day for the tournament. Again, he enjoyed time suspended by the athletic expertise and competitive spirit of the young. When his head hit the pillow just before midnight, he was exhausted but content. He put in a wake-up call for seven and expected to do it all again on Sunday.

Now awake, alert and sitting on the bed, Max was frightened by this dream. His hands and legs shook. The anxiety lingered as he rationalized the dream. Max tried to match the images of the dream with the photographs of the Curtis exhibit. There were no matches, not one.

He glanced at the bold block red digits on the alarm clock that read three forty-eight and mumbled, "What the hell...where did that come from..." He remembered. It was the empty chairs; he remembered Charlie Bay's spirit dream and the empty chairs. It couldn't be. This wasn't possible. This was the dream Charlie Bay described that summer afternoon on Long Neck Island. Max never understood the empty chairs. It was sacred territory. It was the spirit dream of Charlie Bay Burningwater.

Max was angry. He paced the room determined to figure it all out. How could this be possible? You don't get someone else's dream. For the two and half-hours until daybreak, he was lost.

Despite the warm Sunday sunshine and the festival-like atmosphere of the tournament, Max was obsessed by the images in the dream. Unable to distract himself with the lacrosse games, the food or observing people, he replayed the Native American faces in his mind. He still wrestled to link each character in the dream with either the Curtis plates or with something from his professional past. He had to find images in his memory he could make fit the dream. Right off, he knew the faces weren't the familiar Native American photos of popular media and Public Television. They were not Curtis' staged portraits of the noble savage. Recalling other images of aboriginal people, he struggled with the unfamiliar faces. He tried to convince himself the beings of the dream must be individuals whose likenesses he had somehow, somewhere already experienced. But he couldn't explain the empty chairs.

Reconstructing the whole thing as a compilation of Native American images, Max decided it was set off by the days spent with the Curtis exhibit. There had to be a way to make this something other than Burningwater's spirit dream. He had no success with any of it, waking unable to breathe, no air just like Charlie Bay that day on the porch. It was Charlie Bay's dream.

By mid-afternoon, he was nervously trying to decide between driving to Maine for an explanation from Burningwater or returning to Boston for what, he had no idea. To burn some energy, he tried to use his cell to check his messages and home voice mail. But he had forgotten to charge it. With his phone dead, he caught up to Paul and borrowed his smart phone. Max was desperate for information about something that might lead to an explanation, other than it was Burningwater's dream. Max forgot a touch screen was beyond him. After tapping and dragging too many wrong buttons and entering too many wrong passwords, he gave up and gave in. Max returned the phone to Paul, said a quick good-bye, hedged on Maine and headed for Boston.

In the quiet of his apartment Max listened to his home phone voice mail. There were three messages.

"Max, it's Margaret Garret. Ah...it's Wednesday, a little after three. I've been trying to reach you. The departmental secretary said your cell was useless and my best chance was to call you at home. I'm sorry I can't speak with you directly, but I think you should know. I have bad news. Ah... well, Charlie Bay passed away...he died Tuesday. I came up from Philadelphia this morning when I found out. I just thought you should know Max, that's all...I thought you would like to know." Her voice faded. Max sat motionless in the dark. The sadness in her voice was not masked by the background noise on her cell.

He hit the second message. "Max, it's me again, Margaret. It's Thursday, about eleven. I wanted to tell you that the burial of Charlie Bay is on Saturday, sometime in the morning, on Long Neck. Ah...you know, the Casco gravesite by the blueberry patch, you know the place. Any way, I hope you hear this before Saturday and maybe you would be able to come. Bye Max." A third message followed. "I don't know when you'll be back but, it's me again. The burial was yesterday...and ah, it rained some. I'm in Maine a few more days this week. We need to talk about some things, so ah...if you could call me on my cell. I'm staying at my parent's house. And if you're busy, I could drive down to Boston and maybe meet you some place. It's important we talk. Thanks."

Frustrated and embarrassed that he was unable to remotely check his voice mail, he tossed his cell without looking onto his desk and listened to the messages again.

After his Monday morning Human Antiquities class, Max was on his way to Maine. Unable to reach Margaret, he left a message on her phone and another with her mother that he was coming. He expected to be at the burial site on the island by one o'clock. Margaret's mother sounded pleasant, but seemed confused by the information. Max assumed Jim Garret wasn't the only one who told only portions of the family history. Either way, he hoped that Margaret got the message and was there to meet him.

The rail tie bridge didn't appear any stronger to Max as he rattled his Volvo to brown grass and a leafless tree line. Long Neck looked cold but it wasn't empty, he pulled up beside Jim Garret's SUV. Margaret was standing next to some freshly turned soil at the northern end of the burial trough. She was wrapped in a long wool coat and shivered as a chilling northeast wind tugged her hair. After a heartfelt embrace, both stared at the rectangular section of scattered dried grass and light brown sand. Max's nose began to water.

"He died last Tuesday...well you know. The way some of the fishermen describe it, he was digging clams on the late afternoon low tide. His heart gave out somewhere on the sand bar. Evidently, he didn't die right away. He was covered with sand. They said that it was all over his face...chest...legs...like he fell face first... maybe crawled before he got in the skiff." Margaret's eyes were watering and she repeatedly wiped her nose with a tissue. "He made it into his boat but he never rowed. He died on the water and alone. The tide came in and took him up the river into the marsh and then through the night back out into the ocean. No one even knew he was missing. No one missed him." Max reached over and put his arm around Margaret. "Wednesday morning, early...one of the lobsterman...just by chance spotted the skiff on the horizon. They said another hour and the current would have taken him right out to sea. We never would have found him. He was in the bottom of the boat...covered with sand...the oars still across the seats."

Without hesitation Max gave comfort, "He wasn't lost...he's here with his people...you buried him.

How did you find out?"

"My father called on Wednesday morning and I flew right home. Charlie Bay was buried wrapped in silk...the traditional colors...right here...where he asked...beyond the child...over there on the end."

"He asked?"

"Yes he did...that's what I wanted to speak with you about. We talked before I left to go back to Philadelphia. Come on...let's walk down to the work dock. I have some things for you."

They crossed the wind off the marsh and river. It was cold against their skin. Max put his hands in his pockets and Margaret held his arm, sliding behind one shoulder down wind for shelter.

"Before I left...at the end of August...I came out here to say good bye. There was no small talk...he was all business. I got the impression right away he had a list of things he wanted to tell me. He started with...when I die. I think he knew when death was coming and was giving me his will. You were first on the list."

"I was?"

"The Pipeboat...he wanted you to have the Pipeboat."

Max was surprised, then as the pieces began to fall into place, stunned.

Reading the expression on his face, "That's right the Pipeboat and I was to be sure that you got it. So here you are," she extended her right arm, palm open in the direction of the Pipeboat. "I had Bud Walker and some of the other fishermen at the burial carry it up here to the work dock, because I didn't have any idea when I'd see you."

As they stepped onto the platform, Max saw the overturned dory restored. There was fresh red bottom paint on the hull.

"There's no outboard motor well."

"That's the first thing he did after the reburial...rip out the well. I helped him caulk and paint the bottom. The whole time, I listened to him mumble about how this boat was meant to be rowed, just rowed, and how he hoped Earl Alton forgave him." Margaret recalled a wonderful afternoon and smiled.

Caressing the new stem to stern plank Max whispered, "Pipeboat for the dream journey of the Pipeboat People."

"The motor is in the shed...gave it to Bud Walker but he hasn't picked it up yet. The oars for the dory are in there too. They are yours." Ducking into the building, Margaret returned carrying a plastic bag of eight oar lock tholepins. "Max, Charlie Bay dictated something to me that he said you would need. I wrote it on a blue index card. It's in the bag."

Max was distracted by his experience of the spirit dream and the mid-summer discussion with Charlie Bay about the dream journey of the Pipeboat People. Now, they were both his...the boat and the dream. "Thanks Margaret. Thanks..." Without looking Max took the plastic bag filled with the wooden pins. The blue card was in front with the blank side facing out.

"Come on, there's more."

"More?"

"Not for you...but there is more...more you should see."

They walked single file back up the path to the burial ground. As they approached the clearing next to the blueberry patch, Max stepped to Margaret's side.

"You said your father called you?"

Margaret smiled, "Ah, very tactful Max...different for you."

Caught and embarrassed at his probe into Garret affairs, "Well...I know them both as very remarkable men. I wondered if..."

She interrupted, anticipating his question, "There was no reconciliation before Charlie Bay died and my father never made it to the burial.

I made it easier for my father. After the Casco reburial...I told him that I was there the night of your meeting. And...I was with Charlie Bay...we heard the whole thing. We talked a little but not much. He told me how he took his mother's maiden name...why he was always quick to emphasize our Irish ancestry. He asked for some time...the chance to talk with my mother."

"Oh." Max tilted his head and raised his brow.

Margaret didn't volunteer more and Max didn't ask. They stopped walking and stood beside Burningwater's grave. She broke the silence.

"He told me with the same, when I die that he wanted to be buried on the north end about five yards beyond the bones of the child...in silk of Casco colors...in his work clothes with a Casco lobster buoy and his bait iron."

Smiling, Max whispered, "... his Casco buoy and his bait iron."

"He also told me that all the bones weren't here. There were still some Casco bones missing...he said you knew."

"That's why he left the space...for others. He's protecting the north side...on the end." Max pointed to the gap then looked at Margaret. "See...see.

We talked about it that morning on the dock before you came back for the burial."

"Are there?" Margaret already knew there were more.

"I'd say yes...I believe it's true."

"More bones...hmm...it explains why...he asked me to take care of everything here. It seems I got the house...wait 'til you see the house."

"Ya and...I gotta tell you...I...I ah...it seems I got the spirit dream."

"You got what? What do you mean...you got the spirit dream?"

"You remember that day on the porch...when we heard Charlie Bay choking and we ran up to find him just waking up and breathing so hard?"

"Yes, I do...but..."

"You remember him telling us about the spirit dream...his dream...his ancestors...the Ancient One, all unable to move until the bones are returned."

"Yes... I... but how could you have his dream?"

"I don't know...it makes no sense...but I know it's his dream and I'd say for better or worse...it's mine now."

Staring at one another, Margaret broke into a smile. "So, you too, dove three times into waves and surfaced as a harbor seal."

"Heartache of the Hunter..."

"Yes..."Heartache of the Hunter."

Turning his eyes away and squinting to the east, he was angry.

"Margaret...I'm not real happy about this spirit dream. Not only is the experience frightening...I've already had it a couple of times...but I have...or I should say...had plans. I figured I was headed for the banks of the Nile next semester or maybe next summer...you know...to continue the Nubian project. Instead it looks like...thanks to Burningwater...I'm going to have to deal with the coast of Maine for awhile...maybe a long while. That's really not what I want. I was just here as a favor to Sandra...I owed her. And now for some reason...I owe him...I owe the Casco." He turned to Margaret. His left foot rhythmically kicked loose sand in the direction of Charlie Bay's grave. Max unveiled a small portion of his torment. "I mean how did this happen? I'm stuck with this dream until I find the rest of the Casco? That's crazy...I can't talk about it with any one...it's crazier than I already am!"

Max gathered himself and calmed down but continued to ramble, "I have no idea what skeletal material is out there or where to look. We're really not dealing with one excavation here on the Island...if there are more bones...there's got to be more sites...other Casco excavations and somewhere...other collections...

How am I ever going to find a way to break through in one direction if I get pulled so hard in another?"

Max paused, shaking his head with a sigh of resignation, "So I dove three times into the waves and surfaced as a harbor seal." He was still bewildered.

In a barely audible voice, he mumbled toward Charlie Bay, "...don't want to be a harbor seal...don't want...spirit dream..."

Margaret caught the words, seal and spirit dream, she gave him time. "It's a noble work Max...who knows...being attached to this place...finding Casco.

Come on let me show you what's up at the house...maybe that will cheer you up." Again, Margaret took Max's arm and they walked side by side down a fall wind to the home of the Storyteller.

"Take a look under the porch...right here...where this opens." Her voice now excited.

Swinging open a section of the grill panels that surrounded the front porch, Max peered into a small dimly lit space adjacent to the house's stone foundation. On the rough dirt floor were two overturned traditional Native American canoes and one incomplete canoe frame.

"Canoes...that's amazing. Look at these Margaret...they look pretty old...great condition. I don't think he ever would've used them, but he took good care of them."

"Let's go down to the basement Max I want to show you more."

At the bottom of the cellar stairs Margaret plugged in an orange extension cord with four caged hook lights hung from the ceiling. The lamps exposed a large room with walls of fieldstone and lined by wide planked shelves. Each shelf contained section after section of shallow wooden fruit boxes.

Lowering his head to remain standing did not prevent Max's chin from dropping. He was speechless. Beginning on his immediate right, Max worked his way along the shelves. Without missing a surface or a container, he explored the archive of Casco artifacts. The carved stone sculptures and the ritual masks were works of extraordinary beauty. Even utilitarian objects; axes, choppers, projectile points, knives, spoons, ladles and serving bowls were so pristine in character, it disrupted his breathing. His heart was racing. Passing the far wall, he examined the bone carvings, bird amulets and the stone effigy pipes until his eyes fell upon a shelf overflowing with lacrosse sticks. Each carved wooden shaft was unique in size and thickness. Each pocket of woven leather was perfectly formed by the curved frame. Studying one stick, he discovered lightening bolts etched and painted into the wood just a few inches from the webbed pouch. White dots of hail ran the shaft. Max's body chilled. He sat back on an overturned five-gallon clam pail.

"I just have to take a minute. I'm starting to hyperventilate. This is embarrassing. This is what's left of the Casco material culture...he saved it...he saved all this. This is generations of creativity."

Holding the lacrosse stick across his knees, Max leaned forward and took a deep breath.

"Max, are you OK?"

"I'm fine. It's all just so remarkable...I never would have figured him for it. It's all..."

"Max...this is not all."

Regaining his strength and lifting his head toward Margaret, "Are you trying to kill me?"

"Bring one of the lights over here to the fruit cellar" Margaret grunted, as she partially pushed open a thick wooden door.

Placing the light in the available space before peering inside, Max was astonished by the baskets and pottery, stack upon stack. The decorative symbols alone were spectacular.

"How large is the room?"

"I have no idea...I haven't been able to get the door open wide enough to get in there...I don't know how he did it."

Max sat on the stairs and gazed at the bundle of harpoons and fishing equipment, attempting to integrate the treasure. "Are we done?"

"No, we have to go upstairs." Margaret wondered how much more he was able to take.

On the second floor there was a center hallway, three bedrooms and a bath. As they reached the platform at the head of the stairs, Margaret pointed to the closed door at the end of the hall, "That's Charlie Bay's room. Just take a quick look in this first room on the left, so that you'll have some idea of what's up here."

The bedroom was devoid of furniture and filled with woven blankets of remarkable design, rugs with intricate patterns and traditional clothing and festival costumes that hung on make-shift racks across the room.

"It's overwhelming Margaret...truly overwhelming."

"Yes, I know...I got the house remember. But here's the most amazing record of all." Leading Max into the second bedroom, she presented the written and photographic archive of the Casco Nation. "I've just spent a little time here...but it seems to me that he divided it into three sections; photos, family albums, pictographs and paintings in this section, letters, diaries, journals and anything else that look personal in this area and all the legal transactions like agreements, treaties, contracts over here. The most astounding thing is... Charlie Bay couldn't read...he must've just gone on instinct. And here's the best of all...these tapes! "Heartache of the Hunter" wasn't the only story Charlie Bay dictated...there's all kinds of stuff on these tapes. Look...there're Clementine boxes full of cassettes maybe eighty to a hundred of them! And Max, some he did in three languages. There're in English...then what I'm assuming is a translation in Casco...then French. He couldn't read or write but he spoke three languages...my grandfather was a very intelligent man.

I think Charlie Bay recorded the Casco oral history...all he could on all these tapes. He saved and protected it all. My father isn't the only warrior to fight extinction. I think Charlie Bay gave us the Casco story... maybe all the way back from the beginning."

Max picked up a cassette, looked at it and began to circle the room, "since the beginning of time." He caressed the tops of the piles and looked through some of the photographs without another word. They stayed in the room for some time, drifting from section to section. As the afternoon sun moved further from reach, Max finally whispered, "It's a life's work."

Margaret wasn't sure whether he meant of Charlie Bay's, for her or for himself. But instead of clarifying, she asked if he wanted tea or a beer. Margaret already knew it was for her. Max chose beer.

Sitting together at the kitchen table, Max looked to Margaret's eyes, "What are you going to do?"

"I'm going to write Max. It's what I do. I write plays. This is my Pittsburgh...my home."

"You mean DNA Pittsburgh...?"

"No, I mean August Wilson Pittsburgh...my plays...my place...my people...I'm a Casco American."

Max was still a little lost and Margaret just kept going.

"My father has spent his life trying to get away from being Casco. Charlie Bay spent a good part of his life keeping the Casco alive. And I...I have a lot to learn to become more Casco. "

Max raised his eyebrows. He understood and Margaret knew he would.

"Look, this house holds the Casco story...but not as a museum...this is not a place to visit on a rainy Sunday afternoon. It's a story that's living right now... with a past...a present and a future...all now...right here...I believe Charlie Bay is going to help me uncover it. If I write...if I'm faithful to it...he'll take me there...he'll guide me.

This place is of a people...it has an identity that lives ...a people whose stories must be told. Charlie Bay is going to teach me with all those tapes...he expects me to write it and to write it well...to strive for an expression of Casco culture that forces recognition...the recognition of the existence and value of the Casco people...their beliefs. The need for strong Casco ethnic identity among alienated living Casco is profound...our cultural base...it's all here. The Casco aren't going away!

Writing the story is one part...my part. My father has his part...as ironic as that may seem...the Casco Board of Directors...the Tribal Council theirs.

Look Max...if we...with efforts on these different fronts and others to come...keep the Casco as a distinct Nation in the present...a Nation with customs and traditions, religion, the Casco colors and on and on and it's lived...people are living it...it forces fairness. It forces everyone to recognize the issues of American history...the atrocities and injustices...the extermination.

The Casco aren't going to disappear...we have a past and a future...right here...in the present. It's a way to hold a line for my grandfather and all the others. This island is the ground of the Casco. This is the place. And we need your help."

"You're asking me?"

"Yes."

"I think it's going to be hard to fit the Pipeboat into my apartment." Max was trying to peel the label of the beer bottle at each corner, searching for something to say.

"Max, I need your help with the bones...the missing bones."

Margaret wasn't about to let his distraction last. She slammed her open palms on the kitchen tabletop. Max jumped in his chair.

"Max, I know you have Charlie Bay's spirit dream...I believe you. You don't need to talk about it with anyone else. We both know Casco bones are still missing. And I need you to flat out tell me you're going to get them back or none of this is going to work...I believe none of it will happen! The Casco bones must be returned to Casco ground...spirits in order...so they can act in our favor."

He loved passion and she was overflowing. Max looked up.

"You know I've been out of sync my whole life...always a few beats off... remember me and ancient DNA. I was a disconnected academic until Charlie Bay. My whole career I skirted the issue of what people believed. I was always able to bend or twist or sometimes not even advert to other people's beliefs about human remains...they were there but not that important...nowhere near as important as the bones...as the scientific data. I figured that if what I did was in the name of science...seeking and acquiring knowledge...it was more important. People's belief didn't carry that much weight...didn't matter. I could justify it...until Charlie Bay. From Charlie Bay I learned belief can override science.

Something is happening between us...Charlie Bay and me...I have his spirit dream...and I know they're not all here.

Ya...I will keep looking...hunting for Casco bones...but you've gotta know putting them back in the ground is pretty much the opposite of my whole professional life...it's counter to everything I've done and been trained to do. I recover and analyze bones...it's what I do.

Margaret...I don't want to spend the rest of my life as a harbor seal...I don't want to even be a harbor seal.

It's not going to be easy...easy to keep up the hunt...to repatri..."

Max felt this was an awful turn. He needed help. He wouldn't look at Margaret and tried not to think about it.

"You have his fire Margaret." The thought of repatriation lingered. "I just hope I'm able to keep up...to keep up the hunt."

The Casco seated in a circle around Max were silent. Some eyes fixed to his, others stared away. Like before, Max faced the Ancient One and stared back into the eyes of his ancestor. Max was drawn to this man and studied his features.

The Ancient One's shoulder length white hair was parted in the middle. It fell in an arc that paralleled the downward curves of his brow, his eyes and his lips. The expression was sealed into his face. The Ancient One's arms were folded across his chest and pressed a large bird's wing to his left shoulder.

Max let his eyes drift to the woman seated inches from the white wing's tip. A dark blue scarf covered her forehead. A red woven blanket sheathed the curves of her body. Her beauty had hold of Max's heart. The sorrow in her eyes made him uneasy.

A grandfather sat alongside the sad eyed woman. His weathered brow was shielded by a brown felt hat with a starfish pinned to the front. His hair was bundled at the ears by shreds of a blue cotton kerchief. The two streams of gray slid down the back of his shoulders and clung to his faded jacket. A lacrosse stick with dots of hail and lightening bolts on the shaft was at his feet. The grandfather's eyes were tired and glazed. His lids puffed.

An empty chair skewed to the outside of the arch was next to the grandfather. Dust masked its color. Beside the empty chair was a young woman with pitted skin. A crescent scar marked her right cheek and a heron amulet hung around her neck. Her head tilted forward and her eyes were sheltered from Max's view by dark *disheveled hair. A child, swaddled in sealskin, stretched across her lap.*

One by one, Max met his ancestors. He met them eye to eye with strength and an edge of arrogance. He held firm that his choice was the right one. Once again, the empty metal chairs, staggered between the Casco ancestors shattered his defiance. The vacancies haunted him. They were seats of the missing, spirits whose dream journey had been halted. Each empty chair pressed his obligation to act in the favor of Casco spirits.

Max tried to retell his story, but he had no air.

Max woke up choking. He gasped raspy wheezing breaths. His pillow was soaked with sweat and his moist hair was matted to the back of his head. Single trails of water ran from under his chin, through the folds of his neck and pooled on his chest. Max lurched forward and labored to breathe. As his lungs filled, he fell back onto the damp sheets and glanced around the room, muscles beginning to relax. It was his room.

Rolling to his left and reaching for the nightstand light, he read the digits on his alarm clock; three nineteen. There was time. He still had time with the night. With the lamp on and the room dimly lit, Max fumbled through a stack of printed articles and books. After knocking his old yellow sport CD player and head phones to the floor, he gently placed a disc, labeled "Heartache of the Hunter," to one side. Moving a hardcover, he found a clear plastic bag containing a single light blue index card. Angling the card, still in the bag toward the light, he read aloud Burningwater's words, written in Margaret's hand.

"Uh-kosisco, Uh-kosisco rising above me,
look down upon a son of the Nations
...give strength to the hunter,
that I might persevere.
I make this prayer to you Uh-kosisco."

Max slid the bag back onto the table, shut off the light and stared at a thin slice of moon shadow that slipped between the curtain and window frame. Dropping back to the pillow and still staring at the moon shadow, he wondered about this latest turn in his vocation.

He knew that Charlie Bay was acting in his favor and he had to act in favor of the Casco.

He believed that the bones were not all on Long Neck Island and somehow Charlie Bay was going to illuminate his hunt.

But, he still wondered about his ability to carry on, to keep going. He wondered if he had the strength...the strength to persevere.

With a fresh breath, Max chanted his prayer.

"Uh-kosisco, Uh-kosisco rising above me,
look down upon a son of the Nations
... give strength to the hunter,
that I might persevere.

I make this prayer to you Uh-kosisco.

Uh-kosisco rising above me,
look down upon a son of the Nations
...give strength to the hunter,
that I might persevere...I might persevere."

Chapter Fourteen

In the four months since the death of Charlie Bay, Max found few bones and had lots of the dream. He was no closer to recovering Casco bones than the day he kicked sand on Burningwater's grave and acknowledged that it was going to take time, maybe a long time, never expecting this much time.

Max was lying in bed, wide awake again at a little after three in the morning, feeling like he had been here too many times before. He was still angry with Charlie Bay and he still had no idea where to find Casco bones. The hour between three and four used to be productive for him, but that was before Casco repatriation; now nothing, just confusion and worry. He thought he might be depressed. He wondered about an ulcer...wondered why he felt so impotent. This was all on Burningwater. Max still believed that Charlie Bay would illuminate the hunt to find Casco bones. Max also knew that he must persevere. But he wanted Charlie Bay to hurry up with his part.

At Sandra's direction, Max started the search for more Casco bones with the Maine State Archeologist and his knowledge of private collectors. The archeologist was a friend to Dr Walsh and the Anthropology Department. He responded in kind to Max and was supportive from day one. Sandra also found office space back in December two doors down from her own and funds for his travel and expenses. She set up a stipend that began later in March when Max planned to begin a sabbatical year in Maine. He was amazed how she could find money, especially for him, on what was a vague repatriation project. But as always, he was grateful for her assistance and took it.

The private collectors that Max tracked down through the State Archeologist were no help. At his first meeting with one who, on paper, looked to be promising, Max quickly became the enemy. He was the enemy not for hunting Casco bones, but for wanting to repatriate Casco bones. He was searching his only leads unsuccessfully and growing in frustration, frustration like he had known in Burningwater; he just wanted them back. It was one more part of Burningwater's life that was becoming a part of his own. Half way through the State Archeologist's list, the private collector network warning system was in force and all information shut down. From the four-month effort of weekend travel and meetings over coffee in Historical Society one room school houses, he had nothing. It was a dead end and instinct told him to let go. There were no Casco bones, maybe some Native American bones, but not Casco.

Looking up at his bedroom ceiling, he considered failure. It wasn't failure with the Casco or with Charlie Bay; that was stuck but it wasn't over. It was with Linda. The yellow manila envelope had been sitting on top of his bureau for five days. He knew Linda's handwriting, saw the return address and couldn't bring himself to open it. At first he thought that it might be more documents, points of clarification, more documents that confused him. But at this time of the morning, in the darkness, he was frustrated, edgy and documents or not, had nothing to lose. Max got up, found the envelope and shook the contents to the bottom. He sat on the edge of his bed, ripped open the top and turned on the lamp. From the envelope he removed a folded white single piece of copy paper with a handwritten note and a letter-sized envelope addressed to him at his old home, now still Linda's home. The return address on the letter was an unknown street in Tucson, Arizona. Max knew by the way PhD was written in big Palmer capitals after his name that it was from his Aunt Pearl. He also knew that he never told her about his move to Boston and the divorce from Linda. Max hadn't spoken or written to Pearl in almost three years. Feeling a surge of guilt, he read the note from Linda.

"Max, this came from your Aunt Pearl. After receiving it, I called her to let her know you are in Boston. We had a good talk. She is still Pearl and wonderful. Linda"

Max was hoping for a, "love, Linda" or even a, "take care, Linda" but he got just "Linda" so he moved to Pearl's letter on stationary.

"Dear Max,

I hope this letter finds you in good health. Mine is failing. It is my eyes that seem, to me anyway, to be the most pressing problem. I can't read very well, so it is good that you didn't write. But you'll be happy to know I can still hear. However, this herd of doctors that Medicare shuffles me through, without apparently talking with one another, see my overall health as otherwise. I have decided to return to Maine for the last go-around. Biddeford Pool is a good place to die. I've always loved the cottage on Oceanside Drive, the sounds and the air surrounding the front bedroom, my old room. I don't know what your life is these days, but not hearing from you, I don't take as positive. I'm not asking you to visit me but when you do, bring the usual and we will talk.

With all my love,
Pearl"

Max caught a fragrance from Pearl's stationary and wondered if he could catch anything of Linda from the copy paper. He shook his head, disgusted with his drift and decided not to try. Putting both letters back in the large envelope, he walked to his desk and slid it into the top drawer. It was time to see Pearl.

Max wasn't sure about their familial relationship. He had called her Aunt Pearl for as long as he could remember. Everybody did. Even as an adult it was always Aunt Pearl, but Max was driving to Maine to visit someone he knew as "Pearl the Curl". From the first summer they met, she was and always would be, "Pearl the Curl".

As he thought about it, heading north on 95, their relationship was curious. Pearl LaPierre was a thirty-year old philosophy professor with three children of her own, who took a ten-year old summer kid under her wing. She taught him to body surf and then she dragged him to any beach with the right waves to body surf. Apparently her children had no interest in cold water, spending the day in a wet bathing suit and waves. Summer after summer Max grew with a passion for waves and grew in affection for "Pearl the Curl". Any beach on the southern Maine coast between Ogunquit and Higgins was fair game. Depending on ocean swells, the wind and tide, Pearl picked one as the best body surfing beach of the day. And the best waves of the day were picked by curl. Too much, regardless of height, and you would be slammed to the bottom, sucked back into the surf and end up wrestling for air. Not enough curl and the wave would start to die the second it broke, never developing enough thrust to carry you to shore. Through those years, Max spent a considerable amount of time standing, at "Pearl the Curl's" direction, in waist high water and studying waves. For Pearl, body surfing was about choice and the key was choosing the wave with the right curl. She expected Max to learn about break point on his own and wasn't surprised it took him awhile.

Guilt was creeping back as he crossed into New Hampshire. He should have chosen to write Pearl, one more thing he should have done. But, Max did drive past Pearl's place two seasons ago. The outside hadn't changed for almost a half century. He heard that she allowed central heating and insulation installed under the house but never a foundation or paved driveway. The path to a two-story carriage house in the rear of her lot was always crushed clam shells and he remembered that she did her best every summer to keep the top layer fresh. Her oldest son lived there year round for the past decade and Max heard from time to time that he had plans to remodel but it never happened because of Pearl. Everyone knew that he would wait and do whatever he wanted to the place after she died. Max figured that was alright with Pearl. She was grateful for the chance to be in her old room, in her old house, just the way it had always been; grateful for the chance to die facing the ocean.

The Piscatiqua River Bridge came into view, a woven iron bubble on the horizon. He was getting close to Maine and facing Pearl. Guilt was starting to overtake him. He thought champagne might help. He took the last exit in New Hampshire to the State Liquor Store at Portsmouth Rotary and searched for Chandon splits.

After emptying the wine cooler of the last seven small bottles of champagne, he paid what he thought was a fair price for at least some forgiveness. In the liquor store parking lot he took his sax case out of the car and set it on the trunk. He then removed and put back into the car everything in the case but his sax. Around the sax he packed the seven splits of champagne and knew he could get by Pearl's son but wondered about his wife Rachel.

As Max expected, it wasn't hard to walk past Jack LaPierre with his sax case. He was raking the front lawn of a winter's worth of twigs and pine needles. It was apparent to Max that Jack didn't like yard work and knew a pause on the pathway to the front door could become a long distraction. Max was cordial and quick. Jack was disappointed. In the front entryway Rachel was also cordial but not quick. She wanted information and the chance to look Max up and down, for what, he had no idea other than smuggling. He gave her enough, mumbled about a tight time line for a meeting in Portland and expressed his desire to see Pearl. Rachel relented but remained suspect of the sax case.

"So you're going to play something for Pearl? How nice...I hope it's something new."

Knowing the way, he smiled and started up the oak stairs to Pearl's front room. Max had forgotten, from years ago, how much he annoyed her.

At the top of the stairs Max turned and walked toward a window with a view full of ocean. To the left, he knocked on a half open door and pushed through, gently closing the door behind him. Pearl was sitting, S shaped, in a rocking chair pulled up to one of the room's two ocean side windows. Her white hair was collecting the sun while everything else melted into shadows and pastels. Max heard her sigh. In a low tone he said, "Pearl the Curl".

"What's left of me..." without looking up, she continued, "Did you come to see me before I croak?"

Max smiled, "Well...ya...kind of."

"You finally did learn the break point."

"With no help from you..."

"I helped you by keeping my mouth shut but don't plan on it this time around."

Max set his sax case on the made bed and leaned next to Pearl as she raised her head. He kissed her on the cheek. She aimed for anywhere on his face and got him with a kiss on the chin.

"Ah...Max..." They held hands and stared at one another. "You didn't lug that thing in here just to play for me did you?"

"No."

"Well, crack open a bottle."

"It's a little early isn't it Pearl? It's only nine fifteen."

"Max...it is getting late."

Max stared at her for a moment. "OK, I'll get you a cold one, since you'll probably be drinking the rest warm." He twisted off the fake cork and handed her a split. She drank a sip like it was a bottle of Coke.

"I see that you are still wearing your wedding ring."

"I thought you were blind."

"Going blind...I saw the reflected sunlight that bounced across my eyes when you handed me the bottle. I see some up close."

Holding his ring with right thumb and index finger Max mumbled, "Ya, well ah...I didn't..."

After two more quick sips and Max's trying to say something without saying anything, Pearl changed direction, "OK, let's hear *Sweet Soul* and make my daughter-in-law happy and unhappy at the same time."

"She knows I brought you champagne."

"Yes. And soon she'll know you didn't fill up the whole case...that will make her happy."

"And unhappy?"

"You know damn well...same ol' Jr. Walker. Please play."

Max took his sax out of the case and looked into Pearl's eyes, "I hope your hearing is as good as you say it is. I'm playing for only you."

As Max began to play *Sweet Soul,* Pearl rolled back into the S position in her rocker, eyes closed and body still, the champagne split held with both hands in her lap.

Max kept his eyes open, they never left Pearl and he never played better. When he stopped, the room was quiet, the sound of the ocean in the distance.

"You have changed Max. How should I say, it's no longer...mechanical...your soul has the blues...what's going on?"

"You mean besides Linda?"

"Sure Max, besides Linda, that's been a given for a long while. It's been what, three, maybe four years now...heard she was date..."

"Pearl, let's leave it..."

"OK, OK, another day, but remember, I'm not supposed to last long enough to see the leaves fall...your communication record is poor...I'm worried that you'll be slipping a note in my coffin. "

Max slid a desk chair between Pearl and the window to create a silhouette with the sunlight. He was quiet and she waited. It was confession, she said, "You may begin." She took two large swigs of champagne and waited some more...till the flood gates opened.

"Pearl, I've hit the wall on a Casco repatriation project....I've been working on it for almost a year... the last few months I was supposed to be finding missing Casco bones to repatriate...but no bones... I can't seem to get out of my own way...nothing. I know they're out there because I'm still dreaming the same spirit dream...sounds a little crazy...but true. I believe...I owe the Casco...but I'm not able to repay.

I've seen blocks before Pearl...yes maybe with Linda that I didn't work through...but this time it is not the same...it's me, my whole life, it's the Casco...there's something more and I'm locked in and empty.

I don't see a future...I can't get hold of it. Everything ends today, for the first time I stop right here in this moment. This is me and no more." Max paused, feeling that his ramblings made no sense.

"Hmm, Casco, you've been reburying Casco bones?"

"Pearl, yes, but come on, I'm trying to tell you I'm playing blue because I'm lost...I'm not good at talking about it. Repatriating the Casco set me off and without the chance of finding more bones I have no where to go. I can't go back and I'm not going forward!"

"Ah...still the dramatic one...sooo dramatic.

Max, listen to me. You are not only the sum of what you have done and who you have become... you are also the sum of what you could do and who you could become.

You *are* your future."

"What?" Max threw his arms up in the air. "Who are you paraphrasing...Charlie Bay Burningwater...you sound like Burningwater...I am my future. I am a headache, right now, with no sense of future, no sense of self!"

"I don't know Charlie Bay Burningwater...it's Jean-Paul Sartre with a wee bit of "Pearl the Curl".

Max, I'll be blunt, you need a distraction with direction...and I'm it. Let's go out to the carriage house."

He didn't want to go. "The carriage house, why...what about these?" Max looked to the remaining six splits and wasn't sure why he came. The guilt was gone.

"They won't survive long." Pearl pointed to the closet. "Hanging on the inside of the door is a plastic pocket rack for shoes. Just slip them in the pouches. I'll hear them when I open the door. Now come on, help me up."

"Here? Rachel doesn't..."

"She doesn't want alcohol in the kitchen cabinets or the refrigerator...you know, around Jack. He won't even come in my room let alone my closet. Come on help me up. Let's go."

Pearl walked along the clam shell path with short, wide unsteady steps. Max kept her upright by holding her left hand in his left and wrapping his right arm around her waist. The trip to the carriage house was going to take awhile but the Spring east wind felt good to them both.

As they got a little closer Max studied the building. At this pace, there was time. The carriage house had two sliding garage-sized wooden doors, square four pane side windows and a loft with swinging doors that closed to match the midline of the sliders. The steeply pitched roof was topped by two lightening rods. He wondered how they were going to get inside. The tracks were rusted and the doors looked heavy.

"We'll need to split the doors for light...the loft too." Pearl raised her right hand.

"We will?"

"Of course, I point...you do."

It took some grunting and groaning but Max did get the doors apart and guided by sunlight Pearl slipped inside. Max followed to see one bay empty and in the other, resting on a trailer, dusty, ghostlike, was about a sixteen foot sailboat, mast and boom running fore and aft tenting canvass. Pearl was headed straight for the boat's bow, hands forward waiting to touch wood. Hustling to

284

her side Max worried about a fall. Pearl worried about the condition of the gaff-rigged sloop. It had been such a long time. Her hands, now on the hull, followed a single plank aft. They left a trail of finger-tip touches in the dust inches below the brown canvas cover.

"Ah Max…the STURGEON MOON and she needs work."

Max dropped his head, chin to his chest knowing what was to come.

"I saw that, silhouetted…remember. Come with me… over to the stairs…the loft."

In the rear of the space, the stairs to the second floor started up along the far wall to a platform and then turned left along the side wall up to the loft. The platform was the same height as the stern tucked into the right angle. Without a railing, it was possible to step from the platform onto the boat. After Pearl had given Max directions, faster than he could follow, to move the canvass forward, slide the boom to starboard and clear lines from the fantail and cockpit, she was ready for him to somehow get her on board. Max's solution was to pick her up, set her on the bench seat and tell her to hold on to the tiller. It was his turn, he had questions. Except she looked so happy poised to sail right out of the carriage house he was unable to ask for an explanation. All he could do was talk about boats.

"I saw the hull lines and now the cockpit…with the center board trunk…I'm pretty sure this is a Haven 12 ½…your Haven 12 ½ by the look on your face."

"I love this boat Max...I've been dreaming about sitting in this spot...the last ten years in Tucson."

"In your barn...blind and with me?"

"Being back on the water Max…back on the water."

Max knew, and he loved her for it. He sat next to her and waited. Nothing but a smile, so again, he talked about boats.

"Joel White designed this boat didn't he? Based on the Herreshoff 12½...designed for places just like Biddeford Pool. If I remember right... only draws around a foot and a half with the board up, a little over three with it down." Max was showing off.

"When was the last time you went sailing Max?"

"Me? Ah, long time ago...long time."

"To know that about a Haven 12½ doesn't mean you know the STURGEON MOON...it means you read a lot...maybe too much. You have a problem. Anyone who knows that much without sailing a Haven...has a problem, you need to get wet."

Max rambled, "I don't know...I enjoy reading about old boats, old designs...about sailing. But ya, it's a lot more reading than sailing...the last time I was serious about it...I was in my early thirties and crewed during a Soling Race Week...that was it. From there I got distracted…it was teaching, kids, books and bones and on and on to the Nile Valley and now the Casco...who knows where it all went...last time I was on the water...it was with Charlie Bay Burningwater. I did get wet and ...seasick." Max dropped his head.

"Hmm...Burningwater again...Max, I need you to go up to the loft. You'd better open the doors for light. And I want you to bring down a box, a particular box for me. It's supposed to be midway down on the right side as you head to the doors. The carton is a little smaller than a storage-file box and it's the only one sealed with florescent orange tape. I thought I'd have a chance to recover it during the move in but the loft got it first, so it's up there somewhere. I'll wait for you right here..." Shaking her head side to side, "...should have brought champagne."

Max sat still. He wasn't deciding whether he would do it or not. He would, but he wondered where she was headed besides sailing.

"OK, I'll be right back."

"I doubt it, but I'll be waiting."

At the top of the stairs Max mumbled about how much stuff was stored there and no apparent path through it all to the daylight-bordered doors.

Pearl heard Max say, "A flashlight would be good." As expected, he took a tumble.

"It's alright...it wasn't your box that got crushed. No orange tape, no broken leg."

Pearl shook her head again, listened for the loft doors to swing open and hoped they didn't take him to the ground. She caught, "I can see now" and she sighed. After that, all she could hear were the sounds of boxes moving and sliding, grunting and finally words, "I got it."

Once back in the cockpit with the box and the sunlight even brighter, Max took a rusty pocket knife, laid still for ten years in a canvass tool kit and cut through three sections of florescent orange tape. Inside, wrapped in bubble plastic was a walnut box about fifteen inches long, twelve inches wide and six inches deep. Again, he used the knife to free the treasure and handed the box to Pearl. Max could now appreciate what he thought was a chest, it's walnut cover was inlayed with dark mahogany and tiger oak patterns highlighted by silver ribbon, pencil thin and flush to the design borders. Max was curious and the chest was locked.

"What's in there...that's got to be over a hundred years old?"

Pearl didn't answer. She reached into her pocket and removed a key. Placing the chest across her lap, she inserted the key into the lock on the front panel, turned it and lifted the top. The chest separated evenly along a seam in the middle of the vertical walls and opened completely to form a flat surface twice the width. Purple silk covered both sections with the exception of a two-inch compartment running the length of the chest's front panel. In the compartment was an inkwell, a rack for ink pens and two square sections, presumably for extra ink and pen tips.

Max threw up his arms. "It's a portable writing desk...the nineteenth century version of a lap top!"

Pearl paused, she was not amused.

"Max, remember...you need a distraction with direction.

Here's the deal. You know that you and I are not related by blood. Through successive generations of family historians a good portion of my family story has been recorded and organized. Somehow along the way I ended up as the gatekeeper for my lineage. In Tucson, I brought things up to date by studying and sorting through generations of letters before my eyes deteriorated. Some of those letters, and I don't know how they got in my hands, are of your blood line."

Pearl flipped open the silk tops to a paper and envelope compartment in each section. She removed a medium-sized stack of letters tied with a white ribbon and two large stacks tied with blue. Holding up the white she said, "all mine" and then the blue "some yours".

I'll give you the letters, over two hundred years worth of history. In return, I want you to do two things: one, get the STURGEON MOON to float and two, sail with me.

And I know...I know, the boat needs work but nothing major, some of the carvel planking needs to be re-caulked in spots under the water line, sealed with seam compound, painted and here's a key part of the deal, once launched, someone has to stay on her till those planks swell enough to float..."

"But Pearl, why in the world would I take on sorting through two hundred years of different family histories plus your boat! I'm already in way over my head with the Cas..."

"Because there're Casco in the blue pile Max!"

"There're Casco in the blue pile?" Stunned, Max was trying to process the information and speak at the same time, "Deal."

It didn't take Max long to drop his unproductive strategy of the last five months in the search for missing Casco bones and to start planning a new one. On his way back to Boston with the letters and portable desk, he decided to set the lineage research in his Maine State University office. The space was already allocated to him for his coming sabbatical year and specified for Casco repatriation. In Max's mind, even though it was a bit of a personal distraction, the Casco were implicated in there somewhere enough to justify the whole thing. At least, Max thought he could make the case to Sandra for using the space and equipment. But he hoped it never came up.

That night in his apartment, Max sat on the couch and set Pearl's portable desk across his lap. He removed the two bundles of letters. They were faded, some water marked and all brittle. Holding the letters gave Max some energy and as tempted as he was to dive in, he knew this would require discipline. They were all fragile and the more touched the more they were likely to fall apart. His overall plan was to sort them into chronological order and scan everything. He would only work from the digital file. In his lack of familiarity with artifacts, he was afraid that some would be damaged or even worse destroyed. He wanted to scan and return the letters to

Pearl as soon as possible, but keep the desk until she asked for it.

At his university early on Monday morning, he began to wrap up loose ends and put his all night planning in motion. He expected to start the genealogy in Maine by Saturday. The hardware he needed for his new office was a scanner, printer and a desk top, which he signed out for the year with a lot of paperwork from his current Anthropology Department. The other things he ordered from Sandra's secretary; an extra large white board, two large bulletin boards and wall maps of Maine and the northeast. He bought an eight foot folding conference table from an office supply company that delivered on Saturday but never told Sandra that he or any of this other stuff was coming. He wondered about his office size and if it was empty.

Sandra was busy on Saturday and annoyed. The space was available, the budget undefined. The two of them crossed paths during the equipment set up long enough for him to get the look from Sandra. The office, lab and the year were supposed to be dedicated to Casco repatriation. This was the purpose of his position in her department and his funding. She wondered if he had already lost his focus. Max did catch the look but wasn't sure if it came because he was trying to screw into cinderblock or that he was off on another apparent tangent. Neither was of concern enough to slow him down. With everything running by noon, he sequenced, scanned and printed letters into Saturday night, finishing up on Sunday morning. Max laid the reprinted letters in chronological order on the table and identified his first problem. For some of the letters, the dates on which they were written and the dates and people they were writing about were different, very different. Postponing what he suspected was to become a difficulty; he loaded the file into his laptop and was southbound on 95 by one o'clock. He stopped at Pearl's with the original letters, some more champagne splits and gave her an update. She reminded him about getting started on his part of the deal.

Throughout his last work week in Boston Max wrapped everything up fast enough to take Friday off and was headed back to Maine on Thursday night, without a thought to his part of the deal, until now. With his mind wandering during the late night drive, he remembered Margaret explaining how she had re-caulked Charlie Bay's dory. He recalled last October, the hull of the Pipeboat overturned on the island work dock, intact and freshly painted. Margaret had helped Burningwater remove the outboard motor well and replace the stem to stern planks; all with caulking, seam compound and paint, just what he needed for the STURGEON MOON. She had the experience and the skills and he had neither. He called Margaret and then Pearl from the road to set up the boat work for Saturday afternoon. Despite plans, Margaret enjoyed the desperation in his voice and the indebtedness to his Aunt Pearl. She agreed to help. Pearl was just pleased he called.

Friday didn't go the way Max had hoped. The problem he anticipated was even bigger than expected. Most of the dates and places of the letters' origins did not match the dates and places of the letters' subjects. As a result chronological order of the letters meant nothing to the chronology of the subjects. After spending all day Friday and part of Saturday trying to post letters in some order on the bulletin boards and sketching a lineage on the white board, Max was frustrated and thought about a hot dog. What he had projected to look like a gracefully ascending oak with branches labeled by names, gender, dates of birth and offspring leading to other branches, all emanating from one robust trunk, looked like tumble weed, maybe multiple tumble weeds. It was a mess. He had laid the letters out on the table like skeletal material. But these weren't bones and he had no skill or patience for the process. He wanted Casco bones from the letters and he wasn't getting any.

Max wondered how he could get out of working on the STURGEON MOON and disappear for some sax therapy. Exasperated, he leaned on the table and gazed down at a letter, eyes catching the words, "dented skull". It was the second page of two, addressed to Pearl and signed, Josephine Brennen. Pearl made a notation below her name, "JB, friend of paternal second cousin once removed, Harriet Fields". It wasn't Casco bones but he needed a break from the tumble weed.

"Dear Pearl,

I thought that you might enjoy some juicy gossip about some of the characters in our correspondences. Most of this I have cross-referenced and believe it to be true. If you remember I sent you information a year or so ago concerning some folks who I thought may be related to you but it turned out in further investigations that they are not. San Rochelle is the family name, originally from Montreal.

Well it seems, maybe third generation in North America, there was a daughter, Yvonne, born around 1829, who, somehow ended up in Saco, Maine married to a "Jack of all trades" from Boston by the name of Tom Moran. He and two brothers had a cigar and tobacco business with a shop in Saco. The couple had been married a little over a year when their first and only child, a daughter died at a month old. After that Tom was known to drink and take off from time to time. On a Friday afternoon in November, Tom headed for the bank with a week's worth of cash and wasn't seen again. The shop closed and the other brothers left town. The rumors were the usual; ran off with another woman, robbed and killed and his body never found, drank it all away and then went to start over somewhere else. No one ever really knew. Yvonne San Rochelle legally divorced Tom Moran and about three years after he disappeared she remarried. Shortly thereafter, Tom Moran was found, ironically by his banker, on the Portland waterfront unloading cargo ships. He was known as "Topper" and had a dented skull. He had no memory of his past life and was ill with consumption, presumably TB. Yvonne San Rochelle brought him back to Saco where Tom Moran stayed in the attic, cared for by his wife and her second husband. Moran died about two months later.

Now you know why I love investigating genealogies and have another..."

Max didn't read any further, now searching the table for Josephine's first letter to Pearl. He recalled the name San Rochelle and early dates in his initial sequencing. If he didn't have Casco, he still had enough perseverance to try one more time for the solid oak trunk. He finally found it posted in the middle of one bulletin board. The letter regarding the San Rochelle line was included in Josephine's first letter and written by Alice Clark in the mid nineteenth century. It reported a number of blood lines, all unrelated to Pearl or Pearl's cousin, Harriet Fields.

Alice wrote, "Martin San Rochelle was born in Montreal in or around 1778. He was educated in Paris as a physician and returned to Montreal traveling with the Jesuits to care for the indigenous people of the Saint Lawrence River Valley between Montreal, and Lake Ontario. About five years into a mission that took him throughout Iroquois country, he met and married a woman from a remnant of the Huron and they had a son born 1803 along the Saint Lawrence in the small town of Iroquois. There is no record of the death of Martin San Rochelle or of his wife. Presumably she was baptized but Church documents of the region are missing or incomplete. Their son, Jean Louis, however, was raised in Montreal and also sent to Paris for medical education. He followed in his father's footsteps and returned to Iroquois territory; in fact, also marrying into the Heron People."

Max noted the spelling error of the word Huron as Heron in an otherwise well written letter.

"Jean Louis and his wife had four children; three boys and the youngest, a girl, was the only one with a baptismal record in Montreal. Her name was Yvonne Marie San Rochelle. It is believed that she and two brothers later traveled to and were educated in Boston."

Max already knew what was ahead for Yvonne and lost interest in the San Rochelle story. He was disappointed; evidence of Huron but no Casco. Max considered how the Huron and Casco were related. They weren't. Huron were sedentary horticulturalists just beyond the Seneca's western New York border, eventually assimilated into the Iroquois Nation. The Casco were marine-hunter gatherers from the northeast coast of the Atlantic. The only thing that tied them together was being wiped out by a succession of European diseases over four centuries, the Huron People and the Pipeboat People. Max shook his head and wondered if the Casco were really the Pipeboat People or was Charlie Bay just toying with him...he did give him a Pipeboat for the dream journey...he did give him a spirit dream. What about the Heron People...how did they travel on their dream journey?

He whispered, "Heron People or Huron People...?"

Max made the same mistake over a hundred years later. He called the two generations of women married to San Rochelles the Heron. Were the Heron a separate and culturally different group in the Saint Lawrence River Valley, different than Huron? Heron, heron, heron...he remembered the heron amulets in the Clementine box in Charlie Bay's basement. His heart started to pound.

Max sat down at his keyboard and did something that as a researcher was embarrassed he hadn't done at Sandra's almost a year ago. He typed in an online word search; Casco, in the <u>Handbook</u> of <u>American</u> <u>Indians</u>.

"*Uh-kos-is-co*, shortened by Europeans to Casco, meaning heron" was all he needed to read...the prayer given to him by Charlie Bay, "*Uh-kosisco rising above me...for the strength to persevere...*" The Casco, the Heron were in the Saint Lawrence River Valley and marrying San Rochelles for two generations. Yvonne San Rochelle was more Casco than anything else! Casco would have migrated west to the region because of the Europeans-on foot, by horseback, wagon or any other means that allowed escape. Their bones weren't removed from Long Neck to museums or universities. The Casco went to Montreal and upstate New York living and breathing.

Max was starting to hyperventilate, thoughts racing...still having the spirit dream...find still missing bones...out there somewhere in the Saint Lawrence River Valley. Their bones, Casco bones, removed from the ground and gathered in their new homeland...collections excavated in Iroquois country included Casco.

Pacing the room helped Max calm down. He hadn't felt this much energy and a direction to pursue in months. His first step had to be a cautious one: make a list of researchers with expertise and knowledge of the skeletal collection in the area and inquire carefully. Colleagues, in light of current attitudes and sensibilities associated with repatriation, were guarded about information concerning their archived skeletal material. They protected their collections. Max understood. He understood very well Sandra's passion to collect, catalog and hold onto bones for a very long time, and she was not alone in the field. Now however, Max found himself on the other side. His joy in the possibility of repatriating more Casco surprised him. He wanted them back in the ground. Finishing up the contact list, he looked forward to seeing Margaret with a story to tell.

"You're late!" Pearl and Margaret said in unison as Max jogged to a stop in the middle of the carriage house doors.

As Max struggled to catch his breath, Pearl continued, "And obviously out of shape."

Pearl was sitting in an Adirondack chair facing the STURGEON MOON as Margaret, under the hull, scraped out seam compound and caulking from between the planks.

"Sorry I'm a little late but I have some news. Pearl you were right, there were Casco in the blue pile. Margaret, you are going to enjoy this."

"Of course I was right, now can you work and talk at the same time? And it wasn't a little late, it was an hour and a half. But, it did give Margaret and I a chance to get to know one another a bit. She talks and works at the same time very well...should be inspirational for you Max." Pearl's voice, raspy, she sipped from a champagne split.

Max looked at the hull and what Margaret had already accomplished.

"Max, grab that tile cutter, the one with the hook on the end and scrape the seam compound from all the places Pearl has circled with chalk."

"Pearl circled?"

Pearl offended, "By feel Max, where the compound has been squeezed out by the planks then dried, leaving gaps...by feel...you can feel it"

There were five or six circled sections between planks on the aft quarter of the hull. In the largest area, Margaret had already removed the old seam compound and cotton caulking. She was tapping in new spun marine oakum with a mallet and caulking iron. Max was glad he called her and began to talk.

"Remember Max, talk while you work. Pearl and I are listening for both."

Max reviewed Pearl's gift of the letters, his lineage reconstruction inadequacies and the Yvonne San Rochelle story ending with the death in the attic of her lost husband. His voice got much louder and higher as he explained the European alteration of the Maine coast Abinaki word for heron, *Uh-kos-is-co* to "Casco". In detail he presented his hypothesis of Casco migration to the Saint Lawrence River Valley and their subsequent skeletal excavation with Iroquois populations. During Max's story Pearl dozed and Margaret got a lot done.

"You know Margaret, I'm still having the spirit dream...*Uh-kosisco* is part of Charlie Bay's prayer... still Casco bones out there, I know it... now I'm going to find them. I'm close."

With "still having the spirit dream" Pearl woke up.

"The spirit dream of Max Sorensen, I know nothing about it...I'd like to share in that piece before I leave this earth."

Margaret smiled at Max, "I'm happy for you Max. It's been awhile coming...'

Pearl interrupted, "Max, do you know who Yvonne San Rochelle's second husband was?"

"No, I never got that far."

"He was William Sorensen, a boat builder from Portsmouth, William G Sorensen."

"There're a couple of William Sorensens in my fam..."

"Ah huh, the same." Pearl nodded

"You mean one of my grandfathers was married to Yvonne San Rochelle, the Casco daughter...that means...that means I'm part Casco..."

"I thought you might enjoy that..."

Margaret stopped working and turned to Max dead on, "Looks like you just dove three times into the waves and surfaced as a harbor seal again Max."

Max stared at her for a moment, "Margaret...there's Charlie Bay's spirit dream...touching all those bones...Casco bones....my ancestor's bones...I'm Casco." He leaned against the stairway to the loft, his eyes dropped to the floor. "I'll be damn."

Chapter Fifteen

After Max left Pearl and Margaret, he called Sandra and invited himself to dinner; he would bring the food if she supplied the beer. She agreed as long as it wasn't hot dogs. So on route, Max picked up a baked haddock sandwich and cold slaw for Sandra and a fried haddock sandwich with onion rings and fries for himself. Studying Casco bones, being part Casco, feeling guilty and seeking repatriation, all this was not going to be easy to discuss with Sandra. But it was necessary to keep things moving and the fried food would help. Sandra ate, Max talked and ate. To begin, he played it safe, outlining his hypothesis and withholding his intent to repatriate Casco expecting Sandra to lobby for a new archive.

The hypothesis had merit to Sandra, even if she had to sort through multiple points of classic Sorensen speculation. She gave him ten straight minutes of repeating the four key points: Casco migration, assimilation into Iroquoian cultures, burial somewhere in the Saint Lawrence River Valley or upstate New York and skeletal excavation along with other Iroquois populations of the region. She was sold and surprised, after months of floundering; he was onto something she never expected.

Sandra gave Max and herself a break when she left the room for more beer. As she handed him a cold bottle and before she could say a word, Max began the San Rochelle story. He was more subdued, thorough with the details and almost quiet when he ended with, "So ya...that makes me part Casco."

Neither moved until Sandra said, "...that explains a lot...I never could figure out why, after you hit the wall a few months ago, you didn't take off to the Nile Valley like you usually do...leave it all behind, abdicate like so many times before...that was a first for you Max...you persevered...I think the Casco in you persevered."

"I had help...

And that's why...when I find Casco bones Sandra... and I will find them...they are to be repatriated...back in the ground...no studies...no archive."

"You mean when *we* find Casco bones they'll be repatriated."

She was also implicated, some by her departmental position and some by her American heritage. She had six generations of Euro-American ancestry, ancestors who relocated Native American populations, including the

Casco, away from the Maine coast, onto reservations or westward, forcing them to face even harder lives. But most of all she was implicated by her history with Casco bones. This new segment of Casco repatriation was an obligation. She accepted it. Max, surprised at her shift to repatriate the Casco collections unstudied, accepted her help.

Almost four weeks later and with one promising lead, Max found himself in Sandra's office excited to finally be getting somewhere.

Sandra was all business, "OK Max, so now that the I.T. people have us up and running for this video conference call, who are we talking to and what do we want out of this remarkable electronic effort?"

Max, with a fresh cup of coffee, sat down opposite Sandra at the round maple table, his back to a forty inch LED monitor. She had seen the look on his face before, wide-eyed energy.

"...you really need the caffeine Max? You may want to move over to this side before we start... I'm planning on you to run this meeting...please, fill me in before we get going."

Max remained seated, "The call is scheduled with Grant Shivington, a biological anthropologist in Syracuse and the collections manager of an Iroquois historic cemetery site dated between 1775 and 1790. Grant studied with George Lowell who worked with us, primarily you, years ago on some TB bone pathology research pre and post contact. Shivington was the only one who got back to me with a promising lead."

"Sure, I knew George very well, bright guy...was sorry to hear he died..."

Max didn't stop. "The burial site...I think individual graves...he said was around a hundred and twenty adults archived in accordance with the NAGPRA regs but no time line for repatriation. I asked him if there was evidence for marine hunter-gatherers in the sample and he said that he hadn't taken a close look...no one else had either as far as he knew. So I'm hoping that he has something to show us...sounded like he did when we set this up...we can go from there..."

"So the bottom line Max is...we don't know what he has other than Iroquois."

"Correct."

The tech turned on the screen and camera as Max moved next to Sandra. There was a thin manila folder in front of Max containing maybe a dozen pages. As he pushed it out of the way to set down his coffee cup, he noticed the top page stuck out beyond one end by about three inches. It was letter-quality paper with the heading O'Connor and Napolitano, Attorneys at Law, the address line below was cut off. Max had seen the firm's name before...

"We're all set...you're on."

Max looked up to see the backdrop of an osteology lab, human remains in the foreground and their counter part seated behind a human skull resting in foam on the table top. A security badge with a head shot photo above the name Shivington was clipped to the breast pocket of his lab coat. Max mumbled, "...great image..."

Sandra cleared her throat.

"Grant, I'm Max Sorensen...can you hear me OK?

"Yes, I can and I can see you pretty well too."

"I bet...good...good to put a face to your voice. Thanks for helping us out. Grant, this Sandra Walsh..."

"Sure, hello Sandra. George spoke of you often and cited you even more...pretty much most of his publications."

"Good to see you Grant."

"So Grant how about taking Sandra and I through what you have."

"OK...feel free to interrupt me any time with questions or comments. I thought I'd email you the files of the archeologist's site report and the osteological record...any other info that you think would be helpful...let me know and I'll see what I can find...but here's what I thought might be most interesting.

In George's personal papers I found his original notebook...all his notes and observations of his first look at the skeletal collection. As you know, he was very interested in boney evidence for TB in sedentary horticulturalists as a population-dependent disease. He examined one hundred and twenty-six adults. Seventeen had, what was to George, dental findings significant enough to exclude them from the sedentary horticulturalist sample. It's well-documented, both pre and post Euro-American contact, the Iroquois ...had...lots...lots of dental disease...decay, abscesses, missing teeth...the seventeen individuals had none of that."

Max and Sandra both knew where he was going. Max started to squirm in his seat and Sandra leaned toward the screen.

"All they had was dental wear...severely worn teeth. I brought a specimen so you can see for yourselves."

Grant held a skull in one hand and a lower jaw in the other, brought them together to recreate the individual's bite and showed the relationship of the teeth in a close up from three views.

"Can we switch cameras so they can see a close up with the micro video camera...oh, they already have it...way ahead of me Cheryl, thanks...here are the chewing surfaces of the teeth."

"Marine hunter-gatherers..." Sandra whispered.

"Way ahead of *you* Sandra...Casco marine hunter-gatherers."

"...so these seventeen specimens never were included in Lowell's TB..."

"Grant, excuse me." Max interrupted, "Any grave goods with the seventeen?"

"I don't know Max, but I know it's a digital archive so I'll send you images if there are any...but I can tell you this...there is DNA."

Sandra and Max both responded, "DNA?" Max was louder.

George wanted to make sure with DNA they weren't Iroquois, either from the same sample or from other Iroquois groups in the region...they weren't. So they were separated from the rest of the collection...archived in a basement vault until now...at the time, his notes speculate that they were probably a remnant migrating to the Saint Lawrence River Valley from Cape Cod.

A DNA match...either from a living individual or skeletal sample...seems to be the only way we'll know where they belong...do you have any skeletal material?"

Max looked at Sandra and shook his head, "No".

After an uncomfortable pause, Grant became fidgety, anxious to speak, "Max if I could be direct here. I'm well aware the majority of Dr Walsh's work is with the Casco...ah...George had great respect for you Sandra...that's one of the reasons I responded to you Max...when I saw his association with your department...so...ah...if the rumors that I'm hearing are true...you're acting as an advocate Max, to identify Casco and repatriate...your best bet and I'm not telling you anything that you don't know...your best bet to claim these bones as Casco...avoid considerable litigation and cost all around is to get hold of some well-documented Casco DNA; skeletal or from a living individual...the problem is the assimilation through generations of Casco into other cultures...other gene pools...in today's world, living Casco may not be close. In my opinion, to get as close to 100% as you can and make it a sure thing...a sure thing to circumvent all the politics...you're going to need bone...known Casco bones. If you can get some DNA like that and we have a good solid match...these seventeen are yours...George would've jumped at the chance to know who they are and to treat them appropriately.

Grave goods are going to be an awful lot tougher to establish cultural affiliation...DNA is the best bet to expedite the claim on this material...if you can get it...I'm all set on this end."

Max was staring at the screen, focused, but not on the image. Sandra turned to Max, "Slow down Max."

"But I haven't done anything!"

"Slow down before you do."

In keeping with his part of the deal, Max agreed to be at the boatyard on the morning the STURGEON MOON was launched. Based on Pearl's repeated concern of the time needed for the wooden hull to swell, Max expected the boat to leak but he had no idea how much or for how long. The plan was to have the mast stepped on shore along with the rest of the rigging but no sails. Pearl had those tucked away in her house, kept safe for the last decade. Margaret was going to bring them over at noon for Max to rig and also bring a gas-powered water pump borrowed from Bud Walker just in case the boat leaked a lot.

As the yardmen lowered the STURGEON MOON with the travel lift into the water, Max heard, "Yup, she's a leakin."

That was followed by, "Ayup, she sure is. Where's the guy Pearl promised she'd have here for bailin?"

"I'm right here." Max did not have a good feeling about his role in this wooden boat adventure; but a deal's a deal.

"OK good...hop aboard and grab that hand pump and we'll ease you right over to the finger dock...right close here."

Max climbed into the cockpit and watched the two men with a bow and stern line guide the Haven away from the travel lift to the closest float.

"You best pump rather than stand around watching us...'cause you're sinkin."

Lifting a floorboard to get at the bilge, his feet were already wet and the May ocean freezing. Without thinking, Max stuck the pump's shaft into the water next to the hull's centerboard casing and draped the six foot corrugated tubing over the side unsecured. As soon as he had water up into the pump and out the tubing, the tubing jumped back into the cockpit like an out of control garden hose. Bilge water was spraying all over the floor boards, bench seats and back into the bilge. Along the way, Max was getting soaked and the STURGEON MOON was continuing to sink. Knowing he was in trouble, Max looked back to the travel lift for help from the yardmen and saw Margaret carrying sail bags and Bud Walker lugging a gas-powered water pump. Trying to recover the end of the tubing and get it overboard, he reached aft, the water in the hull followed his weight and the boat shifted. On the slippery floorboards Max's feet went out from under him. He splashed down into water and slid aft.

All Margaret could do at first was laugh, and then, after realizing what a mess he was in, she yelled, "Hey Wet One, Wet One, don't worry we're coming." She turned to Bud, "Keep an eye on the Wet One. It's endless."

Bud Walker had the pump set up and running in no time. The amount of water pouring in from open dry seams was about equal to the amount being pumped out. Bud figured it would be that way for awhile so he volunteered to stay long enough for Max to get a change of clothes. He also knew it meant lunch with Margaret.

In the parking lot, before Margaret went for sandwiches and Max to get dry, he asked her for a minute to talk. She said yes, but Margaret knew the Wet One was up to something.

"A few days ago Sandra and I had a good video conference with a collections manager from Syracuse...helpful guy and I believe he has some Casco skeletal material archived...seventeen individuals. And the good news is that there is DNA for all seventeen...DNA Margaret."

"Oh."

"Ya and all we need is a solid match on this end to claim them as Casco and repatriate."

"And the match is going to come from where?"

Max looked away, "Well...the best match I know...as close as we are ever going to get to genetically 100% Casco...is...Charlie Bay."

"What!" Margaret spun in a circle and slapped her palms to her thighs. "What...are you crazy...crazy Max.

Charlie Bay is dead...he is buried. What do want to do exhume him for some DNA."

"Well...ya...that's..."

"No Max, absolutely not."

"But Margaret he is the closest one I know to being all Casco...next is your...your father."

"Good, my father...good...go with him." Margaret got into her car and drove.

Max yelled at the cloud of dust from the dirt parking lot as she pulled away, "It's to repatriate...repatriate..." It made perfect sense to him until Sandra's slow down came to mind.

It was a quick lunch and easy to find a yardman to keep an eye on the water pump until Max returned. Margaret took Bud to the Co-op and dropped him off before she called her father. She was surprised to catch him at the bridge to Long Neck Island. Rather than talk on the phone, she drove over and met him on the mainland side.

There were two pickup trucks and her father's car parked just off the dirt road and before the bridge. Margaret turned in next to his car as two men, one with a clipboard and the other with a tablet were walking to their trucks. Jim shook hands with both and Margaret waited until they climbed into their cabs before she walked over to her father, now standing in front of the bridge.

"Hey Margaret...what's up?"

"I was just wondering the same thing. Were you going to fill me in later...maybe much later? What's going on? Who were those guys?"

Jim laughed. He was not defensive. "I'm still getting used to that, fill you in part...I'm seeing what it would take to put in a new bridge to the island."

"You mean a new bridge to the casino?" It never took long to tap the edge with her father when she felt him withholding information.

"The casino and Long Neck will never be connected...connected physically anyway. I'm worried about safety...maybe with increased traffic...this is pretty old."

He was right, "yes it is."

"And you...what's going on Margaret?"

"It's Max. You know he's still working...working on finding Casco remains and plans on repatriating here...the island burial grounds. He's made some progress and believes he has some skeletal material that's Casco and there's DNA associated with it."

Jim winced. She wished she had never used the word material but tought it was probably DNA that got to him.

"So?"

"So, he wants to exhume Charlie Bay...desecrate his burial for a DNA match...because he is the most Casco person we know. I said no as loud as I could and now, since it is well established that you are his son...he wants some DNA from you. I thought I should warn you..."

"He's persistent...I'll give him that..." Jim shook his head.

"He's over at the boatyard in Biddeford Pool trying to keep his aunt's wooden sailboat floating long enough to swell...I don't know how long...but he'll be calling."

"Biddeford Pool...maybe I'll go see him..."

"Why would you do that?"

Jim answered but not her question. "He's an entertaining character...hmm DNA...it is endless with him...thanks for the warning."

Knowing his response was all she'd get on why see Max, she would let it go if he'd give her something on the bridge. "I'd like to get a look at the plans for a new bridge."

Jim gave Margaret a smile and a lot on the bridge, "You'll be the first to see them."

As Jim walked down the ramp to the float, Max looked up from the bilge. "Ah, Margaret got to you first..."

"She did." Jim leaned over the gunnel and stuck out his right hand but didn't climb aboard. "Dr. Sorensen, how have you been?"

"Are you ever going to call me Max?"

"OK Max, I will now."

Max wasn't sure what he meant or how much Margaret had told him about the past few months but before he could ask, Jim continued, "She told me that you were looking for some Casco DNA, as close to 100% as

315

it gets...you wanted to go for Charlie Bay...the most Casco man I know...tribal roll included."

Max pounced. "That's what I was thinking...that's what I need for more Casco skeletal remains...to get them back...would you give permission to..."

"No."

"Well then, how about you..."

"Max, how about late this afternoon, you and I take a ride? Get someone to cover for you here because..." Jim looked at the transom for the boat's name and at the waterline, "because it looks like the STURGEON MOON is going to be leaking for awhile."

"Sure, but where're we..."

Jim turned, waved over his shoulder and started back up the ramp, "Good, I'll pick you up, the University, your office building at five and bring your DNA collection kit...the swab kit for someone living."

This guy baffled Max, "my office, how'd you know my off...swab for someone living?"

The red Cadillac Seville with the vinyl cabriolet roof was parked curbside and Jim, unrecognizable in a Scally cap and aviator glasses was tucked in the red leather seat behind the wheel. Max got in, lower jaw hanging and speechless.

"Max, you like Dean Martin?"

"No...not really."

"One song, just one...on these speakers...the best the eighties had to offer." *Volare'* came from the bulging speakers, loud but, not so loud that they couldn't talk.

"Where're we going?"

"An eldercare facility with a geriatric psych unit for Alzheimer's patients...about twenty minutes from here." Jim didn't volunteer more and Max didn't ask.

It was a long fifteen minutes for Max until Jim spoke again.

"We're about five minutes away...so...here's some background.

I had a half sister...her name was Molly...she passed away a few years back of pneumonia...but mostly she fought depression for a long time...in and out of places...group homes...hospitals...because of her mental illness. She needed help so, as she got worse, I became her guardian because I was never able to locate her mother. I hired an agency specializing in finding relatives, birth parents...but nothing until about three months after Molly passed. We found her...Molly's mother. She and Charlie Bay were Molly's parents....all Casco...Molly's mother was about as close to 100% Casco as Charlie Bay. Her American name is Justine Thompson and after she was found, I became her guardian, healthcare proxy, power of attorney...you name it; she needed one. She had been diagnosed with end-stage Alzheimer's and I had her moved from a nursing home in Camden, New Jersey to this place...so that she could spend her remaining days in Maine and be buried with her people. She said she remembered me when I told her I was Seal Swimmer, from the Casco Reservation back in Maine...because of Molly, we knew each other before she left the Casco. I told her all this when we first met in New Jersey. I'd say she remembered the name anyway. So now, I tell her every time I visit...it's me, Seal Swimmer and most times she does remember way back...hopefully she will again today...because lately...it's not so good, she is losing ground." Jim wondered if he said too much, but still with concerns.

"I don't want her to be frightened. If she is, we won't do it.

When we get to her unit, I'll let the Nursing Supervisor know who you are and what's going on...sign any forms. She knows that I'm her health care proxy and POA and that we're going to take a mucosal DNA sample...I'll get the sample at your direction. You OK with all this?"

Max was able to get out a quiet yes and considered why Jim was doing all this.

"Max look at it this way, it's not a dark warehouse in the middle of the night, you didn't come by way of the ocean and you don't have to explain this...to Margaret...I will."

Jim left his Scally cap and sun glasses in the Seville. By the way he positioned them on the dash, Max got the impression it was where they belonged. As they walked side by side from the parking area to the main entrance Jim presented a quick breakdown of the large facility.

"We are going to pass through an Independent Living section before we get to the elevators that take us up to the Skilled Nursing Units. I don't know how many apartments there are in this independent section but the place, in general, is huge. It was a big learning curve for me to find a good place for Justine... I'm still learning a lot. Assisted Living is over there in the wing that heads north but I've never been in it. Most of the residents in this independent wing will be on their way to dinner.

Come on, we'll cut through a common room to the elevators."

They passed down a long corridor, lined with offices and services that opened into a large recreational area. On Max's immediate left were four elderly men of varied shapes and sizes sitting at a poker table playing cards. The pot in the center of the table was pills, different colors, also different shapes and different sizes.

"Lou, I see you one Viagra and raise you one Viagra."

"Vic, come on. You can't raise me with that Viagra. I bet a Flomax...we said one Flomax is worth two Viagra. See me with a Flomax and raise me with another one...I'm eighty-nine years old and ugly...what the hell do I want with Viagra...I need Flomax...Flomax is the new Viagra...get some perspective."

As Max slowed down and considered the game, he mumbled "They're playing for pills...they are gambling what has the most value...which pills have the most value...relative currency in the elderly..."

Jim pulled ahead, amazed at how easily he was off track, "Let's go Max we can make this elevator...remember why we came."

Max snapped out of the distraction, "Why? Why we came? Why...is a very good question."

Justine was standing next to her bed wearing a light blue nightgown and dark blue sweatshirt with Hilton Head in white block letters across the front; grey straight hair touching shoulders, wrinkled face, no eye brows.

"Max, please wait here by the door and give me a chance to say hello."

Max thought that Justine looked lost and confused, he was. Jim eased in front of her.

"Hello Justine, good to see you...it's me, Seal Swimmer."

She didn't acknowledge him, no movement. Jim leaned toward her left ear.

"It's Seal Swimmer. Max and I have come for a visit."

"Seal Swimmer...Seal Swimmer...ah good, how's Bobby?"

Jim turned to Max, "We're going to be OK today Max...but we're starting in Philadelphia."

"Philadelphia?"

Jim stayed with her left ear, "Bobby Vinton?"

"No, no, Bobby...Bobby Rydell. I danced with him on Bandstand, danced a long time. Dick Clark said I was pretty good."

"Did you sing with him too Justine?" Jim knew what was coming.

"Back up. I sang back up for him, Bobby Rydell, on Bandstand." She did some shuffling dance moves and began to sing. *"Forget him...forget him because he doesn't love you. Forget him...forget him because he doesn't care."*

"Beautiful Justine, Bobby was lucky to have you. Sit down on the bed and let me check your cheek so you can keep on singing."

"Singing with Bobby, sure...check my cheek, sure."

"Bobby Vinton?" Jim waved for Max to give him the cotton swabs, took them and ran one along the inside of each cheek as she said *nooo...oooh...nooo.* He gave them back to Max. Jim rubbed her back. "You're a good woman, Justine. I believe that you just helped a lot of Casco souls."

Max felt like he violated her trust. He backed away, eyes still on her face.

"Seal Swimmer, I saw Bat Player yesterday. We were planting trees...Spruce trees...all three of us over there...on the north side, where they're supposed to be. Did you see them?"

Jim raised his shoulders and eyebrows to let Max know he didn't catch the references. "We should go...she's off to somewhere else...it's time for her dinner." He turned again to her left ear and rubbed her back, "I did and they are growing well. It's me, Seal Swimmer Justine, it's good to see you...I'll see you soon."

Justine sat still on the bed, no response.

Neither Max nor Jim said a word until they were alone in the elevator, both staring at the door.

Max spoke, "Did she really sing backup for Bobby Rydell on Bandstand?"

The doors opened and Jim exited the elevator without responding. Max followed and realized his question made no sense.

In the car, it was quiet for most of the ride and again it was Max who broke the silence, "Can I ask you just one question?"

"Just one?"

"No...no, probably more."

Jim didn't answer.

Max spun on the leather front seat toward Jim, his back now to the passenger door, arms reaching to the dash and seatback, "When you said to Justine that you believed she helped Casco souls...did you mean the same thing that Charlie Bay said to me a number of times. He was always talking to me about acting in the favor of Casco spirits...return their bones to the ground...we must act in the favor of spirits. Because you said Casco souls...never heard Charlie Bay say souls...but matching the DNA and returning their skeletal remains to Long Neck Island is certainly acting in their favor...you acted in their favor...the favor of spirits."

"I was raised Casco by Charlie Bay; rituals, ceremonies, seasonal cycles, beliefs. At the same time I was raised Irish Catholic by my mother, same things; rituals, ceremonies, beliefs, plus Sacraments...sometimes I get them confused. It was a constant source of tension and anger between them. I raised Margaret Catholic.

Spirits or souls...maybe I'm just coming to terms with acting in their favor."

Max dropped his arms and leaned in, "You know that you are putting at risk everything that our deal that night in the warehouse buried back in the ground forever. You were so adamant not to create a Casco DNA profile and with a mucosal swab we probably just did. We have a match between Justine and the DNA data from the collection in Syracuse and you created what you asked me to bury away with Sandra's University collection last summer. Why the dramatic change of heart?"

Jim looked at Max for a couple of seconds, slight smile, a man at peace with his action and didn't answer.

Curbside at the Microbiology Building, Max outlined the tentative time line for the DNA comparison. He also let Jim know that he planned to work with Margaret on the documentation of lineal descendancy and cultural affiliation for Justine Thompson, expecting a DNA match. Jim nodded.

Max said, "Thanks" frustrated that he didn't get more of the why.

Jim put on his Scally cap, sunglasses and said, "You're welcome Max."

Chapter Sixteen

Max was surprised with Margaret's reorganization of Charlie Bay's home on the island. The living room furniture had been removed and in its place were some old oak library tables, a desk, some straight-back chairs and brand new hardware including a scanner, much better than his.

"Nice stuff Margaret, this is a great work space."

"Sandra helped with a grant for all the equipment and she was able to get the furnishings from a University storage facility. I don't know whether she had to buy it or what...but I didn't ask."

"She sure can find money. She helped me a lot funding this sabbatical year."

"So as you can see, this is some of the archival material from upstairs and I have found a fair amount on the Thompson family. But before we go over it, let me show you the old dining room, because I have help."

With Max still surveying the room, they drifted into the dining room. The table was reoriented to catch light from the room's double window. It had sewing machines stationed at each end, the center piled with fabric.

"You sew?"

"Of course not, I don't sew...I shop...that's where the help comes in. I met two women from the Tribal Council who are extremely talented seamstresses and we are going through all of the garments, costumes, rugs, blankets...all of it that Charlie Bay saved upstairs. When it's in order, it's cleaned and stored in protective covering and hung over here...not sure where it is going next."

The opposite wall was lined with mobile garment racks. Max smiled, "Margaret...you are making some progress."

"I'll show you what I found on the Thompson family and Justine."

They walked back into the living room office, sat at one of the tables and Margaret opened a file of copied documents.

"Before we start Margaret, is it OK if I ask whether or not you have spoken with your father about Justine?"

"Yes, he did call and we talked...yes, I was upset I never heard about Molly's mother until now. He came here and I showed him what was in the Casco archive from Charlie Bay on the Thompsons."

"He came over here?"

"Yes, he did...he had no idea what Charlie Bay had saved...yes, he was upset that he never heard about it until now.

And we did talk about our unique father-daughter dynamic...I'd say we are working on it. We are going to visit Justine together and I'm going over the inventory with him of Casco Nation artifacts."

"I think this whole hoarding information dynamic you two have going on is remarkable...you're just like..."

Margaret interrupted, "Do you want to see what I have...?"

Max nodded, "OK, let's have a look."

"The first section is Thompson lineage, late nineteenth-early twentieth century. It's diverse and to me anyway...confusing. The big thing for the more recent documentation is baptismal records. By the beginning of World War II the Casco were locked into Christianity. So for Justine and her siblings church records mark their name changes. Her Casco name was Sand Piper Diving, sometimes shortened to Piper Diving or just Piper and later her Christian name was Justine Ann Thompson. There is a notation in Tribal Rolls of Piper Diving giving birth to a daughter. She was unwed at the time and later showed up in a reference of three: Seal Swimmer, Piper and their daughter, Molly."

Max wondered if Justine remembered Jim as Seal Swimmer or Charlie Bay as Seal Swimmer and thought she was talking to Charlie Bay. Margaret knew by the look on his face that she had lost him. So she slapped the file folder to his shoulder and brought him back.

"Sorry, sorry Margaret. This is great...good work. I'll write it up. This is nice timing on the cultural side because I think we have a lead on another collection... I'll find out more this week." Max stood, turned to leave and saw an adjacent table covered with neatly organized cassette tapes.

Margaret caught his gaze to the table, "Glad we have another lead...yes Max...the jackpot. It's a wonderful gift...from my grandfather. I've already started to outline two plays from some of what I've been listening to...these tapes are the Casco story...story of cultural and biological disintegration...all embodied in the arc of Charlie Bay's life."

Max was happy with the file information on Justine Thompson and left Margaret's dive into the Casco story untouched. He thought maybe she should be called Playwright Diving but didn't mention it. Instead he invited her sailing, "Pearl and I are headed out on the STURGEON MOON tomorrow around lunchtime. Are you interested?"

"No, sorry I can't. I'm going to Boston. *Shadowcatchers* has a reading coming up this weekend and I have a lot to rework...this is a good break for me...I don't want to mess it up...but thanks, I would like to go sometime."

"Pearl would enjoy that Margaret, hopefully soon." Max knew he would enjoy it too but, he didn't mention that either.

It was an incoming tide that would be high in an hour, perfect for the ramp angle, almost horizontal from pier to float. Max had no doubt Pearl, at her own pace, could get down the ramp knowing the STURGEON MOON was waiting for her docked on the leeward side. But as a precaution he walked in front of Pearl and backwards down the ramp. Two yardmen looked on, both expecting something to happen to Max. They remembered the Wet One. Max disappointed them but not Pearl as he lifted her aboard the Haven 12 1/2 and positioned her at the helm.

"Deal's a deal Pearl! Let the record show the boat is floating and we are going sailing."

"Margaret's the one who got her floating Max."

Max was glad Pearl brought up Margaret. He wanted to give Margaret the antique portable writing desk and was about to ask Pearl's permission.

"Max, speaking of our deal, you returned the letters but not my desk. Am I ever going to get that back...I want Margaret to have it. I'd like to give it to her soon."

Starting to set the mainsail, he looked at her for a long moment and said, "Sure, I'll bring it over."

Pearl couldn't see his face but there was hesitancy in his voice. She waited, waited, then tested, "You rascal, you wanted to give it to her."

"No, no I didn't...'course not, it belongs to you."

His tone the second time around confirmed it.

He changed subjects. "I brought some champagne splits, fruit, cheese and crackers. Are you hungry?"

Pearl let Margaret and the gift slide, "You are going to have champagne and cheese?"

"No, I have beer and a baloney sandwich."

"Before sailing Max, I'd just a soon stay away from drinking and eating...I don't want to be dulled...miss any of the feel. This is as good as it gets for me...I want every bit of this...I'll drink champagne when we come back...might even eat a little too.

So...you can go ahead and set the main Max...the jib...drop the centerboard halfway...cast us off as soon as you are ready, 'cause I'm ready!"

"You are going to sail us out of the harbor?"

"Ten years in Tucson...you bet I am...tell me if it looks like we're going to hit anything."

In the harbor, it was a light to moderate breeze. The channel was a straight shot across the wind and against the tide. Pearl sat on the leeward side of the cockpit, eyes closed, first three fingers of her right hand touching the tiller. On the windward side, Max pushed off the bow, grabbed and trimmed both main and jib sheets. The boat took off and Pearl, eyes still closed, smiled.

"Max, take the board up all the way. We're not going to need it till we get outside. I want to go closer to shore and get out of this current in the lighter air."

"Closer to shore?"

"You do want to get out of here and into some good air don't you? I'm only going to last a couple of hours...I'd like it to be in some wind. Speaking of wind...tell me about the wind Max."

Max knew his lesson was about to begin. He had never hesitated in the past with Pearl and wasn't going to start now. He responded with no idea where she would take him.

"South-southwest at ten to twelve knots."

"How did you get your information?"

Knowing it was a poor assessment, partially influenced by his early morning check of the marine forecast he mumbled, "Coast Guard station flagpole."

Pearl interjected"...which is on a hill and about a mile from where we are right now. Close your eyes and feel the wind."

"So...we'll both be sailing with our eyes closed twenty yards from shore."

"Close'm Max."

He did and immediately let out the main and jib sheets, conceding to Pearl, "It's more westerly at around eight knots. Can I open my eyes now?"

"Yes."

"Pearl you better head off a little more, we're coming up on the jetty." Max watched as the three fingers of Pearl's hand eased the tiller to windward. The STURGEON MOON picked up speed and they were out of the harbor and past the bell in no time.

Pearl turned her head into the wind, "Let's go across open water on a broad reach to round Green Island...hope the wind picks up a little more and we'll have a beat to windward all the way home."

The smile on her face was enough for Max to go with whatever she wanted.

Pearl did get what she wanted, taking turns with Max at the helm, sailing on the wind and feeling a long forgotten side of Max Sorensen return to her with each puff of air. As they eased into the dock, Max knew he just had the sail of his life. He had recaptured feel.

With the STURGEON MOON put to bed, Max handed Pearl a champagne split.

"Thanks Max. And thank you...that sure beats DNA doesn't it?"

Surprised, Max looked at Pearl, paused and then issued a quiet, "Yes it does."

This was the first chance Margaret had to see Max's lab since he moved to Maine. After a funding meeting with Sandra on the seventh floor of the Anthropology building, she was drifting through basement corridors and trying to find his lab when she heard the high notes. The door was open, she knocked anyway and walked in.

"Sax therapy Max... *Sweet Soul?*"

"Of course, what are you doing here Margaret?"

Max set his sax to one side on the lab table as Margaret looked around. The space was about one third the size of the Casco repatriation lab of last summer and without equipment. There were cataloged storage boxes on the floor surrounding the exam table, each box with packing removed and left open to expose human remains. Max was seated in front of two long bones, one in two pieces, apparently sawed three-quarters of the way through and broken, the other bound in the shaft's center with clay and wet red silk wrapping. Next to the bones was a bowl of water, strips of red and blue silk and a small mound of the clay.

"The bones of each individual in this collection have borings, saw cuts like this one, some are broken...all to harvest DNA. I'm putting them back together...filling in the holes before reburial." Max, voice low, was staring at the broken long bone.

"Thanks for the message Max, about the DNA match on this group of Casco...hope you got my message...my father was pretty happy..."Margaret paused for a response but didn't get one. She went to Max's initial question.

"I just had a meeting with Sandra and she said that you had a second collection...maybe Casco...you turned down DNA to confirm...funding for it and everything. What's going on with you...is this why?"

Max tilted his head up, pursed his lips and raised his eyebrows, "...can't be burned or broken...can't interrupt the dream journey...dream journey for all these Casco..."

Margaret caught the reference but knew Max had been to a place in the spirit dream she never experienced. She met him the only place she could.

"Are you going to put all these broken bones back together...you want help?"

"This is it...last one...but thanks Margaret." He paused. "I never felt harvesting DNA was desecration, until now."

"What are you going to do?"

"Get'm back without DNA...the way I've always done, lumps and bumps on bones, marine hunter-gather ware and tear...on teeth...some grave goods...I'm getting them back...I can do it without DNA...I can...plus a little help in my favor from Charlie Bay..."

After an eye to eye pause, Max started fresh, "The second collection of possible Casco is listed as an ossuary collection...everything is co-mingled..."

Margaret interrupted, "I don't know what ossuary means."

"Sorry, come on sit down for a second..." With his favorite student as an audience, Max was perking up, "well...ossuary burials were practiced by some of the cultural groups in the regions of Ontario and upstate New York. For the Huron, not to be confused with Heron...because I've done that, it was called Feast of the Dead and documented by the Jesuits traveling through the Saint Lawrence River Valley. It occurred every dozen years or so when relatives of the deceased would either, exhume their loved one or at the time of their death remove the flesh, boil it off, bundle the bones and carry them around in a sacred...honored fashion until the Feast. When the time came those participating would select a spot, dig a pit large enough to accommodate those to be buried and then erect a scaffold around the pit. The pit was lined with furs and sometimes ceremonial copper kettles...other significant possessions of the dead...all put in the center. After prayers and feasting the bones of the dead were thrown onto the furs and skins from the surrounding scaffold...more prayers and then it was all covered up...but the bones of all those individuals were mixed in together...co-mingled...no individual burial or individual sites."

"So that's what you're dealing with in this second collection?"

"It was presented to me that way, but I don't think so. First of all it's a much smaller number of individuals; thirty-one, unlike most ossuary burials...well over one hundred. I think the burial site is a mass grave of individuals killed by disease...probably something simple, but deadly, like a new strain of influenza, maybe from the British army on the St. Lawrence and this group was without resistance... throw in some bad weather and little food and they were wiped out...maybe in a week... radiocarbon date for the sample is somewhere around 1775...they were buried near the St Lawrence just inside the New York border...all at about the same time... probably by a group resistant enough to survive the outbreak.

I read the site description and artifact inventory...no post hole evidence for scaffolds, no copper kettles or ceremonial goods, no fur lining of the pit...just a mass grave of co-mingled individuals with utilitarian objects and a few amulets."

Margaret was thinking about the awful death of possibly Casco until she heard amulets. "Amulets, what do you mean, amulets?"

"Great question Margaret...take a look at these photos." Max took three photos from a folder on the table and placed them in sequence facing Margaret. "Here's a heron amulet from Charlie Bay's collection in the Casco archive. Here's a photo of one of the amulets that I requested from the grave goods of the Syracuse collection, now confirmed Casco by DNA..."

Margaret whispered, "They match...there're both heron."

"By the way, all of those artifacts from Syracuse are soon to show up on the island archive's doorstep for you.

But...but take a look at this photo of one of the amulets from the mass grave burial site...the archeologist in charge e-mailed me this an hour ago."

"Max, it's the same carving of a heron...they match...the three are almost identical."

"And that's not all that matches! Look at these bones." Max removed three more photos from the folder. "The first is one you and I took during the Casco repatriation exam and inventory...approximately eighteen year-old female...look at the wear patterns on the teeth...classic marine hunter-gatherer. And the second is from the DNA confirmed collection...also about an eighteen to twenty year-old female...classic marine hunter-gatherer wear...the dentitions match. And from the third co-mingled site a mandible, presumably female, based on the angle of the jaw...gracile form of the bone ...the age is similar to the others...eruption of third molars...dental wear and tear...identical.

Margaret, we have an ethnographic record of known Casco in the area during the period in question, thanks to the San Rochelle family, cultural evidence with the matching heron amulets in three samples and skeletal evidence of marine hunter-gatherers...the primary method of subsistence for Casco, with the Long Neck archive as the known baseline.

I know we can bring them home for repatriation. What do you think?"

"I think that I should start planning the reburial for all of them on the island."

"Plan what Margaret...how are you going to do that without Charlie Bay?"

"Well...the most important thing is...they're returned to Casco ground...the rest...we'll figure out together...I need your help...what...did you already forget you're part Casco Max...these bones a part of you...us?"

Max hesitated. He had forgotten.

The return of the ossuary collection took longer than Max planned, but his request for the return, the evidence and the accompanying narratives were well received by the curator and collections manager. There was discussion, no argument and lots of paperwork. It was the practical of getting the bones back to Long Neck that dragged on from the end of May until the end of June. Finally, the week after the Fourth of July, Max became so frustrated with the pace of the process; he packed a bag, rented a van and with Sandra's blessing headed off to retrieve the remains of thirty-one Casco. Neither he nor Sandra expected it to go well. They were both wrong. A day to get there, a day to inventory and pack the collection and he was on his way home.

During the weeks of waiting for the second collection, Max and Margaret bundled the individuals of the Syracuse cemetery and archived them in Max's lab, anticipating the repatriation ceremony would include both collections. They also planned the burial location for internment. The grave design continued Charlie Bay's trough to the south for individual bundles with the end opening into an ovoid pit running east to west for the co-mingled remains. Considering the size of the collections, there was not enough space on the northern end between last summer's repatriation and Charlie Bay's grave to bury either group of remains. So they left the space between the child's skull and Charlie Bay undisturbed. When they weren't digging, they were dying parachute silk and following Charlie Bay's protocol as much as remembered.

Upon his return with the remains of thirty-one Casco, Max settled into a schedule to organize by bone type and to bundle accordingly the entire ossuary collection without Margaret's help. She was tied up in a two-week run of *Shadowcatchers* at a small summer theatre in Kennebunk. Max kept saying he would make it down to see the play but never did. Margaret was glad he didn't. He was doing the work of two and the sooner completed the sooner reburial. She felt guilty but took consolation in Max's determination to have everything ready by the time she returned.

The morning preparations were few on the day of repatriation. Margaret and Max were meeting Bud Walker at Charlie Bay's work dock to review food for attendees after the ceremony. Bud had everything set to go, including folding tables on the dock which surprised Margaret. He was efficient and off to take care of a couple of last minute errands before the noon ceremony. With a few extra minutes, Max and Margaret sat on the edge of the platform, feet dangling just above the sand, watching Charlie Bay's dory swing in the shifting light air.

"Margaret, I've been thinking...maybe we could get some seaweed and place it on the bones...bones haven't been burned or broken...well, no longer broken...before we have everyone shovel on the sand...I know Charlie Bay didn't do it but..."

Margaret interrupted, "Heartache of the Hunter."

Max still pressing for seaweed, "I just don't know around all this sand where to collect it."

"See those two black plastic bags next to Charlie Bay's traps...I got it yesterday at low tide...from the rocks on the northeast tip of the island."

Max smiled, "I forgot about that little section of ledge...yes "Heartache of the Hunter."

...time to get Casco remains Margaret...it's time for another Casco repatriation."

By noon the sun was high in a cloudless sky and the southwest wind had reached a cooling twelve knot breeze. Max had opened all of the collection archive boxes and set them in even intervals on the eastern edge of the trough and pit. Invited guests and members of the Casco Nation began to make their way from a parking area to the burial site. Jim Garret was walking behind Sandra Walsh and two other anthropology departmental members. He was quick to catch Margaret's eye and nod hello. Soon after, Jim slowed and let Sandra's group drift ahead to the southern end of the burial site while he remained alone on the western side. Max was just about to climb into the pit, now lined with parachute silk, when he saw Jim, lost his balance and stumbled into the center but didn't fall. Margaret saw the near tumble as she began the welcome and wondered how this was going to go. After continuing with thanks to all those who helped in the preparation for the repatriation and a brief history of the Casco to be reburied, she made a tobacco offering in the four directions and to the earth and sky. She then climbed into the trough on the northern end and began lifting bundled bones into the grave with help from any one who wanted to participate. Orientating the bundles with skulls on the east and facing west she worked her way toward Max. With more help than he expected, Max was also placing skulls on the eastern side followed by bundled torso bones in the center and loose long bones on the silk to fill in the western section. Once the deposition of Casco remains was completed, Margaret invited all to cover the bones with seaweed, followed by shoveling sand to fill in the burial sites. After making another tobacco offering in the four directions and to the earth and sky Margaret, feeling that a closing prayer was needed, bowed her head. She whispered an inaudible "Our Father". She was uneasy with the choice, knowing that Charlie Bay would not have said an "Our Father", but it was a part of her people, it belonged.

At the prayer's completion she lifted her face to the gathering and spoke, "Max and I would like to thank you all for coming to return these Casco to sacred ground that they might take their place among the ancestors and the living...present and future...of the Casco Nation."

Margaret looked at Max to see if he wanted to add anything. He shook his head no.

"Now, if we could all move down to the beach and Charlie Bay's work dock we have a feast...a clambake prepared for everyone to enjoy and celebrate this day!"

Margaret was on her way to her father. "Are you coming to the clambake?"

Jim was trying to get away but knew it wasn't going to work. "Clambake? I hadn't planned on that but...OK.

By the way Margaret what prayer did you whisper at the end?"

"You saw that? I wasn't sure what to pray...an "Our Father"...seemed to fit."

"Good prayer...Charlie Bay answered in your voice."

Margaret knew what he meant, "He's not done."

Jim had no idea what she meant and let it linger unquestioned.

On the work dock Bud and Margaret were dishing out soft shell lobsters, clams and sweet corn. Max was drinking beer with Sandra when Jim walked over.

"Hello again, Sandra."

"Jim, how are you?"

Max was puzzled, "You two know each other?"

Sandra paid no attention to Max and excused herself to get clams.

"Taken the Seville out for a ride lately?" Max was still nagged a little about their trip.

"Yes I have. I took it down to Kennebunk to see Margaret's play...don't say anything to her...I'm wrestling with her as a playwright...but she can write. It was good."

Max continued edgy, "Still withholding information from one another?"

"There's an old guy in the play Max, the old publisher who falls in love with a young and beautiful photographer...the old guy wouldn't be you would it?"

Max smiled, he liked this guy, masterful at deflection. "I haven't seen the play, but I think she wrote it before we met."

Sandra returned with clams. All three sat at a table, drank beer, ate clams, lobster and corn and had a wonderful afternoon made even better by Max figuring out who funded Casco repatriation and the Long Neck Island archive.

On his way out Jim took Margaret aside for a few minutes and gave her a photo of Justine that once belonged to Molly. On the back, written in Justine's hand was a prayer and signed: to Molly with love, Mom. Margaret remembered the prayer; one that Molly recited from time to time at the eastern tip of the island. Margaret slipped the photo in her pocket, distracted by the memory.

Jim hugged and kissed her goodbye. He wanted to say, "I love you" but couldn't get out the words.

Sitting in the Pipe boat anchored in the northeast shallows of the Casco River, Max was enjoying midmorning sun after two days of damp cloudy weather. The sun felt so good he was in no rush to start rowing. It had been three weeks since the Casco repatriation ceremony and Max wasn't sure what was coming next. It was only the middle of August and teaching a couple of fall courses as a favor to Sandra was around the corner, but not a concern. He was uncertain about Casco bones. With the reburial of just two small collections did he get them all? There had been no spirit dream since the internment ceremony. But there had been gaps in the dream's frequency before, maybe as long as a month. Max saw not having the dream as meaning simply that he didn't have it for awhile, but not that he would never have it again. As usual, when he over analyzed the spirit dream, he gave himself a headache. Today his response to the confusion was to row.

Max had been rowing in Charlie Bay's dory a few times with the intention of exercise and the hope of handling the boat well enough to fish some of

Burningwater's traps in September for soft shell lobsters. He knew it was an unrealistic expectation to catch anything but an attractive reason to exercise. Max felt old, fat and at a loss to explain how it all happened so fast. In the warm sunshine with an unusually tropical east wind, Max had passed on pondering the spirit dream, accepted old and fat and decided to tackle a more practical problem. Should he row facing aft and see where he had been or face forward and see where he was going. For a biological anthropologist who had spent his whole career looking aft, where human beings had been, he was perplexed as to why looking forward, where he was headed, was so appealing. He decided to row standing and facing forward.

As Max removed the dory's middle seat and made ready to pull the anchor, he checked the tide; outgoing at about mid tide and running strong. With this much current and his limited rowing skills, Max had no intention of leaving the river headed for Spain. He would first row against the current in the shallows going west and then he could drift back east to the work dock if exhausted. Moving to the bow for the anchor line, he faced a steady and getting fuller east wind. Max looked to the horizon and saw what appeared to be huge waves at the mouth of the river, on the rocks to the north and the sandbar to the south. To get a closer look Max pulled his binoculars from the LL Bean bag on board that also held a baloney sandwich and a life jacket. Peering through to the bell at the channel's entrance, he was amazed at the size of the ground swells. The storm off shore that had traveled up the east coast over the last week must have come closer than the marine forecast indicated earlier this morning. The twelve foot high bell at the channel's entrance almost disappeared between swells. As he followed the horizon south, Max caught the even larger breaking waves rolling from the tip of the sandbar forty to fifty yards up onto sand. The center of the channel had ground swells held up by the stiff ocean east wind to form an angry looking curl topped with intermittent breaking foam. It was a rip tide in full force; water pouring out, swells and wind powering in. It was nasty looking from a distance; Max had no desire to see it up close.

Panning further to the south along the sandbar, for afew seconds, he wasn't sure what the gray, U-shaped objects were on the crest of the bar. Harbor seals sunning on the sand, that's what they were, maybe twenty or thirty of them. Harbor seals with their heads and tails in the air; U after U. Max laughed. He had never seen anything like it.

As he watched the seals, doing nothing but sunning, a human head, moving right to left, drifted across the binocular image. Max pulled the glasses down. Kayaks, two of them, just off the edge of the bar and moving seaward, he yelled knowing they would never hear him, "Get out of there! Hey, get out of there!"

In each kayak was an adult and a child, both kayaks heading to a mess; current, wind, waves all in a gigantic rip. Max mumbled as he cut the anchor line with his pocket knife, "This is bad...very bad." He never rowed faster or straighter. Getting close, he saw both adults working hard to get their boats to the sandbar. The seals didn't move. The four people, as Max now made them out, a man and boy in one kayak, a woman and girl in the other, were being drawn out and into the rip. They were panicking. Max could see it in their strokes. He was a hundred yards away. The woman was loosing ground faster than the man. Max went for her first. When he got there, they were in six-foot swells but not breaking. He pulled the girl by the collar up and onto the floor of the dory. The woman tried to climb in, rolled her kayak, fell into water still grabbing the gunnel with one hand. Max pulled her inboard by the shoulders. The dory, broadside to the swells, now with curl, tipped toward the trough by the push of wave and wind. An oar slid through the thole pins into the water. Before it drifted too far, Max kicked off his flip-flops, dove overboard and retrieved it. After pushing the oar into the boat, Max tried to climb back into the dory but couldn't hoist his body. "Too damn old...fat..." He whispered into the side of the hull and held onto the rail.

The second kayak, now ten yards away, capsized in a rip curl. Both man and boy were in the water, the boy was closer. Max had him to the dory in no time. The women grabbed him from Max's arms and jerked him by the life vest into the boat. A wave crested and broke. The dory, bow first, rode over it with Max holding on aft. The kayak was pushed away by the wall of water and the man disappeared. Max saw his silhouette inside the curl of the next wave. He went for him. The man's inflated flotation device brought them both to air. Riding out two more waves, they were back to the dory. The man, unresponsive, was grabbed by the woman, Max pushed, she pulled and he flipped into the dory.

They were being sucked out further into the surf. One hit from a crashing wave and the dory was turned broadside, Max in the water holding on to the leeward rail, weakening. Second crashing wave and the dory capsized, four bodies falling toward Max, under water, up and four heads by his side. "Hold onto the boat, don't let go!"

The man, more alert pleaded, "Save my children...my wife...my family!"

Max saw the Harbor Master's Whaler trying to get close, two on board, one, on the bow with line and harness. The dory rode over the crest of a big wave, good for the five of them, broke bad for the Whaler. Motor still running, the boat was swamped and headed in the opposite direction to bail as much water as possible as fast as possible. They were back, the Whaler still floating. Max, with harness in hand was yelling to the mother, "get in...under your arms...take her with you...you, don't let go of your mother!"

Mother and daughter were off. The dory rolled upright, full of water as the waves were getting bigger, meaner. The Whaler was having trouble getting close. The dory and the three hanging on went further into the rip. Things were slowing down. The dory capsized again. Max hit on the forehead, bleeding warm blood into his eyes. The Whaler was back, Max harnessing father and son...both gone. Max, now slipping under water...pulled under water...his t-shirt torn, riding up, covering his face...pulled it off...quiet.

He bumped bottom sand, not fighting the current, waiting to bounce up, remembering Pearl's words, "let it take you down... wave lets go... push up." But it didn't let go. This wasn't a wave...this was a rip...Max tumbling across the bottom...not up.

At the crest of a backwards summersault, as Max faced the sand, a harbor seal swam underneath him, big eyes rolling to the top of its head, staring up at Max, Max staring back at the seal...darker...the seal gone. Continuing to tumble, upside down now, Max's right hand floated in front of his face. His fingers, close to his forehead but he couldn't move them. He rolled upright, almost sitting in the current, riding backwards, looking somewhere; somewhere back there. Max was bumped just below his left shoulder blade, a glancing blow...felt like Charlie Bay.

Chapter Seventeen

Margaret had spent yesterday's remaining daylight on Bud Walker's lobster boat as part of a large land and water search; no Max.

In the day's morning paper there was a front page article about the rescue on the river and Max's disappearance. Usually reading the Portland paper on line, she saw the story, but couldn't look at it. The article was under the column, News Briefs. Margaret left it on her screen as she headed out before sunrise for the Co-op and Bud's boat to search for Max.

Boston man missing during family rescue

A man from Boston, MA was reported missing from the mouth of the Casco River during the rescue of four people yesterday afternoon. Aaron Cohen, his wife Beverly and their two children, all of North Conway, NH were pulled from the unusually heavy current and surf. The couple's two kayaks capsized in a rip tide a half mile west of the Casco bell near the southern shoreline of the Casco Indian Reservation. The missing man was last seen in the water aiding family members to the Harbor Master's patrol boat. Search and rescue operations are to resume today.

When Margaret got to the Co-op Bud was waiting at the entrance to the fishermen's pier and talking with the Harbor Master. As she approached, she picked up the Harbor Master's side of the conversation, "Twice Bud, he just handed over the harness...not a moment of hesitation...he just handed it over...mother, daughter; father, son...last time around looked like he was bleeding from the top of his head..."

"Morning Margaret...this is Alan Craig, the Harbor Master. Al, Margaret is a friend of Max

Sorensen's...worked together on some Casco reburials...over on Long Neck..."

They shook hands. "Pleased to meet you Margaret, we can use the help...should have the Coast Guard chopper here today...so long as the fog don't roll in. I should get going Bud...sun's coming up."

Alan Craig left for his office and Bud, with Margaret by his side, walked down the fish pier, gray sky, no wind. Bud looked to Margaret, "You sleep?"

"No." Margaret remained facing forward.

"Me neither." Bud wanted to be realistic with her about the chances of finding Max, not raise too much hope. He knew with each passing hour Sorensen's chance of surviving in deep water became less and less. Bud experienced the ocean as cold, beautiful and unforgiving, but said nothing.

Bud and Margaret had covered about half of the nautical miles in their search grid when fog rolled to the mouth of the river. The whole region was socked in with thick fog, no sun and ground swells. The water search and rescue was suspended for the remainder of the day. With word from Al Craig calling it off, Margaret finally broke down. She sat on the first step of the companion way to the cabin, face in hands, rocking front to back. Margaret sobbed off and on to the mooring.

Once Bud had the boat secured and was back in the cockpit, Margaret stood. "I'm OK...I'm done...for now anyway. I think I'll walk the State Park shoreline while there is still some light. I know you have work to do...see you at sunrise tomorrow?"

"Sure Margaret, sunrise."

Casco Indian Reservation

Search and rescue suspended due to fog

The search and rescue of a man missing from the mouth of the Casco River for two days was suspended yesterday due to heavy fog. US Coast Guard Commander Paul Hartwell stated that weather permitting, operations would resume today. The man was last seen in the water during the rescue of a family of four from North Conway, NH.

On Friday before sunrise, with coffee and the morning paper, Jim Garret found in *Around the Area,* the article about Max he dreaded. He never touched the coffee.

Missing man believed drowning victim

by Jake Taylor

Casco River-A man missing since Monday is presumed to have drowned in the waters off the mouth of the Casco River. Authorities have ended a search and rescue mission that has been hampered for the past three days by dense fog. The man is thought to be Max K Sorensen, a university professor from Boston MA. Dr Sorensen was last seen in the water assisting in the rescue of Aaron and Beverly Cohen and their two children. Mr. Cohen stated shortly after his family's rescue that an unidentified man "saved them all" after the two kayaks in which the four were paddling capsized in a rip tide on the Casco River. Alan Craig, the River Harbor Master classified the rip as "the worst in recent memory, every condition required to make the most dangerous rip possible was present...Sorensen rowed his dory right into it to help those folks". Local Harbor Patrol, volunteers and the Coast Guard will begin search and recovery operations today.

Jim was out the door and headed for Margaret on the island, the words, is presumed to have drowned, replaying in his head.

Margaret was sitting at the kitchen table, lap top open, eyes red, sweats and a T-shirt, crumpled Kleenex everywhere. She heard the car pull up and saw the headlights run the wall even with fresh sunlight.

"Margaret, it's Dad. Can I come in?"

"It's open." She stood as her father walked into the kitchen, hugged him and sat back down.

"I came over...did you read today's... on Max?" Jim saw the screen with the newspaper page. "So you saw it."

Margaret nodded.

"I'm sorry Margaret...it's a recovery."

"It damn well better be. His body belongs on this Island...I'm going to help find it...the ocean's not that indifferent that it won't give him back...it did Charlie Bay...we just have to hunt for him."

"Who are you going out with?"

"Bud found me an inflatable dingy to borrow...if I go on the water it will be to check the marsh and feeder streams...I'll walk the mud flats...the rocks of the State Park and any other place I can think of...because I don't think he's in open water...he's going to show up some place on shore...at least that's what the lobstermen say...they know more than anyone else...I'm listening to them...have to try."

"You OK alone with the outboard on the inflatable?"

Margaret nodded. Jim was not convinced.

"It's been awhile Margaret...with an outboard...

If you need anything let me know. I'll be on the Pointer whenever I can...along the northeast with Al Craig...he's using my boat...the Whaler is out of commission...keep in touch won't you." There was worry in his voice.

This was the third time she walked the River along the southeastern tip of the State Park; once at high tide, again at mid tide and today dead low. A few hundred yards down the wet shore she found a four-foot piece of the Pipeboat's gunnel, thole pin holes included. The jagged, splintered length wood was wedged between two shivs of granite protruding from the low water line. Margaret's heart was pounding. It was the Pipeboat, the gift from Charlie Bay to Max. It was the gift for the dream journey, now in pieces, smashed for days against the rocky Maine coast. This was a bittersweet piece of Max and Charlie Bay. She teased it from the rocks and caressed old, familiar wood.

After reporting her find and location to the Coast Guard, she wrapped what was left of the Pipeboat in Casco colors and placed it on a shelf in Charlie Bay's basement.

Margaret gave Sandra a call to let her know about finding a small section of the Pipeboat. It wasn't so much that Sandra needed to know, it was an excuse to talk with her about Max, the Casco, anything to help integrate the loss. She missed Max and she needed to talk. So did Sandra and that evening, she invited Margaret to dinner, day six of search and recovery.

After a small meal of grilled chicken, corn on the cob and salad, they sat in Sandra's living room, each with a bowl of vanilla soft serve ice cream topped in raspberries.

"I find soft serve ice cream soothing when stressed, which is most of the time."

Margaret smiled and knew that Sandra would not take long to go somewhere specific. It came fast.

"Margaret, I plan to resign as chair of the Department as of September 1st and take an indefinite leave from teaching. It's been in the works awhile, not just since the loss of Max. With all the funding development for you and Max as well as other Casco projects, I've directly or indirectly created a position for myself. I didn't really plan it all out...it simply evolved and it fits...remarkably at this time in my life and career it fits. The killer is...I thought it would fit for Max as well..." Sandra's eyes filled and her voice cracked.

Before Margaret could respond, Sandra's cell rang. She checked caller ID.

"Excuse me, I have to take this.

Hello Stan, how are you...That's right. I forgot all about it... I'm so glad you called...sure that'll be fine. It's a week right? Sure...sure will...have a good time. Bye, Stan.

That was Stanley Chevinski the CME."

Margaret looked puzzled.

"The State of Maine's Chief Medical Examiner, I'm a consultant for the Office and with the end of the summer he has some coverage conflicts and wanted to make sure I'd be available for forensics to consult...I forgot all about it...good he's on the ball.

So...Margaret, bottom line, it looks like you are going to have some help."

"I can't believe it Sandra...this is great. You know I've been pretty overwhelmed since that first day I walked through the place...Charlie Bay saved everything and I've been making decisions...without really knowing what I'm doing."

Sandra said with a smile, "I know."

Margaret laughed, first time in a while, she laughed hard and her eyes filled with tears. Sandra reached into her pocket. Margaret thought it was for a tissue. It was for a carved heron amulet.

"I walked in on Max carving this one night in his office...looks like he almost finished it...not bad. I don't think Max ever carved anything in his life. He told me...when it was done he'd wear it...so he would never forget...he was part Casco...found it when I was clearing out his desk." Sandra gave the heron amulet to Margaret.

Her father's concerns with the inflatable were justified. She was rusty about the outboard. Before her first time out, Margaret was reviewing the sequence she remembered as a kid; pump gas, choke, neutral, pull, and adjust throttle. At least she was tied to the float and not drifting in the river. She felt eyes on her, pulled the cord and the motor started. She heard applause, looked up to the pier and saw Bud with another fisherman smiling and clapping. Life was sliding back into moments of normalcy, everyday events waiting uncomfortably to meet the next wave of sadness. Margaret gave them no response. She cast off, spun the inflatable around with the engine in a tight space and took off full throttle. She smiled knowing that it all came back in a heartbeat, but the two on the pier never saw the smile as she headed up river.

There was one decent-sized feeder stream that ran into the north branch of the Casco River. Margaret could make it out from Long Neck and on day eight of recovery, she wanted to check it. Unlike most of the river's smaller estuaries this one, for some reason, was deeper and lined with sand, not mud. Margaret figured deeper therefore stronger current and more chance of carrying Max into a secluded patch of sand and sea grass. As Margaret moved into the shallow water on an outgoing tide, she was careful not to beach out the inflatable. She anchored the boat in a reasonable amount of water to give her about a half an hour to search the area on foot. Margaret was wading toward wet sand when her phone rang. It was Sandra.

"Margaret, they found Max."

By Sandra's tone, she knew Max was dead. "No."

"Yes Margaret...I'm sorry to tell you...Max is dead. We need to talk. As soon as you can come on over to my office, I'm not going anywhere. I'll be here."

"OK. I will." She shut off her phone, walked to dry sand and sat facing the warm sun.

"Margaret, would you like coffee or anything? You hungry...cause I could order out for something?"

"No thanks Sandra, I'm really not hungry."

"Me either...your father know?"

"I got him on the way over...the Harbor Master gave him the news this afternoon. He was on his way back from Providence...business trip. I also got hold of Max's Aunt Pearl...she's not doing that well herself...fading...Max truly loved her." Margaret seemed to drift.

"Margaret I spoke with Max's ex-wife Linda, who lives in Albany..."

"Ex-wife? Max still wears a wedding ring. I thought he was married...I didn't..."

"Long story...it's been about five years. I spoke to her when Max went missing and she let their two sons know about the search and rescue...her youngest left Baltimore for Albany and they were planning on coming here if anything broke...the older son is in San Diego. Anyway, I've spoken with her a few times this week and then again today with the news of finding Max's body. She asked me to call her with the positive ID."

Margaret cringed with the words, Max's body. Sandra read her face.

"About Max's body Margaret..."

"What about it?"

"Well...because the ME's Office is short-staffed, I'm the only one around to do the ID from..."

"You would do an autopsy?"

"Do you want to hear this, about Max's remains?"

"Yes I do." Margaret wanted to know and Sandra wanted to tell her.

"As you know Max was in the water a long time. Apparently, when he was swimming during the rescue, he took off some of his clothes; shoes, probably sandals or flip-flops, his shirt, maybe swim more easily and his pants were torn either by getting caught on the boat or later on the rocks.

Bottom line, when a human body is in the water a long time with a lot of exposed skin, flesh...it is attacked by scavengers, mostly crabs...where there were no clothes, Max's body was...in those places, consumed to bone by opportunistic scavengers. There are no prints...facial recognition isn't possible....markings may or may not be present...like a..."

Margaret interrupted, "So what happens?"

"The ME's Office takes a DNA sample, a look at the lungs, autopsy of soft tissue...the rest of the body is skeletonized, cleaned and sent to me. Max's bones will be at my lab tomorrow around ten...for examination, dental x-rays...the comparison films from Max's Boston dentist arrived today by e-mail...for ID."

Margaret had the look that this was all a little strange.

"Margaret, he would do it for me."

Margaret thought of Max's body scavenged by crabs and felt nauseated.

Body found near mouth of Casco River

by Jake Taylor

The body of an unidentified man was found yesterday afternoon by a fisherman a mile northeast of the mouth of the Casco River. The body was discovered in a tidal pool by Andre Willette of Sanford while surfcasting off the rocks of the State Park. The remains, believed to have been in the water for some time, were sent to the Medical Examiner's Office for autopsy and identification.

Eight-thirty came early; she had been awake and pacing until three before finally falling asleep. But she didn't feel tired and knew that she still had plenty of time to be at Sandra's lab by ten. Studying the article in the morning paper on the recovery with her first cup of tea in awhile, Margaret wondered where the tidal pool was on the shoreline and how she could have missed it. She had a second cup, showered and was knocking on the lab door at quarter to ten.

"Margaret, I wasn't expecting you here this morning." Sandra was surprised and cautious. "Why are you here?"

"To help you."

"Are you sure you want to do this?"

"Max would have done it for you."

Sandra had just unpacked Max's remains and was distracted. She had no idea what Margaret meant by the comment but was happy she came. Sandra opened the door wide enough for Margaret to see Max's bones on the exam table as she whispered, "OK. We'll do this together."

Margaret's eyes were fixed on the remains. Sandra had placed Max's bones in no particular order next to the shipping container. As Margaret walked to the table she commented, "His bones are so white...there's not a spot on them...so sterile looking."

"Part of the cleaning process, before they are sent to me...cleaned by soaking in bleach."

That his bones were so white troubled her but at least they weren't broken.

"Margaret if you need a minute before we..."

"No, sorry Sandra, sorry...I just expected them to look more like the Casco...I'm OK, what can I do?"

"Well, since your computer skills are probably much better than mine, I'd like you to deal with the images as I capture them. I plan to confirm the ID first and we'll do that with teeth. I've set up two screens; one has his most recent x-rays from his Boston dentist, the other will show the images I take...so I need you to size both sets of radiographs the same for comparison...it may take me a couple of tries to get the angle on my images to line up with the existing films."

It didn't take many tries and Margaret had matching images on each screen in no time. However, Sandra wanted matches, which she got, in all four quadrants of the jaw before she picked up the phone. First she called the ME's office following a standard verbal protocol for positive ID, faxed a hard copy and then called Linda. Margaret asked if she wanted her to wait outside and Sandra shook her head, "no, but if you want to...you can start arranging Max's bones for the digital exam and archive..." She dialed the second number on the landline.

The phrase, Max's bones, lingered with Margaret, no doubt left; they were Max's very white bones. She started to tear. It was another wave. She wondered if she could hold herself together until she heard, "Linda, this is Sandra Walsh." Margaret knew that listening to one side of an important conversation was never a good thing but she did anyway.

"We have a positive ID on the remains...I'm sorry to tell you that it is Max...you'll make those arrangements from the road...good...the Medical Examiner's Office can forward that paperwork for you...I'll make sure that's done...I'll have everything prepared here for the pickup later on this afternoon. How long will you be in Hartford...oh at Bradley Airport... then you'll be here tomorrow morning. Good we'll see you then...goodbye Linda." Sandra had tears in her eyes.

"You OK, Sandra?"

"I'm still mad as hell at him.

Let's take a break...get outside...you call Pearl...I'll call Jim...ah your father...meet you back here in an hour."

By the precise alignment of Max's bones on the exam table it was clear to Margaret that Sandra had been back and working for some time.

"Hi Margaret, I thought we'd follow the exam and recording protocol you and Max used on the other Casco." She was all business and distant. Margaret followed her lead and their words were functional until Sandra spoke, "I spoke with Linda again...she had talked with her sons...they've decided to have Max cremated...sprinkle the ashes in the ocean off Biddeford Pool...someone from the Harborside Crematorium staff is coming by here at four...to pick up Max's remains."

"What!" Margaret set down the digital camera wand, stretched both arms onto the edge of the lab table and leaned over Max's bones, looking down but not looking at the bones. "What...cremation...burn them to dust and dump them in the ocean...we just got him back from the ocean...Max is Casco...why would anyone do that..."

"Margaret, I don't think she knows Max is part Casco."

Margaret began to mumble, "as long as the bones are not burned or broken...can't be burned or broken...they aren't going back." She picked her head up. I'd like to talk with Linda...can I have her number?"

"That might be tough, their picking up her oldest son...flying in from San Diego to Hartford about now and headed to the coast for some time alone, together as a family... in New Hampshire or southern Maine...she said she'd check in early tomorrow."

"But..."

"Margaret, the boys just lost their dad."

Margaret was embarrassed. She was thinking of Max, who he had become, what she wanted for him. She felt selfish, not thinking about his sons. "I'd like to try anyway...maybe I can still catch her...fill her in on the last year or so...maybe my request not to cremate would make more sense."

Sandra gave her the number. "I'll keep on working...so we can get this done."

No sooner had Margaret left the lab than she returned. "You were right...straight to voice mail...hopefully she'll call...sometime."

There was a tone to her voice; it caught Sandra who was looking for it. Margaret was plotting, already with a plan. Sandra would have been disappointed if she didn't. Their conversation continued as functional, productive, another Casco exam and archive nearing completion. But this was Max Sorensen and Sandra didn't buy Margaret's compliance. It prompted a story as they finished up.

"You know Margaret, when I was trying to talk Max into repatriating the Casco collection with you last year and he was arguing for continued research...new technologies...human bones as simply objective data...he got so desperate that he said...as only he could have said, that when he died...if he were interesting enough...he wanted to have his bones cleaned and kept right here." Sandra started chuckling and Margaret's mouth dropped open. "Ya...he wanted them kept right here so students could study whatever it was that made him interesting enough...right here with the rest of our collection of human bones...but we already have plenty of bones from Euro-American males in their late fifties...of course we didn't know he was part Casco" Sandra paused, "...ah Max, you know I loved you...I loved you Max." Sandra sniffled and mumbled "...too bad Max, those draws are already full of interesting bones..." Her voice trailed off to quiet.

Neither woman moved. They were done.

"If you want me to Sandra I'll clean up and shut everything down...wait for the crematorium pick up...if you need to go."

Without looking at Margaret, Sandra regained her tone and energy, "Good, because Linda asked me to write Max's obituary for tomorrow morning's paper...think I'll head to the ocean...haven't been in a while...write there...

Please turn off the lights and lock the door when you leave."

Lock the door was the first thing she did. If the crematorium driver came, he'd have to wait. With the lab to herself she methodically replaced every one of Max's bones with a matching counterpart from the bone drawers. There were now two sets of bones on the lab table; Max's and a composite. She cleaned a top end drawer, laid a foam pad as a liner and placed Max's remains inside. Before closing the drawer, she set the small plastic bag containing his wedding ring next to the bones of his hands. "This is temporary Max. I'll get you to Long Neck."

She packed the container from the ME's Office with Sandra's bone collection and sealed the cover. Margaret tried Linda again, still straight to voice mail. After taking some breaths and disciplining herself not to rethink what she had just done to buy time, she unlocked the door and waited.

OBITUARY

Maximilian K Sorensen, 57; Anthropologist

Casco Nation-Dr Max Sorensen drowned on August 17th while aiding in the rescue of four people from the Casco River. His body, after missing for eleven days, was recovered by the Coast Guard and identified by the Medical Examiner. Dr Sorensen was 57.

Max was beloved by his students as an educator who consistently taught wildly popular courses in Biological Anthropology and Human Evolution. Somewhat eccentric and always entertaining, he filled entry level anthropology courses in numerous colleges and universities throughout the Northeast during a long academic career.

Dr Sorensen's research focused on the Nile Valley and the study of an elite ruling class present prior to the Pharaohs. Most recently, he returned to Boston and additional research with the Casco Nation in the repatriation of ancestral remains.

"Max was passionate about acquiring knowledge, utilizing technology, passing it on to students and equally passionate about his sons' lacrosse," said colleague Alice Lowery.

Max Sorensen was married to Linda Roberts of Albany. Their marriage ended in divorce. He is survived by two sons; James, of San Diego, CA and Paul, of Baltimore, MD.

Funeral services, at the family's request, will be private.

Margaret had read the obituary twice before her cell rang. The only person that either called or showed up at sunrise was her father. She almost didn't look at the ID. But she did and was surprised, this time it was Sandra.

"Margaret, there was a fire last night at the Harborside Crematorium."

"Well, isn't that the idea?" She was on her second cup of coffee and had a quick edge from the last two paragraphs of Max's obituary.

"Margaret some of the bones you switched for Max were plastic...resin duplicates...they melted. Smoke everywhere...no one was injured...they just had to shut everything off and air the place out before the sprinklers...you gave them plastic bones!"

"Oh...I did? They all looked the same to me...all so white."

"I need you to speak with Linda before the crematorium director does...get this straightened out one way or the other...you didn't bury him on the island did you?"

Margaret hesitated knowing she thought about it, "No."

"Are Max's remains still at my lab?"

"Yes."

"Good.

OK Margaret, you got the time you wanted to protect Max...now talk with Linda...lead with your heart like you always do and let she and her sons make the decision. You know I'll defend and protect you with every one else...but you talk with Linda."

Chapter Eighteen

"Hello, Linda Roberts?"

"Yes."

"Linda my name is Margaret Garret. I'm a friend of Max and Pearl. I left a message on your voice mail last night. I wondered if we could talk...maybe meet. There are some things about Max that I think you and your sons should know...I can drive to some place that will make it easy for you. I won't take up too much of your time...I realize this is a hectic and difficult..."

"Unfortunately Margaret, this morning there is another issue that I have to take care of first... there was a message, right after yours, from the Director of the Harborside Crematorium...he needs to speak with me about picking up Max's ashes. Evidently there was a problem...I'm...ah...not...not sure what's going on so I need to take care of that this morning."

"Linda, I am responsible for that problem and I'd like the chance to explain face to face...before you go to Harborside." Margaret paused to no response. "Linda, Max was my friend and I care about him greatly...over the last year and a half he became a very important person to the Casco Tribe...there are things you need to know...about Max."

"Well...my sons are still sleeping and the message asked me to call back after nine so..."

"Where are you?"

"Kennebunk."

"There's a clam shack at the junction of Rt. 1 and Rt. 9 in Kennebunk, just before you get to Biddeford...I could meet you out front in thirty minutes...they won't be open...there's some picnic tables in a grove to the side of the building."

"OK, OK Margaret I'll meet you there but, I won't have a lot of time...I have to pick up Max's ashes."

"Thanks Linda, meet you in the parking lot."

Linda appeared a little puzzled but mostly sad as they walked to a table. She was tall, maybe taller than Max. Margaret was feeling guilty about withholding Max's remains from Linda and her sons. She was also nervous about where to start the story; she said the first thing that popped into her head, "Well, Max would've liked talking here...you know, when he was anxious...fried clams, onion rings...all the disgusting, salty, greasy stuff."

Linda smiled, "You knew him well."

They sat down facing one another at a picnic table in the shade, pine trees still in morning cool. Margaret had no script, no plan, just talk and hope she hit the right parts of Max.

"Max and I met over a year ago...I was helping my grandfather rebury members of the Casco Nation that had been removed from their burial grounds on Long Neck Island...not too far from here. Sandra Walsh was in charge of the collection of Casco skeletal remains...over a hundred individuals...for the University and she asked Max to help her..."

Linda, did you know Max was part Casco?"

"Part Casco...part Native American...no, no I had no idea."

"He found out about three months ago...once Pearl heard he was working with Casco bones she led him there...enjoyed every bit of Max's self-discovery. The thing that was so remarkable about a very complicated sequence was...up until the University collection was reburied...Max was the enemy, of my grandfather, to me, even to Sandra...he did not want to rebury any Casco bones. He was always fighting against knowledge lost. Max thought they belonged in an archive for students, researchers...for DNA. He was the enemy, knew it, even liked it. His insensitivity to Casco belief drove me crazy. He was oblivious to the spirit world, what turned out to be our Casco spirit world...but he changed...Charlie Bay Burningwater, my grandfather changed him."

With the thought of the spirit dream and how much Max changed, Margaret started to drift. Her eyes filled with tears, another wave hit.

"Margaret?" Linda saw her struggle.

Margaret pulled the heron amulet from her pocket and set it on the table. She sniffled and rubbed her nose but left her eyes alone.

"With the University collection repatriated, my Grandfather told Max to keep hunting for more Casco remains...in other universities...museums. There were still Casco out there that needed to be reburied...place their spirits in order. Max found two more collections, one with DNA. He was always rambling on and on about DNA...how it could do what lumps and bumps on bones couldn't do. When he chose not to pursue DNA with the second collection, I went to see him in his lab. He was repairing broken bones with clay and Casco silk...the DNA harvesting sites. He was distraught...said it was a desecration of the Casco...they must be repatriated...bones not be burned or broken...so that their spirits might live again.

Linda, Max rediscovered belief...he discovered his Casco heart. Of course, classic Max, he got distracted and forgot he was part Casco from time to time...that's why he carved this...a heron amulet...a Casco amulet."

Margaret picked it up and showed the unfinished carving to Linda.

"He carved this?"

"I have an eye witness. He was planning to wear it ...never forget he was part Casco.

I would ask you and your sons...to consider having Max buried in the Casco burial grounds on Long Neck...his bones not be burned or broken...buried according to Casco traditions."

"But the cremation...I'm supposed to pick..."

"Ah...that...that is where I meddled...I meddled into your family's affairs...I'm the problem...there was a fire at the crematorium...to buy time and the chance to speak with you...I gave the pickup driver from the crematorium other human bones...lab specimens...evidently some plastic bones...Max's remains are still in Sandra's lab...I don't believe that Max ..."

Linda leaned to the center of the table, "You had no right to do that."

"Yes and no. I had no right to make that decision without you and your sons. But, I do believe I have a right to act in favor of Max's future...act in the favor of his spirit. In Casco belief...no bones shall be burned or broken to block the dream journey...they must be buried."

Over a weathered and grease-stained picnic table they both leaned to center, eye on eye, angry for all kinds of different reasons. After what seemed to Margaret a very long time, she made her final reach.

"If you'd be willing, I'd like to take you and your sons to Long Neck Island, to the burial site...you decide."

Margaret left them standing on the ridge, next to Charlie Bay's grave facing the sun in a southwest wind. They were three visitors against blue sky and brushed clouds. Margaret looked back over her shoulder to see Linda bury her face in her hands, body shaking as her two sons surround her in open arms. Back at the house, Margaret slid into the rocker on Charlie Bay's front porch and waited.

Before they climbed the steps to the porch, mother and sons looked east to the mouth of the Casco River and let their view drift south to the sand bar. Linda pointed and spoke a few words meant only for her sons. Margaret didn't move until they started up the stairs and onto the porch.

"Margaret, we all feel this island burial ground is where Max belongs. If you would, we'd like you to make the arrangements with the Casco people in charge for Max's burial...we were hoping soon."

"How's this Saturday morning around ten...gives us a day to get ready? I am the Casco people in charge." Margaret smiled.

Linda looked to her sons, both nodded and smiled at Margaret, "Saturday at ten is fine then...thank you. We'll be staying in Kennebunk if you need to reach us. Tomorrow, I'm planning on visiting Pearl." Linda was headed for the screen door.

Margaret following, "I'm sure she would enjoy that very much. Can I get you anything before you go? Are you hungry...how 'bout a blueberry muffin for the road?"

James and Paul both said, "Sure."

At the same time Linda said, "No thanks, we're all set. We have to go."

Even though it was more than a week until Labor Day, the Canadian air made it feel like fall. Margaret was standing at the southern end of the Casco burial ground to greet all who arrived for the ceremony. Sandra, James and Paul waited on Charlie Bay's work dock for their procession to the grave site. Still a little uneasy about Casco traditions and prayers for a burial ceremony, Margaret was pacing when she saw her father and mother walking arm in arm toward her. "Mom...I'm glad you came."

"I shouldn't have worn sandals with heals. I didn't know what to expect...of course your father was no help."

"But those are nice...you look good. I think you'll be fine...the ground is harder up here...hi Dad." Margaret gave them both a kiss on the cheek and Jim surveyed the burial site.

"Who dug the hole?"

"I did."

"I thought you might have Margaret...next to Burningwater."

Margaret was surprised her father knew Charlie Bay's grave, but let it go, "Digging the grave isn't the hard part...I'm still not sure about what to say and when."

Jim looked to his wife, "Terry, that's Dean Columbo and Marie...you remember from the fund raiser with the Parkers. Sandra asked me to watch for them. Would you invite them to come stand with us. I have some things to discuss with Margaret before they come over."

"I'll go and get them. They look a little lost...give you a minute."

"Thanks.

Margaret, if it makes you feel any better...and I've been through enough of these with Charlie Bay...the "Our Father" is a good prayer for you to say in the same spot you did before...after Max's bones have been laid in the grave."

Margaret looked at her father, mouth open, stunned. "What?"

Jim opened his palms and tried to look innocent, smiling, "Seal Swimmer's son...remember...ten-year old kid...apprentice to one of the keepers of the western burial ground...on Long Neck...like my father and his father before him."

He was rescued by the Dean, "Dean Columbo, I'd like to introduce my daughter, Margaret."

Margaret, on her way to shake hands with the Dean, mumbled to herself, "Max truly would've enjoyed this one...never would've heard the end of it."

As Margaret walked toward the path to the work dock, she was amazed at the number of people present: Aunt Pearl on oxygen, with a walker, son Jack by her side, Casco tribal members including the seamstresses, academic friends and colleagues, lobstermen, a lot of lobstermen, the Harbor Master, the Cohen family, the grateful father already with tears in his eyes and Linda with a man, a tall man. Margaret was happy all of these people came to honor Max but hurt for him, knowing he would be hurt by the man at Linda's side. Considering it had been five years and Linda looked so happy, at ease, and that Max probably had more than his share of chances to work on their relationship, she let the thought go. She held tight to knowing that Max was going to be buried next to Charlie Bay, his bones not burned or broken, in place for the spirit journey. Margaret was thankful to Linda and their sons for that gift. She gave Sandra the signal to begin.

Paul Sorensen was the first to emerge from the path by the blueberry bushes. He was carrying a wooden lacrosse stick, woven leather pouch, lightening bolts and dots of hail painted on the shaft. James Sorensen followed with the recovered section of the Pipeboat for the spirit dream journey. More than a few steps behind, breathing heavy, slow up the path, was Sandra Walsh, Max's mentor, colleague and friend. She was carrying Max's bones wrapped in silk of Casco colors. Margaret caught Sandra's eye, smiled it was OK, there was no rush. Sandra eased up and fell even further behind. Paul and James stopped at the edge of the grave and stood by

Margaret. With Sandra's arrival next to the three, Margaret made a tobacco offering in the four directions, to earth and sky. Then holding James' hand, she climbed into the burial pit. Sandra handed down Max's remains and Margaret oriented them in an east-west direction. Bending over Max's bones, Margaret reached into her pocket and removed the partially carved heron amulet and tucked it into the bundle. She then received the lacrosse stick from Paul and the piece of the Pipeboat from James and laid them on each side. She adjusted the bundle one last time and reached for Paul. He helped Margaret out of the grave as James moved a large woven basket close to the pit's edge. Margaret took a handful of seaweed from the basket and threw it onto the silk. James, Paul and Sandra followed as Margaret invited anyone who desired to add seaweed. The Casco Tribal members didn't hesitate nor did Jim Garret. After the seaweed, Bud Walker, other lobstermen, Aaron Cohen now sobbing and Al Craig covered Max's remains with sand. Pearl made her way to the grave with her walker. Margaret gave her a handful of sand that Pearl spread like seed over fresh ground.

Margaret decided not to eulogize Max. No need. Instead, bowing her head she whispered a quiet prayer and ended the ceremony with a tobacco offering. Before the gathering dispersed, Margaret extended an invitation to all for coffee and blueberry muffins on the front porch.

Standing beside Margaret, Sandra leaned to her ear, "The amulet...I saw you put the amulet into the bundle...did you slip his wedding ring in there too?"

Margaret leaned back, "Yes...Alice Lowery in the obituary...that was you wasn't it...you just made her up?"

Sandra looked straight ahead, eyes watery, "Yes...thought Max would enjoy that."

Getting the answer she already knew, Margaret was on an agenda, they would have their time for tears later, "I need to catch those two...I'll see you at the house...my mother is here...I'd like you to meet her."

Margaret chased after James and Paul, "Hey, guys, wait up...I didn't want to miss you." As she caught them, she reached into her pocket and took out her phone, "Here is a gift for each of you...it's my grandfather telling a Casco legend that was very important to your father...the seaweed might make a little more sense after you hear this...sorry I didn't get it to you sooner...you know you are always welcome here."

James responded, "Thanks Margaret we know that."

Margaret held up her phone. Paul and James took out their phones and in succession, gently bumped Margaret's. The story is called, "Heartache of the Hunter". She considered hugging them both until she saw Pearl and Jack getting ready to leave. The moment passed, "I'll see you up at the house."

She was on her way to Pearl and wondering if Linda, the tall man and the rest of the Sorensen family would stay around.

"Ah Margaret...Jack's off for the car.

If you could, I'd like you to stop by the house sometime soon...there's a portable antique writing desk at my place that Max wanted you to have." Her speech was labored.

"Max wanted me to have...?"

"Yes, he did." She paused and Margaret waited as Pearl gathered her strength to speak. When it came, her voice was clear and strong, "Take consolation Margaret...Max became who he was...he hunted long...we both must remain faithful to doing the same...he became who he was Margaret...you must remain faithful to the same."

Margaret froze, ingesting each one of Pearl's words. Jack came with the car and they both helped Pearl get into the passenger seat, oxygen in her nose, canister in her lap. Before she closed the door, Margaret, still on her words, "Max became who he was..." gave Pearl a kiss on the cheek. With the door shut, Pearl had Jack lower her window.

In a soft voice with very little facial expression Pearl said, "Margaret...I'm leaving you the STURGEON MOON."

Her head tipped back as she sucked in oxygen. The window rolled up and Jack drove off.

"I brought lunch; grilled chicken on pita, no mayo for you and steak and cheese with peppers for me!"

Margaret laughed at her father's enthusiasm for lunch. This was an important event. Jim Garret had called his daughter, without prompting, to be first to review the plans for the new bridge to the island. He had the sandwiches and drinks set up on the tailgate of his old SUV and he was pulling out architectural drawings as Margaret walked from Charlie Bay's truck.

"Do you want to eat first...or look at plans?"

"Eat...I'm starving!"

"Good choice...this steak and cheese isn't going to stay warm forever...here you go...here's chicken."

After food and small talk about a wind shift and some bad weather moving up the coast, Jim spread the plans out on the tailgate.

Margaret was surprised. The new bridge was so much larger than the old. It was wider and arched. "It's much bigger..."

Jim was excited to discuss it, "Four main points: two-way traffic, railed off bike and pedestrian path on the right, a channel arch so boat traffic can still pass underneath at high tide...there's a great tidal pool and beach up river... and last, expanded parking with the bike and walking path beginning over there...extending all along here...what do you think?"

"This is a big bridge..." Margaret paused, looked into the SUV and back to her father, "I think you're up to something. What are all those other plans rolled up in the truck...those all can't be of the bridge...what's going on?"

"It didn't take you long did it...I guess it's better sooner than later, hop in."

When they pulled up in front of the collapsed salt marsh hay barn, Jim walked behind the SUV and looked west, across the knolls of Long Neck and onto acre after acre of marshland. Margaret stood next to her father and followed his view.

"Look at that would ya...almost three thousand acres...

I'm going to stop development on the Casco Casino...pull the plug on the whole thing...casino, hotels, roads...boats, all of it...haven't told anyone yet...but I've been thinking about this for a while...it's time...time to change direction and let it go."

"But..but, last I heard, you were just about to start."

"Good thing we didn't." Jim smiled.

"Why?"

"Short version or the long one?"

This didn't happen often and Margaret wanted all of it, "Long."

Jim opened the tailgate, "OK. We might want to sit."

They both sat on the tailgate, feet dangling, Jim still gazing over the marsh, Margaret's eyes on her father.

"Since the night I met Max on the dock and we agreed to rebury all those Casco remains...maybe even six months before that...the casino gaming landscape had been changing...changing fast...not just in Maine but all over the northeast. The shift has been driven by money...the states and municipalities...once happy to get a cut from Native American Reservation gaming saw the revenue potential without Indians. If they changed the law...circumvented the feds and the need for reservation land...they'd get a bigger piece of the pie."

Jim looked at Margaret, "bottom line Margaret, there is only so much money to go around in the gaming business. Foxwoods saw a decrease in revenue with the competition from Mohegan Sun....Rhode Island is down and Massachusetts's legislature has put the state in the middle of everything. Maine has also made it possible for a municipality like Bangor to have Las Vegas style gambling...racino at the Downs. The trend is away from federally recognized Indian gambling to state reconstructed gaming laws...all designed to generate revenue for the states. Massachusetts is the model that has capped the industry...I don't think Maine is far behind...plus then you add on New York, New Jersey and Pennsylvania, the whole region has become saturated. These guys are dreaming if they think they are all going to survive...but not me, not with the Casco future. That's a different dream."

Jim turned to the marsh as Margaret responded, "You're protecting the Casco Nation."

"Maybe...but I'm definitely preserving the marsh. I already rubbed it out once when I agreed to the landfill. I'm not going to rub it out again with a casino. This is the land of the Casco people, it requires preservation...it's the center of the circle." Jim looked back to Margaret, "...ah, maybe there is more Seal Swimmer in me than I thought."

"So, what are you going to do?"

Jim reached into the back of the truck for a roll of drawings, "Let's start here."

The SUV was parked facing the collapsed roof. Circling around to the front of the truck, he spread out a set of drawings on the hood. As soon as she caught a glimpse, she knew; barn theatre.

"These are preliminary but you'll get a feel for some of the initial ideas for this structure and the others."

"The others?"

"Yes, but we'll start here. The theatre is bigger than the footprint of the barn. As you can see it still looks like a barn but inside it is a black box theatre that seats a little over two hundred. The wall to the east, the barn doors, pick up the contour of the hill rise and with the doors open, there is additional lawn seating. Dressing rooms, prop storage all that stuff is in the walkout ground floor to the west. There is pick up and drop off on the south side that meets all accessibility requirements. This building and the others are designed to physically fit the island...look like a part of Charlie Bay's home.

Same thing for the Casco Cultural Center...we'll use the footprint after the fire, including the fireplaces...it will look something like this..."

Jim rolled up the theatre and rolled out the Casco Cultural Center.

Margaret whispered, "Cultural Center?"

"Yup...with classrooms, meeting rooms, a Tribal Council room, a kitchen...all accessible...parking to the north to serve this building and the Casco Burial Grounds that overlook the whole thing.

And then, here's an addition and remodeling of Burningwater's home..." Jim spread out more plans, "...all remodeling is on the inside of the house...to become the Casco Archive and Research Center...inside climate-controlled storage and preservation rooms...part of the addition on the north is a wood working and boat building shop...large enough to build a Bank Dory. The porch gets expanded to the east and wraps around to the south...accommodates four times as many people.

From there we'll see how things grow...maybe housing...expand Charlie Bay's work dock..." Jim thought Margaret had enough and was surprised by her question. She was thinking differently.

"How are you going to fund all this without gambling?"

It was a good practical question but he didn't say so to Margaret.

"I didn't let go of gambling completely...not yet any way. Six years ago I bought a slot machine software company...expanded it and hold a considerable number of game patents...with some in the pipeline...for slots sold all over the United States. The money may not be in building a casino...but they all have to have slots...for a while any way...but I won't hold onto that company for long."

Margaret shook her head and Jim laughed.

"Margaret, one thing I learned from Sandra about our people...marine hunter gatherers...we have always had a diverse economy...if one resource failed there were others that overlapped enough to keep the Casco alive. For hundreds of years a diverse economy kept the Casco going.

A casino is one big egg...if gaming is down, everything is down...everything fails. It's going down.

I have a plan to move a few of my profitable companies...the slot software, seafood processing, including frozen foods and the plastics facility...which as of this month is making blades for wind turbines...orders already in place. I plan to move them all to a non-profit called The Heron Foundation.

Second phase is right up your alley...not too high risk...shoes. I bought a Maine shoe factory at auction because they were practically giving it away...between you and your mother I couldn't resist...hired some young designers and materials people with one requirement...the shoes had to be of recycled materials. They came up with sandals made from netting and lobster pot rope...some other recycled stuff... belts for both women and men.

Another area on the horizon is to expand the food division to include some gourmet seafood products, clam chowder...oyster and lobster stews...my grandmother's recipes.

Then in this river...long term...I'd like to bring back the oyster beds...Casco oysters...all profits from all products go to The Heron Foundation...same mission as the casino...education, education of the Casco people."

Again, Jim expected Margaret to be done. He was.

"Who's going to run all this?"

Jim switched to the short version.

"Sandra has agreed to direct the Archive. I'm going to run, with a Board and staff, The Heron Foundation. We need to find someone for the Cultural Center...I was hoping University consultants and a strong Tribal Council. That only leaves...leaves the Casco Theatre...I was thinking..."

"To do that right, you need an Artistic or Managing Director with experience in summer stock theatre...it's not me...I'm a playwright...but I can help recruit."

"I saw *Shadowcatchers*...you are a good writer Margaret. Maybe you could do something for here..." Jim now stumbling "...hope to be opening next summer...working on any..."

"Yes, "Heartache of the Hunter" for the stage."

Jim knew the story, "Charlie Bay's "Heartache of the Hunter"?"

"Yes..." Her eyes drifted toward Charlie Bay's home to remember.

It was an unusual day for early October, warm and breezy from the south-southwest. Margaret was quick to take advantage of it with the STURGEON MOON, straight off the mooring and headed east past the bell. This was the second time sailing the Haven since Pearl's death and the first alone. Bud sailed with her to bring the boat from Biddeford Pool to the harbor in the Casco River. But this was the sail she had been waiting for; alone in Pearl's STURGEON MOON, with Max's hand against the hull, on Charlie Bay's open ocean. They were with her.

Moving across the wind, the Haven began to heel. Margaret settled into the leeward side and pulled the photo of Sand Piper Diving from her pocket. Turning to Molly's prayer she whispered,

"Uh-kosisco, Uh-kosisco rising above me.
Look down upon a daughter of the Nations.
And give strength to my Casco heart
that I may remain faithful.
I make this prayer to you Uh-kosisco.

Uh-kosisco, Uh-kosisco rising above me.
Look down upon a daughter of the Nations.
And give strength to my Casco heart
that I may remain faithful.
I make this prayer to you Uh-kosisco."

Margaret closed her eyes and touched the tiller with the tips of her fingers, "...that I may remain faithful."